The Experimental Mind in Education

Exploration Series in Education

*Under the Advisory Editorship of
John Guy Fowlkes and Edward A. Krug*

The Experimental
Mind in Education

BOB BURTON BROWN

UNIVERSITY OF FLORIDA

HARPER & ROW, PUBLISHERS

NEW YORK · EVANSTON · LONDON

To my wife Evelyn and our offspring
Tandel, Michel, Deborah, and Scott

CONTENTS

EDITOR'S INTRODUCTION

IT SEEMS LIKELY that anyone who has had contact with education at any time during the last half century, particularly during the period 1950–1968, has been aware of the need for improving education programs. The new recognition of the importance of schools is heartening because there is an awakening to the potential of education. Suggestions and prescriptive recommendations for more effective educational offerings are being issued by a variety of publications, governmental agencies, special committees, and commissions.

Staffs of schools, from kindergartens to graduate schools, urge changes in all curricular programs. Reports of studies by special committees urge drastic shifts in organization. One report, known as the Coleman Report, "Equality of Educational Opportunity," 1966, financed by the Federal government, indicates that things easy to change in a school (number of books, teacher-pupil ratio, number of days in a school calendar) seem to have little effect on student achievement; factors which produce better results (teachers' verbal facility, willingness to teach children from slums, the quality of preparatory programs for teachers, teachers' attitudes to racial integration) are tougher and less likely to change.

Temporary interest gained from difference or change holds no guarantee for basic improvement. Staffs and teachers know that no segment of school curriculum is perfect. Perfect answers for stimulation and assistance to learners have never been found and may never be, but unceasing effort is essential.

This book deals with major patterns of the experimental mind, its operation, and some implications and suggestions for its cultivation and encouragement. Whatever one's focus of interest, contact, or obligation, this volume is of value towards the improvement of educational programs.

JOHN GUY FOWLKES

PREFACE

SOMEONE MAY MISTAKE this for another book about John Dewey's philosophy of experimentalism. Someone may even choose to use it, as I do, as a textbook in teaching a course in the philosophy of education. If so, I will be flattered. While the book is full of Dewey and presents a detailed analysis of both his general and pedagogical theories, it is not intended as a study *of* or *about* his philosophy. Instead, it is intended as an *application* of Dewey's philosophy—to be *used* as a way of thinking about and dealing with some of the most persistent everyday problems of teaching.

THE EXPERIMENTAL MIND IN EDUCATION is essentially a book on general methods of teaching examined from an explicit philosophic point of view. It is designed to help the reader find out whether he agrees with John Dewey's philosophy at the beliefs level, and then shows him precisely which teaching practices logically and empirically go with those beliefs. No attempt is made to convert anyone to the beliefs and practices advocated by Dewey. All that is hoped is that we learn to be clear about Dewey, and learn to use that clarity to make sense out of our own educational beliefs and practices.

This book represents the culmination of an effort of many years and involved the help and encouragement of many persons. I wish to express my indebtedness to those at the University of Wisconsin who helped me begin the study of the relationship of experimentalism to classroom practices: Lindley J. Stiles and John Guy Fowlkes, who provided the opportunity and continued personal support; Paul W. Eberman, who directed my initial inquiry into this topic with warm and sure understanding; Edward A. Krug and the late Virgil E. Herrick, who contributed to the understandings of educational theory used in putting together the framework of this study; Chester W. Harris, who gave invaluable advice regarding procedures used in collecting and analyzing the data in the early stages. For their participation in the development of the instruments used for the measurement of experimentalism, I wish to thank B. Robert Tabachnick, Merle Borrowman, William Hay, Donald Arnstine, Haskell Fain, Julian Stanley, Frank Baker, and John Withall. For their assistance in data collection special appreciation is due Eleanore Larson, Thomas C. Barrett, John Newell, Tom Faix, James Godfrey, George Cheong, and Rodney Johnson.

Throughout the preparation of the manuscript during the past two years I am grateful to my colleagues at the University of Florida: Dean Kimball Wiles, for providing a climate of freedom for creative thought; Arthur Combs and Ira Gordon, for sharpening my thinking about educational theory; Hal Lewis, for giving me an opportunity to teach the philosophy of education; Robert Curran, for critically reading parts of the manuscript; philosopher Charles W. Morris, for furnishing feedback of the warmest kind on the measures of experimentalism; William Mendenhall, Robert Beaver, and James McClave, along with Douglas Scates, C. M. Bridges, and Wilson Guertin, for their guidance through the maze of statistics. For the kind of help only graduate assistants can give, I am grateful to Winston Summerhill, Nicholas Stoffel, Tom R. Vickery, and Jeaninne Webb.

I am most appreciative to the 19 well-known educators who responded to the beliefs inventories, particularly to Harry S. Broudy, Arthur Combs, Carl Rogers, B. F. Skinner, and B. Othanel Smith who graciously permitted certain details of their scores to be reported, along with excerpts from their personal correspondence. Without their cooperation Chapter 7 would not have been possible.

I am indebted doubly to Edward A. Krug and John Guy Fowlkes, first, for convincing me that I could, and should, write the book, and, then, for providing penetrating editorial criticism which enabled me to do it. For their unusually helpful assistance in typing the manuscript, my deepest thanks go to Marion Terry and Marie Smallwood.

Finally, and above all, I wish to express my gratitude to my wife and my four children, who contributed so much so regularly to the writing of this book that they may not realize they helped at all. But I do.

Bob Burton Brown

Gainesville, Florida

pARt I

Introduction

TEACHERS MUST make choices. They have to decide what to
do and what not to do. They must decide which steps to
take first, second, and so on. They must pick some books and
pass others by. Of all the possible things to do, steps to take, and
instructional materials to use, only a relative handful can be
worked into any given teaching situation. Teachers must choose
between all such alternatives.

In making these decisions, the teacher shares the dilemma of a
child in a candy store: The alternatives confronting him are overwhelming. There is an almost endless variety of flavors, colors,
shapes, and sizes to choose from. A child may decide such things
simply by closing his eyes and reaching in the dark, or by flipping
a coin, or by playing "eenie, meanie, minie, moe." Or, he may
let the storekeeper decide for him, and blame him if that turns
out to be a bad choice. Or, he may ignore all the possible choices
and pick the one piece of candy he knows tastes good—the only
one he has ever tried. However, the capricious devices of childhood lose their charm when employed in decision-making by
teachers. Choices regarding teaching practices need to be grounded
in critical awareness of theoretical alternatives underlying the various practical alternatives available.

Teachers, like everyone else, can behave only in terms of
what seems to them to be so. Their classroom practices are related
to their beliefs. What teachers believe and do about educational
problems in the classroom depends to a considerable extent upon
their fundamental beliefs about (1) people, and why they behave

I

as they do, (2) reality, or the world in which people live, and (3) knowledge, its nature and relationship to what people do. Such beliefs are called a person's philosophic point of view or frame of mind. Within the traditions of our culture different people deal with these basic philosophic questions in different ways and arrive at different answers. What each teacher believes about such questions in theory makes a difference in how he teaches in practice.

In this book we will explore the relationship of theory and practice in education primarily along the dimensions of the *experimental mind*. By *mind* we mean the complex of such mental functions as perceiving, remembering, considering, evaluating, deciding, and, of course, believing. The *experimental mind,* as used here, indicates a state or habit of mind characterized by beliefs, dispositions, inclinations, or intentions which are compatible with John Dewey's philosophy of experimentalism. In subsequent chapters we will describe in detail the characteristics of the experimental mind, but we will first look at some general problems involved in the relationship of beliefs or theories and practices.

1

THEORY AND PRACTICE

IN A FREE and open society we pin our faith on continuous argument, discussion, and disagreement as the method for deciding which policies and practices are most useful and valuable. Our national character has always been one of enormous differences within a framework of disharmonious union. We do not believe that people should be forced into common agreement. Instead, we believe that many conflicting points of view should be tolerated and encouraged. Under this scheme, diversity and pluralism have abounded, providing a natural system of checks and balances among the various special interest groups concerned with any particular problem. The conflicting viewpoints provided by such groups make for healthy controversy and debate of public issues, the stuff on which creativity, experimentation, and freedom thrive.

In some quarters there seems to be a growing impatience with the old-fashioned virtues of decentralization and diversity. Faith in the many to participate in and assume responsibility for making decisions about educational policies and practices, among other things, has given way to belief that the wisdom of a centralized elite is superior to decentralized backwoods wisdom. Democracy is too slow and clumsy, it is argued, to meet the demands of the urbanized space age and the threat of competing totalitarian systems. However, unless we wish to turn into a closed or totalitarian society by default, our decision-making processes ought both to reflect and to nourish the traditional variety in our national character, no matter how exasperating it may seem in our desire for something we call "efficiency" and "progress." In teaching, as in all other aspects of American life, we must constantly be on our guard against those who would have us swap decentralization, disharmony, and diversity in our beliefs and practices for some central, unified, monolithic structure which promises to relieve us of all our burdens and problems.

So long as we cling to our democratic traditions, teachers will continue to be confronted by incessant pressure from economic, ideological, political, and other power groups (including educators) to mold the curriculum and instruction of the school in the direction of their interests. Teaching practices viewed as right and good by some are viewed as wrong and bad by others. Teachers need to have an understanding of the values of such special interest groups as they bear on educational decisions. They need to become skillful in analyzing and criticizing the propositions put forward in debates between competing special interest groups. Operating within such a system, teachers cannot avoid making value-loaded judgments and decisions which stem from issues regarding fundamental ethical, moral, philosophic, and religious principles. Arguments about teaching practices are extensions of arguments about beliefs which for most people are accepted as unexamined premises or self-evident "truths." People disagree about relative merits of various teaching practices because they hold conflicting beliefs about what is "right," "good," or "true."

Teachers are often overwhelmed by the variety and proliferation of practices available to them, and confused by the controversy about which of them they should choose and use. Intelligent evaluation and clarification of the vast jungle of teaching practices is possible only if the concealed cultural and philosophical roots of the competing interests in the controversy are raised to the level of consciousness and are opened for public inspection. This requires teachers to make a serious effort to identify the values they use as guiding principles in making judgments about teaching practices. Likewise, they should learn the value positions of the people who advocate or impose certain teaching practices. The controversy will not be resolved, nor the discussion ended, when underlying issues are properly examined and understood, but relative positions should be clarified sufficiently to permit teachers to devise and choose teaching practices with some personal sense of direction, organization, and confidence.

Even though educational research is still in its infancy, it has already produced a great many facts, or data, about teaching behavior. Those of us who come to look into this sea of data for help in understanding and improving our teaching practices find the water level more than high enough for drowning. Indeed, we find almost more information about teaching than we know what to do with. Our problem is to discover what it all means. For this we need theory.

A theory is nothing more than a way of looking at pieces of knowledge in order to make some kind of sense out of them. Individual facts, swimming around by themselves in a whole sea of data, are easily lost or obscured. Looked at one by one, they have little or no value. It is only when the pieces are put together or connected in some pattern or theoretical framework that they become understandable and useful to us.

A theory is analogous to a simple line drawing of something that cannot be differentiated clearly in the raw, just as it comes in nature, camouflaged against a plethora of details. The cartoonist constructs a theory when he looks at a famous politician and sees past all the richness of texture and detail of his face, as well as the dynamic of his gestures, and represents the essence of his character and personality in just a few bold strokes of the pen. A theory, like a cartoon, is a highly compressed and simplified way of organizing and transmitting otherwise very complex information. A theory eliminates all the nonessential details in order to emphasize some particular feature, thereby improving the legibility of the picture presented in the mind's eye.

Theories and the people who make them can be deceiving. They must necessarily "screen out" much of what is available to include in any given picture. The screen which is used for this purpose is of crucial importance, and must be taken into account. No fact exists independent of knowers or the circumstances in which it becomes known. And all of us, as knowers, must wear the spectacles of our own experience and individual circumstances in order to see any thing. The color and shape of the glass through which we look, and where we stand when we look, makes a difference in what we see to be the fact.

There is an almost unlimited number of ways in which facts can be organized and looked at. The same facts looked at in different ways, from different angles, through different lenses, lend themselves to different interpretations, each of which may be "true"—depending upon the orientation and purpose of the observer. No theory is ever "true" from every point of view, under all conditions, or for all time. What we believe to be factual varies, depending upon the varying frames of reference from which we make our observations. For example, not everyone by a long shot agrees with the relativistic theory presented here. Many people hold beliefs that certain things are absolutely true under all circumstances and conditions, now and forever. They hold that there is a fundamental, permanent and unchanging reality or truth behind what is given to us in experience. Of course, according to such absolutists, all theories which do not agree with this one true theory are false.

Theories vary in scope and size. Some theories connect only a few facts within a highly specialized area, and others pull together a great many facts covering broad areas of our experience and knowledge. Generally speaking, the bigger the theory the better. That is, the more details a theory helps us understand, the more useful it is to us. Theories which do not hold all the facts in the situations they are designed to explain, or which are contradicted by obvious facts in those situations, are said to be theories that do not "hold water."

Some theories are more fundamental than others. Theories grow out of other theories. The first screens or glasses we peer through are themselves frames of references, viewpoints, or theories. They color all subsequent theories we develop and use. Sometimes we change the lenses of our original or basic frameworks but we cannot erase completely our memory of the old ones. These persist in "fogging up" our view of the world from time to time thereafter.

Such fundamental frames of reference are called *principles*.

Principles are the attitudes and beliefs that exercise directing influence on our lives and behavior; they are something from which other things take their origin—the rudiments or seeds which impart a characteristic quality to everything we are or become.

Principles, theories, frames of reference serve as guideposts and road maps which save us from becoming hopelessly lost in an utterly chaotic and incoherent mass of disconnected details. They permit us to ask intelligent questions of the data presented to us about the world of nature in which we live, and gives us a background for understanding, interpreting, and using the answers which result. In short, such frameworks are the means by which we find our bearings, make our soundings, and chart a course which makes this changing and uncertain world an understandable and predictable place in which to live.

THEORY AND PRACTICE

Every teaching practice is based on some theory, whether that theory is consciously recognized and explicitly stated or not. Teaching practice which is unconnected or unaware of its underlying theory is usually dull, routine, and stupid. It doesn't know what it is doing or why. It lacks specifiable direction, purpose, and reason. To be intelligent, or imaginative and exciting, practice must be deliberately related to theory. Failure to make this vital connection between theory and practice is a glaring weakness in American education.

Having culturally inherited some faulty theories, theory and practice have gotten separated, divorced, placed in opposition to each other in the minds of many of us. The traditional patterns of thought in our culture make theory remote from and oblivious to practice, and make practice ignorant of and hostile to theory. Both the theory and practice of teaching suffers because of this unnecessary and artificial separation.

In intellectual circles the notion has long been held that theoretical knowledge is derived from a higher source and has a more spiritual worth than does practical activity. What is theoretical has been exalted as pure, of value in and of itself, quite apart from any reference to its possible practical use in applied art or science. What is practical has been depreciated as intellectually narrow, trivial, mundane, clearly inferior to things of the mind.

On the other hand, among practical people it is not uncommon to find an earthy sort of reverse snobbery which looks down its nose at theory as a lot of fancy, abstract, egg-headed malarky. What works in practice, what proves to be useful in getting the necessary, obvious, dirty old everyday job done counts most. What is mere theory is discounted as so much far-fetched, high-flown nonsense which can be regarded only with doubt and suspicion.

How one looks at theory makes a difference. If we limit our picture of theory to include only an ideal or hypothetical set of facts, principles, or circumstances, we are likely to perpetuate *in our thinking* the separation of theory from practice. We restrict theory to an ideal realm of abstract knowledge and unprovable assumptions which can be connected to the real world of practical affairs by nothing more substantial than mystical moonbeams. With theory thus idealized we assure ourselves of the failure in practice of what looked so promising in theory. On the other hand, if we can widen our thinking to permit theory to be seen as belief, policy, or proposed procedure to serve as a basis of action, we will be able to reunite theory and practice. Theory might then be seen as the intelligent explanation of practice, which permits theory to follow practice as well as lead it. Theory, in this broader view, is always developed in association with practice and serves as its frame of reference.

The Theory-Practice Dilemma

The establishment of the unnatural split between theory and practice has led to a discrepancy between what teachers say they know and believe in theory and how they teach, or fail to teach, in practice. We call this the theory-practice dilemma.

Even the most casual observer of the educational scene is familiar with evidence of this dilemma. Students are well aware that their teachers don't always practice what they preach. Teachers announce their good intentions to teach youngsters to think creatively, but test them almost exclusively for recall of specific facts. Parents notice that teachers' marking and reporting practices frequently bear little relationship to the statements of policy which appear on the cover of report cards. Fervently advertised theories of discipline to the contrary give no assurance that Sammy will not be rapped across the knuckles for violating his teacher's standards of conduct. Teachers in training are likely to discover a perplexing lack of agreement between the theory advocated by their professors of education and the practices demanded of them by the cooperating teachers selected by colleges of education to direct their student teaching experiences. In many textbooks on teaching methods the discussion of theoretical issues and backgrounds in the beginning chapters is not related to the treatment of practical problems of teaching which follows in later chapters. And rarely do the professor's own teaching practices approach those he advocates to his students. It is difficult to find a teacher who does not pay lip service to the desirability of providing for individual differences among pupils. Yet, it is far more difficult to find one who actually does anything about it in the classroom.

Even the best of teachers experience the theory-practice dilemma. They have trouble applying in practice what they know and believe in theory. A wise and effective teacher once remarked to me as we drove toward a state educational conference: "I don't know why I keep going to meetings to learn more about becoming a better teacher—I already know how to teach ten times better than I ever can." The problem of dealing with the theory-practice dilemma has stumped educational leaders for as long as anyone can remember. It is often shrugged off by muttering some old saw about the "best of intentions." Perhaps it can be explained more satisfactorily by questioning what we say we believe, and by inquiring more thoroughly into the nature of the relationship between theory and practice.

Perhaps the most noteworthy example of the discrepancy between theory and practice is the failure of American teachers to fully live up to their promise to challenge youngsters to think. Official statements of educational philosophy all across the nation avow that the most important task of teachers in a free society is to develop citizens who are committed to and skilled in the process of thinking—independently and reflectively. In a culture in which it is generally assumed that children should, above all, learn to make up their own minds and to think for themselves, it would seem reasonable to expect, as we observe teaching in classrooms the country over, to find students engaged in situations which call for reflective thinking. But we don't. Instead, we find students jumping through teachers' hoops like so many trained puppy dogs, dutifully performing the required tricks as efficiently and as thoughtlessly as possible.

Reflective thinking is the method of solving problems by which science has progressed in its conquest of nature. It is also the focal point of John Dewey's philosophy of experimentalism which is supposed to have thoroughly influenced what teachers in America believe and do about education. If this is so, why don't we find teachers providing students more thinking experience than we do? The obvious answer is that teachers have neither understood nor agreed with Dewey so well or so completely as is commonly supposed. While teachers may agree with Dewey about the importance of fostering in school good habits of thinking, they do not agree with Dewey that this is *all* the school can or should do for students.

Dewey equates an educative experience with a reflective experience; most teachers we have studied do not. Teachers do not seem to have recognized or accepted Dewey's belief that acquisition is always secondary and instrumental to inquiry. Instead, they have clung to the more conventional notion that reflective thinking, or experimental inquiry, is secondary and merely a means to the acquisition of a certain body of knowledge, skills, and attitudes which adults in the culture wish to preserve and pass on to their offspring. This insistence that students acquire a predetermined curriculum is why the glorification of reflective thinking and inquiry has been little more than idle talk. In order to give children the freedom to think independently and reflectively, to engage in experimental inquiry, it would be necessary for us to run the risk that they might not end up in possession of the cultural heritage we want so very much for them to have. Teachers, reflecting the mood of the culture, have generally avoided the risks and uncertainties of the experimental alternative and have been satisfied to play it safe, maintaining education as an essentially thought-immune "turkey stuffing" operation.

John Dewey observed that while "no one doubts, theoretically, the importance of fostering in school good habits of thinking . . . acknowledgement is not so great in practice as theory." His explanation of this state of affairs was that "There is not adequate theoretical recognition that all the school can do for pupils, so far as their minds are concerned . . . is to develop their ability to think."[1] He traced the source of the theory-practice dilemma back to the faulty theories of traditional philosophy and religion, which are dependent upon the presupposition of a split between a real physical world and an ideal mental world. What is more, he blamed all evils in education (and society) on the fundamental beliefs of such systems. Since most of us were born and brought up in a culture whose social, political, and religious institutions are rooted in traditional philosophies, it is little wonder, if Dewey's analysis is correct, that we bring beliefs with us into teaching which virtually guarantee that we will become hung up on the horns of the theory-practice dilemma.

CONFLICT BETWEEN BELIEFS

All teachers possess beliefs which enter into or affect choices made in the performance of their teaching tasks. However, teacher beliefs operating in particular choice-making situations may not always be consciously recognized or associated with the practices chosen. Where this is so, we may expect inconsistency and conflict to creep into the method of classroom operation. In choices made on the basis of unconscious beliefs, irrelevant and unwarranted assumptions may be pulling practices in the opposite direction to which the teacher says he wants them to go, and, perhaps, honestly believes they are going.

For example, in investigating the relationship of teacher beliefs to classroom practices, we have discovered many teachers in just this sort of predicament. Most teachers we have studied think of themselves as democratic, flexible, open-minded, and experimental. Teachers' responses on the *Teacher Practices Inventory* indicate that the majority of them are in moderately high agreement with the educational practices advocated by John Dewey. However,

[1] John Dewey, *Democracy and Education* (New York: The Macmillan Company, 1916), p. 179.

when research teams observed the actual classroom practices of these same teachers, they found relatively few of them using such practices. This, of course, is further evidence of the theory-practice dilemma. Searching for some explanation, we attempted to measure the underlying philosophic beliefs of the teachers, using the *Personal Beliefs Inventory*. Most teachers were found to be in moderately low agreement with the fundamental philosophic theories in which the teacher practices advocated by Dewey are grounded. Although they were inclined to agree with Dewey on beliefs about what teaching practices should be, they were inclined to disagree with him on general philosophic questions. The non-experimental basic philosophic beliefs of teachers often contradicted their experimental educational beliefs. And when this contradiction occurred, the observed classroom practices of teachers tended to be pulled in the direction of the underlying philosophic beliefs. Basic philosophic beliefs seem to be powerful enough to overpower or cancel out conflicting or logically incongruent beliefs about teaching practice. This study, which will be described in greater detail in Chapter 12, offers at least a partial explanation of the theory-practice dilemma.

Our beliefs about fundamental philosophic questions lie beneath our beliefs about teaching practices, and are often disassociated with them. In order to understand, to evaluate, and to intelligently reconstruct conflicting theories and practices it is necessary that we first of all raise our basic philosophic beliefs to the level of critical self-consciousness. The beliefs we have acquired about the meaning of life, the nature and destiny of man, and the nature of the world in which we live are often buried deeply at the innermost center of our belief systems.

If we are to bridge the gulf that separates the theory and practice of teaching, we must inquire into (1) theories which help us understand why people behave as they do, and (2) the structure and organization of belief systems or frames of mind. This we will attempt to do in Chapters 2 and 3.

2

BELIEFS, PERCEPTIONS, AND BEHAVIOR

IT IS NOT POSSIBLE to consider the relationship of beliefs and practices in education without getting into both philosophy and psychology. While psychology is the child of mother philosophy, the two have become estranged. The child ran off on its own, and the mother disowned the child. In order to look at the relationship of beliefs and practices (or behavior) it will be necessary to construct some difficult-to-build bridges between psychology and philosophy. In this book, as we have already indicated, Dewey's experimentalism anchors the philosophy or beliefs side. On the psychology or behavior side we will attempt to establish connections with what is called the "perceptual," "personal," or "phenomenological" frame of reference.

THE PERCEPTUAL VIEW OF BEHAVIOR

Human behavior may be observed from the point of view of the outsider, or from the point of view of the insider—the behaver himself.[1] Typically, research on human behavior is conducted from the "external" or "objective" point of view. The behavior of others is observed and explained in terms of the interactions of individuals and the situations in which they are seen operating.

[1] See Arthur W. Combs and Donald Snygg, *Individual Behavior,* Revised Edition (New York: Harper & Row, 1959). This discussion of the perceptual point of view has been extracted and adapted from the work of Combs and Snygg, and is included here with their permission.

It is possible, however, to observe and explain the behavior of individuals in terms of how things "seem" to them. This is the "personal," "subjective," or "perceptual" point of view.

The perceptual psychologist takes as his fundamental assumption that people's ideas, emotions, opinions, and beliefs have an effect upon their behavior. Consequently, he is alert and sensitive to them. On the other hand, the more conventional *S-R* psychologist in his quest for "objectivity" is highly suspicious of such "subjective" variables and goes out of his way to avoid them. When his attempts to eliminate them fail, he simply ignores their presence. Although the perceptual psychologist accepts "objective" data as important for understanding behavior, he points out that people do not behave according to the facts as *others* see them. They behave according to the facts as *they* see them. What governs behavior of the individual are his unique perceptions of himself and the world in which he lives, the personal meaning things have for him.

Another basic concept of perceptual psychology is that all behavior is caused. It is purposeful. It always has a reason. When the purposes or reasons are confused, vague, and uncertain the behavior is equally confused, vague, and uncertain. When the rationale is extremely clear and definite, so is the behavior. Whatever we do seems reasonable and necessary to us at the moment we are doing it, or we wouldn't do it. Whether one is painting his house or committing a crime, at the time of behaving a person's actions seem to him to be the best and most effective acts he can perform under the circumstances—no matter how silly or irrational or irresponsible that behavior may look to other people from an external, objective point of view, or, in retrospect, from a subsequent point of view of the behaver himself.

The Perceptual Field: A Private World

For the perceptual psychologist all behavior is determined by, and pertinent to, the perceptual field of the person doing the behaving. The perceptual field might be called the private or personal world of the individual. The "reality" of this world lies not in physical things and events, but in the individual's experience of those things and events. To each individual the private world of his perceptual field *is* reality—at least, the only reality he can know.

The perceptual field is fluid, continually changing. Even so, the perceptual field does not lack organization or stability. How the field is organized and stabilized is what enables us to differentiate one type of personality from another and to predict how each may behave under varying circumstances. In this sense, there is a striking similarity between the concept of perceptual field and the concept of "frame of mind" or "belief system."

In identical sets of circumstances the perceptual fields of different individuals will differ. The perceptual field of even the same person varies during successive presentations of the same situation. Even so, the perceptual field always has some sort of direction, i.e., it is always organized into what might be termed a "Gestalt," a configuration, or pattern. A person's perceptual field never approaches being identical with the field which is potentially available in the observable environment. It is both much more and much less. It includes some things not physically or currently present. And it includes only a few of the practically infinite number of detailed objects and meanings which are or might be present in any given physical situation or set of circumstances. The perceptual field of a given individual at a given time is organized according to his purpose and the behavior by which he is trying to accomplish that purpose.

Figure-Ground Relationship

The relationship of figure and ground is essential to the understanding of how the perceptual field works. The *whole* of the perceptual field represents "ground." Only that *part* which is taken, extracted, or perceived out of this undifferentiated background is called "figure." We say that the fabric of the drapes hanging at the window are "figured" or "patterned" when we perceive some shapes which are appreciable and separable from their surroundings. The figure is usually that part of the total which is most clearly perceived by an observer, and to which he responds. The ground is the area surrounding and delineating the figure or design. It is usually the plain or background portion of the patterned fabric of our drapes.

The charts used for testing color blindness are a good illustration of figure-ground relationship. These charts are covered with a myriad of dots of varying sizes and colors. Persons with normal vision, for example, may see green and blue dots forming the figure "76" on an undifferentiated ground of red and purple dots. Color-blind persons may differentiate only the purple dots which form the figure "59," or fail to perceive any recognizable figure at all. Likewise, some people look at the myriad of stars in the sky and perceive only a mass of bright spots against the black background of night. While most of us manage to pick out the "big dipper" or the "tea kettle," some very experienced and imaginative sky watchers are able to perceive all sorts of figures, including bears, lions, dragons, hunters, water carriers, and, no less, virgins.

Anyone who has had a beginning course in psychology, or who reads the Sunday funny papers, is familiar with optical illusions, perceptual games, oddities, or tricks which illustrate the figure-ground relationship. When we focus on one part of such objects we see one thing, but see something entirely and surprisingly different when we change our focus. For example, what at first may appear to be the outline of a candlestick or vase may also be seen as two faces. One emerges into figure as the other fades into ground, and vice versa.

The process of emergence of figure from ground is known as *differentiation*. Anything in the perceptual field can become figure, but, as Gestalt psychologists have pointed out, two events may not appear in figure simultaneously. Persons with normal vision may perceive on the color-blind test either the green and blue "76" or with slightly more difficulty the purple "59," but not both at once. Although we sharpen our perceptions by differentiating figure from ground, it should be remembered that the meaning of any perception is the product of the relationship of that figure to the total ground of which it is a part.

Like children looking for familiar shapes among clouds in the sky, each of us is constantly searching his perceptual field for details and meaningful patterns. The constant rise of new characters into figure and the consequent lapse of other characters into ground creates continual change in the perceptual field. Differentiation enables us to become aware of an object or pattern of objects.

Change in behavior occurs with differentiation in the perceptual field. Thus, learning, problem-solving, remembering, forgetting, and the like are all aspects of the process of differentiating figure from ground in the individual's perceptual field.

Perception: A Word for all Occasions

Perceptual psychologists give the word "perception" a considerably more comprehensive meaning than do the more conventional branches of psychology. Ordinarily, the word perception refers only to "a mental image, concept, or meaning obtained through reaction sensory stimulus." To describe acts of knowing, understanding, or forming ideas, psychologists customarily use the words "conception" or "cognition." Perceptual psychologists, however, use the word "perception" to refer to *any* differentiation the individual is capable of making in his perceptual field. They claim that differentiations which result in perceptions of seeing, hearing, smelling, or feeling are much the same as those differentiations which are made in conceiving, learning, knowing, or understanding. Although the subject matter varies, the process is the same. The differentiation of an idea or concept is not basically different from the differentiation of a sight, a scent, or a sound. Therefore, to the perceptual psychologists, there seems to be no need for more than one process to explain these events—and "perception" is the word for it.

This enthusiasm for perception as both a process and a concept is also extended to account for such abstract processes as synthesizing, generalizing, integrating, and evaluating. The perceptual approach to understanding behavior is concerned solely with the problem of how events are experienced by the behaver. Thus, what seems like integration, synthesis, or generalization observed from an objective point of view, becomes simply another form of differentiation when observed from the behaver's own frame of reference.

In other words, any and all so-called mental functions and their relationships with behavior can be explained in terms of perceptions. If this is the case, the word "perception" might be used instead of the word "belief," and one's "viewpoint," "philosophy," or "frame of mind" might be subsumed as merely an aspect of one's "perceptual field" or "perceptual organization." Perceptual psychologists do not necessarily deny the continued usefulness of these traditional words within the frames of reference from which they stem. Instead, they simply offer an alternative frame of reference which they believe more adequately accounts for such events and processes—and within the perceptual framework they find the words perception, differentiation, and perceptual field more precise and more inclusive for their purposes.

The Variables of Perception

If perception is such a fundamental and all-pervasive factor in determining human behavior, we need to understand as clearly as possible the variables which control and limit the processes of perceiving and the function of the perceptual field. Some of the variables influencing perception have been known and studied for many years by several disciplines, including both philosophy and psychology.

WE SEE WHAT WE NEED TO SEE

According to the perceptual view of behavior, man is an insatiably striving organism seeking the maintenance and enhancement of the self. Man's basic need is his need for adequacy. This means that there is a driving, striving force in each of us by which we are continually seeking to make ourselves ever more adequate to cope with life. Interestingly, this is somewhat similar to John Dewey's position that a basic drive of man is to maintain his equilibrium[2] in a life characterized by change and uncertainty. This need to maintain ourselves in some sort of upright or "adequate" orientation to our world has profound effects on our perceptions.

Out of all the things we *might* perceive, we perceive what we think will help us to maintain and enhance the organization of our perceptions of self and, thus, to satisfy our basic need (or, what is threatening to that end). For example, we do not see the cobbler's shop we pass everyday until our shoes need fixing. Even

[2] John Dewey, *Human Nature and Conduct* (New York: Random House, 1950), pp. 178–179, 252. See also Dewey's essay "Some Stages of Logical Thought," *Philosophic Review, IX,* September 5, 1900.

though we have traveled to a place in the country as a passenger in a car, we do not know the unfamiliar road home because we were not paying attention to it on the way out; it was not part of our need. We see what we need to see.

We also see what we want to see. We tend to perceive the favorable characteristics of candidates from our own political party and the unfavorable characteristics of those from the opposition party. We tend to overlook or fail to perceive the shortcomings of those with whom we identify sympathetically. Sometimes we see what we fear or worry about. A colleague of ours once began to worry about dying from cancer. He perceived every bump and blemish, every ache and pain, as a sign of cancer. Fortunately, medical examinations proved his worries to be unfounded. He had seen what he had most feared to see, or, in a sick sense, what he had wanted to see. We pay attention to, or perceive, only what touches our personal wants and worries.

People behave in any given situation in ways that protect their feelings of adequacy. Most women do not feel adequately prepared to be seen in public unless they cake their faces with cosmetics and crowd themselves into girdles. A young beatnik feels somehow more adequate to cope with his hopeless world if he wears a bizarre beard, long hair, and dirty underwear. Ambitious people think it enhances them to be associated, if only by name dropping, with the successful, the famous, and the celebrated. Most of us who hail from rural areas perk up our ears at the slightest mention of our home town on a radio or television newscast. We gain a feeling of increased importance because the relatively unknown town with which we identify makes the national news. We respond to the sound of its name much as we do to our own.

WE SEE WHAT WE CAN SEE

The most obvious factor affecting perception is the physical organism in which the process of perceiving occurs. We see with our eyes, hear with our ears, taste with our taste buds, and distinguish odors with our olfactory organs. Whatever limits the functioning of these organs of the body necessarily limits our perceptions as well.

We can perceive only those things which we have the physical equipment to perceive. Human beings cannot hear high-frequency sounds which dogs and birds can hear. We lack the built-in radar systems which enable bats to navigate in the dark. We cannot find our way home like pigeons. Even so, human perceptions can be extremely varied and extensive. Our perceptions extend far beyond our experiences of sight, hearing, smell, taste, and touch. For example, we have foresight—the remarkable ability to perceive remote events. This makes it possible for us to be aware of time as well as space. We are also able to perceive ideas, values, and relationships of meanings that far transcend the limitations of our sense organs.

Although what we see may be limited by the necessary physical equipment for seeing, what we see is affected relatively little by the structure of our eyes. The structure of the eye tells us *whether* one can see, but nothing about *what* is seen. Our bodies provide the vehicle of perception, but they do not explain it. We are broadly limited by our fundamental physiology, but the variety, the richness, and the almost limitless patterns of human behavior cannot be fully understood exclusively in terms of the physical organism.

WE SEE WHAT WE HAVE TIME AND OPPORTUNITY TO SEE

What a person is able to perceive in any situation may depend upon the length of time he has been exposed to that situation. The longer one looks, the more he is able to see. A classic example of this is the story of Samuel Scudder's experiences in learning ichthyology at Harvard in the laboratory of the famed naturalist Louis Agassiz[3]:

Agassiz began on the first morning by pulling a fish from a jar of yellow acid, laying it before Scudder, and saying: "Take this fish and look at it . . . by and by I will ask you what you have seen." Whereupon Agassiz departed, leaving Scudder alone with the fish. After ten minutes Scudder had seen all that he thought could be seen in that fish. He could not find the professor so there was nothing to be done but to keep on looking at his mute companion. As Scudder reports: "Half an hour passed—an hour —another hour; the fish began to look loathsome. I turned it over and around; looked it in the face—ghastly; from behind, beneath, above, sideways, at a three-quarters view—just as ghastly." After

[3] Samuel Scudder, "In the Laboratory with Louis Agassiz," *Every Saturday* (April 4, 1874), pp. 369–370.

lunch there was nothing else for Scudder to do but to again look at that hideous fish. He pushed his finger down its throat to feel how sharp the teeth were. He counted the scales in the different rows. Then he decided to try drawing the fish, and to his surprise he began to discover new features in the creature. At this point Agassiz returned. Although he commended Scudder on his discovery that "a pencil is one of the best of eyes," he was disappointed at Scudder's brief recital of what he had seen the fish to be like. Agassiz bawled him out for not having looked very carefully, saying: "Why, you haven't even seen the most conspicuous features of the animal . . . look again, look again!" The next day Scudder reported that he noticed that the fish has symmetrical sides with paired organs, and ventured to ask what he should do next. "Oh, look at your fish!" Agassiz urged, "Go on, go on." So for three long days he placed that fish before Scudder's eyes forbidding him to look at anything else, or to use any artificial aid. "Look, look, look," was Agassiz' repeated injunction until at long last Scudder learned to see everything that his professor saw in the fish, a lesson in perception which Scudder believed was the best legacy the professor left to him.

Opportunity and place in space, as well as time, are important variables in controlling the nature of the perceptual field. As the vehicle of our perceiving, our bodies provide the platform from which we make our observations, and important changes in the location of this platform inevitably affect our perception. We may get up too late in the morning to appreciate the sun rise, or be seated at the wrong end of the football stadium to see the touchdown scored, or, in another sense, be standing too close to the trees to see the forest. Ability to change or control our vantage point in time and space is essential to overcome many limitations restricting the scope and precision of our perceptions.

WHAT WE SEE DEPENDS ON OUR GOALS AND VALUES

Goals and the techniques of reaching them are differentiations people make to achieve need satisfaction or, as the perceptual psychologists put it, the maintenance and enhancement of the self. Some goals and techniques are perceived as positive or satisfying and, hence, to be sought. Others are perceived as negative, destructive, or humiliating to the self and, therefore, to be avoided. In the beginning, for young children, differentiations of goals and techniques are highly specific, but as we grow and develop we begin to perceive that some of them are more or less alike in their effectiveness to yield or inhibit need satisfaction. The differentiation of goals and techniques that have common value serves as a kind of frame of reference for making further differentiations. Perceptual psychologists call such frames of reference "values."

Whereas goals and techniques apply to specific aspects of behavior, values are differentiations of a generic rather than a specific character and, thus, affect a much wider field of behavior. For all students of behavior, including both psychologists and teachers, a person's values are, therefore, of great importance in understanding the behavior of others. When a person's values are known it often becomes possible to predict with great accuracy how he may behave in given situations.

In less technical terms, a person's system of values are part of his belief-disbelief system, philosophy, or frame of mind. Values are those beliefs one holds about the relative worth, utility, or importance of various goals and techniques. A system of values implies that some degree of excellence or some sort of status in a scale of preferences has been established. We know what the value of something is to an individual by the way it is sought, shunned, or protected by him.

An individual often is not able to identify his own values. He doesn't know "what to think" about the value of some things. And he cannot "put into words" much of what he does believe about values. Values differ greatly in the degree of clarity with which they are perceived. Some values will be crystal clear in the individual's perceptual organization so that he is able to identify them precisely and to talk about them aptly and succinctly. Others will be so vaguely differentiated that he is unable to recognize or report them. In many instances outsiders may be able to observe a value affecting our perceptions which we, ourselves, may be unable to identify clearly.

When goals and values have been differentiated and have successfully served the person in the satisfaction of his need for adequacy, they *tend to persist* as a part of the field of organization of that person. The more strongly values lead to satisfaction of need, the greater is the differentiation from the remainder of the field, and the greater is the likelihood of persistence. It is a curious fact that negative values—our "don'ts"—are usually stronger and last longer than positive values—our "do's." Negative values are things which threaten the organization of the individual, and are perceived as objects to avoid. For example, a teacher may give up the practice of giving out gold stars to motivate her pupils to greater effort when someone points out the harmful implications of this practice, since the dispensing of such minor awards was only mildly related to making her feel adequate anyhow. But ask the same teacher to give up her practice of punishing children who are caught stealing or cheating, which she clearly perceives as unacceptable behavior to be stopped at any cost, and her reactions will be drastically different.

Once differentiated and established, values exert a selective effect on later perceptions and, consequently, on behavior. In other words, what we see and do is strongly influenced by our values. The peculiar *patterns* imposed upon perception by goals and values produces much of the uniqueness of behavior that is called the individual's personality or, in other terms, the individual's frame of mind.

CONCEPT OF SELF AFFECTS WHAT WE SEE

Perceptual psychologists make a big thing of what they call the "phenomenal self." They think that the self is the most important variable affecting perception. What we believe and how we behave are largely determined by (1) how we perceive ourselves, and (2) how we perceive the situations in which we are involved. The self, according to this view, is the most basic and most stable part of the individual's phenomenal field and is the point of reference for everything he does.

Human beings are continually and insatiably engaged in a never-ending effort to achieve an adequate self. If this is true, it follows that the self perceptions we possess have a tremendous influence in determining every behavior. The phenomenal self gives continuity and consistency to each individual's personality. It provides the central core around which all other perceptions are organized. When the individual's phenomenal self is understood, the various and diverse behaviors of people often become consistent and predictable.

The self concept results from present and past perceptions of himself. We might call it the map which an individual consults in order to understand himself, especially during moments of crisis or choice. The self concept is the means by which an individual can symbolize and reduce his own vast complexity to workable and usable terms. In this sense, it represents for the individual his generalized self. It is himself from his own point of view.

The self provides the frame of reference from which everything else is observed. The more closely related an experience is perceived to the phenomenal self, the greater will be its effect upon behavior. Education has been reasonably successful in making information available to students, but has been far less successful in helping students to make that information so much a part of themselves that they would behave differently as a result. Much of this information "goes in one ear and out the other," as we sometimes say, because students do not see that it has anything to do with them. No relationship is perceived between it and the phenomenal self.

BELIEVING AND PERCEIVING

As we have seen, perceptual psychologists recognize that beliefs (often called "values") have a great deal of influence on perception. Psychologists in general seem to have an aversion to the use of the term "belief." Perhaps they object to the religious and philosophical connotations usually associated with that word. For some perceptual psychologists the term belief is synonymous with meaning or perception, which may explain why they prefer to talk about value instead of belief. "Value" is a limited or specialized term. Properly, it refers to only a single aspect of our beliefs—about what is more or less worthy, beneficial, desirable, or good. The study of value from a philosophical point of view is called axiology, which represents only one of several branches of philosophy. The term "values" cannot be stretched to account for our beliefs about what is so, true, or real (metaphysics), or about what is beautiful (aesthetics), or about what is the right way for people to behave (ethics). Values fail to cover all of the several different kinds of beliefs which exert a selective effect on perceptions. Therefore, because it is a more inclusive term, in this book we prefer to use the word "beliefs" rather than "values."

If beliefs and perceptions are not synonymous, at least they are very closely related. A person believes what he perceives to be so. And in return, what one perceives is strongly influenced by what one already believes to be the case. For example, most people today believe the world is round rather than flat. However, as small children we came to believe this because our parents and teachers told us so. Later, we learned that an approaching sailboat appearing to rise up out of the water was evidence that the earth really is a sphere, just as portrayed by our schoolroom globes. However, recent photographs of the earth's curved rim taken from orbiting space ships invariably bring forth such exclamations as, "See, the world really is round!" Prior to the availability of these remarkable pictures, for most of us the belief that the world is round involved about as much faith as perception.

"Seeing is believing," the old saying goes, and there is considerable truth to it. But believing is more than just seeing. Although it helps, we do not first have to see things in order to believe them. Frequently, quite the opposite is true; we first have to believe things before we can see them. People who believe in ghosts usually see more of them than people who don't believe in them. Those who see ghosts do so as the result of believing that such things can and do exist—just as others are unable to see ghosts on grounds that they couldn't possibly exist. When we think for more than a moment about what is believing and what is seeing our heads begin to spin.

Seeing affects believing, and, likewise, believing affects seeing. The relationship between seeing and believing is intimate and transactional. Which comes first or wields the stronger influence doesn't matter. All that matters is that we keep in mind the two act and react upon each other so unceasingly that we cannot consider one without taking the other into account.

As much as they may overlap, believing is not exactly the same thing as perceiving. Believing indicates some sort of evaluation of what is perceived. Beliefs are perceptions about what is taken and held as true, valid, or genuine. Likewise, disbeliefs are perceptions about events which are judged false, invalid, or unreal. Beliefs and disbeliefs are convictions or persuasions about which perceptions should be accepted in faith and trust, or rejected in doubt and suspicion. Believing involves our giving or not giving credence to perceptions. It is something *done to* perceptions, much as we sort our mail and put it into various piles and pigeonholes.

Beliefs, like perceptions, may be defined as predispositions for action. Our beliefs are the bases on which we are ready and willing to act in a certain manner under appropriate conditions. In this sense, believing and perceiving are synonymous—to the point that one might easily be used in place of the other. If we define beliefs as "evaluations of perceptions" we might modify the basic concept of the perceptual view and say that the behavior of a person is the result of (1) what he *believes* about himself, (2) what he *believes* about the situations in which he is involved, and (3) the interactions of these two.

BELIEVING AND BEHAVING

How a person behaves in any particular situation depends to a considerable extent upon how he perceives that situation. And how a person perceives any given situation involves his outlook, or point of view. Coloring the perceptual lenses through which an individual views the world around him (and this is the point we wish to stress) are his *beliefs*. What is more, the beliefs which are most powerful in their influence on behavior are the person's fundamental philosophic beliefs pertaining to the nature of man, reality, knowledge, values, ethics, and the like. In short, believing and behaving are closely related.

In education, a teacher's beliefs may give direction to his classroom practices. Or, it is just as likely that his beliefs are drawn from his experience, developed to explain and justify his actions in the classroom. A teacher may accept or subscribe to a set of beliefs (or philosophy) simply because it supports what he is already doing. Believing may lead behaving, or follow it.

The practices of a particular teacher may be consistent with the philosophy he espouses, or it may not. A teacher doesn't always practice what he preaches. He may pay official homage to one set of beliefs but base his practices on quite another one. The discrepancy between what teachers say they believe about education and what they actually do, or fail to do, in classrooms with pupils is called the beliefs—practices dilemma, which we have already discussed.

The beliefs on which a teacher actually operates in the classroom may be unknown to him or unrecognized by him. A big portion of teaching is carried on in what appears to be a theoretical vacuum. When teachers are asked, "Why did you use this practice in this situation?" or "What did you expect students to gain from this experience?" they give you, more often than not, only blank stares or vague responses. Apparently, some teachers make important teaching decisions capriciously, for no reason they can think of. They simply "feel like" doing this rather than that. Many teaching decisions are made routinely, with no more explanation than "I do it this way because that is how others do it" or "I've always done it like that" or "That's how I was told to do it." Such teachers abdicate all responsibility for what they do by leaning on some external authority. They do whatever "they say," and let them take the blame if it fails. This being the case, they see no need for theoretical explanations of their teaching practices.

Teaching which lacks any recognizeable theoretical orientation is usually poor teaching. Teachers who are unable to relate their practices to beliefs are lost, adrift, and forced to snatch at passing straws, which may account for the rapid succession of fads in American education. However, it would be a mistake to conclude that poor teaching is theory-less. It is based on some sort of theory, even though the teacher is unable to identify, recognize, or talk about it. Unseen, unacknowledged, unspeakable theories are usually faulty. Poor teaching is always based on poor theory, or, at least, theory which is poorly put together and poorly related to practice.

Even when a teacher is made aware of the discrepancy between his beliefs and behavior he may dismiss it by rationalizing that "what sounds good in theory does not always work out in practice." A charming characteristic of the American mind is that it seems to be able to lie down beside logical inconsistencies and go right to sleep. Toleration of logically incompatible practices and philosophy is the source of much of what is wrong in our system of education.

Given a particular philosophic position, one teaching practice is *not* as good as any other. Some practices can be squared with that point of view and others cannot—because they belong, logically, to a different and opposing philosophic species. Each teacher needs to develop patterns of teaching practices which are logically consistent with *some* coherent philosophy if his teaching is to make any sort of positive or purposeful impact.

Like the fat lady who ate the best things off six different diets and wondered why she couldn't lose weight, a teacher cannot employ just any old teaching tricks and techniques that appear attractive, disrespective of the philosophic assumptions underlying them, and expect to make educational headway. There are undoubtedly as many different philosophies as reducing diets. Each of them implies a different educational menu. True, some of the same items of educational practices may be included on two or more, or even all, of the possible philosophic diets. However, there can be an overlap of individual items and yet be important differences in total patterns. Specific acts of teaching behavior can be understood clearly only in relationship to total patterns of different philosophies or belief systems. In Chapter 3 we will examine some of these patterns.

3

PATTERNS OF BELIEF

PEOPLE HAVE BELIEFS of many kinds. We have sets or systems of beliefs, which have both depth and breadth. We have deep-seated beliefs and shallow-rooted beliefs, far-reaching beliefs, and beliefs of limited scope. We have beliefs about knowledge and beliefs about action, or theoretical beliefs and practical beliefs. All of the different kinds and qualities of beliefs are mixed together in complex systems of beliefs. If we are to make any sense out of our patterns of beliefs, we must examine some theories about how belief systems are organized and structured.

STRUCTURE AND ORGANIZATION
OF BELIEF SYSTEMS

We have already reviewed Combs' and Syngg's theory regarding the organization of the perceptual field. If we can use the terms belief and perception interchangeably, as they suggest, then one's perceptual organization may be viewed as a belief system. Another interesting theory of the organization and structure of belief systems is offered by Dr. Milton Rokeach, who has done much research into the nature of beliefs and personality.[1]

Rokeach sees three layers or levels or regions of beliefs within a system: (1) central, (2) intermediate, and (3) peripheral. In the *central* region we hold our basic beliefs about the nature of physical

[1] Milton Rokeach, *The Open and Closed Mind* (New York: Basic Books, Inc., 1960).

reality and such beliefs about the social world. For example, this is where we hold our beliefs as to whether the world is basically a friendly or unfriendly place to live in, whether our authority figures are loving or punishing, whether people in general are characteristically to be trusted or feared, and whether the future is to be regarded with security or apprehension. In the central region we also hold self-beliefs about our relationship to physical space, beliefs about our self-identity, our autonomy or dependence on others, and beliefs about our self-worth. In the *intermediate* region we hold beliefs about authority, ranging from tentative reliance on authority at one extreme to arbitrary, absolute reliance on authority at the other extreme. Here, too, are the beliefs we have about other people who have beliefs—our acceptance or rejection of people who agree and disagree with us. In the *peripheral* region we hold specific and detailed beliefs about politics, religion, sex, and, among other things, education.

Most of us are conscious, in the everyday course of events, only of our peripheral beliefs and, to some extent, our intermediate beliefs. These are the beliefs we state openly, such as: "Democracy is the best form of government." "There is a God." "Girls who run around with married men get into trouble." "George Washington crossed the Delaware." "It is going to rain tomorrow." "George is nuts if he believes that." "You can't trust anyone." "Capital punishment should be abolished." "Money isn't everything." "Rock-and-roll is noise, not music."

Some of these beliefs we can trace to related beliefs in the central region, but most we cannot, or usually do not. Our central beliefs may be so deeply buried we cannot verbalize them. We may keep them a secret even from ourselves. Some of these central beliefs can only be inferred from our behavior, a slip of the tongue, a compulsive act, an expressive gesture, the choices we make. Or, they may be expressed in our expectations and in our predispositions to act in certain ways. Rokeach calls such beliefs "primitive" beliefs, a term he means to be roughly analogous to the primitive terms of an axiomatic system in mathematics or science:

Every person may be assumed to have formed early in life some set of beliefs about the world he lives in, the validity of which he does not question and, in the ordinary course of events, is not prepared to question. Such beliefs are unstated but basic. It is out of some such set of "pre-ideological" primitive beliefs that the total belief-disbelief system grows.[2]

Sometimes we say we believe something when we really don't. Some of our beliefs are merely "official" or "formal," something we accept or reject merely to satisfy the expectations of others in order to win approval or avoid trouble. Such beliefs may relate to our intermediate beliefs about authority. Knowing this, we can tell what each other honestly believes only by taking into account everything we say and do. As the old saying goes, "It is not what you say but what you do that counts."

Belief-disbelief systems, Rokeach suggests, are more psychological than logical. The difference between the psychology and logic of belief systems is simply this: Psychology describes how people *do* organize and relate their beliefs, while logic establishes how people *ought* to organize and relate beliefs. In logical systems, individual beliefs are inter-related or in communication with each other according to the rules of logic. On the other hand, in psychological systems individual beliefs may be inter-related without necessarily being logically connected. If our belief-disbelief systems had to be logical ones, very few of us could be said to have them.

Most of us permit beliefs within our individual systems to contradict one another. We do this by allowing little or no communication between the parts and the regions which make up the structure of our belief-disbelief systems, even though the potential for communication is there. For example, one of my maturing daughters once confessed, "I know there can't possibly be a real live Santa Claus, but I believe in him just the same—because I want there to really be one so much." Likewise, many of us demonstrate the ability to separate our Sunday from our weekday beliefs, failing to see any contradiction between our theological belief in man's original sin and our everyday faith in his inherent goodness. This same mechanism, called compartmentalization, is used in education: believing we should foster creativity, but also believing children should not be allowed to color cows purple; being for individualization of instruction, but believing that there is no practical alternative to having all students work on the same page of the same book at the same time; believing that interscholastic football

2 *Ibid.,* p. 40.

should be abolished, but believing that the faculty should get first crack at the seats on the fifty-yard line.

Our need to see ourselves as logically consistent, however, usually blinds us to our contradictions. Whenever our attention is called to such inconsistencies we are likely to be resentful, to feel threatened, and to clam up. We must keep such pairs or sets of beliefs isolated in water-tight compartments in order to prevent the force of logic from washing one or both of them away. So we close them off, not only from each other, but also from any and all pressures to submit them to questions or critical analysis. We take our beliefs seriously, regard them as deeply personal, and become extremely proud and protective of them—which makes it difficult, indeed, to be dispassionately intelligent about them.

There are any number of ways of looking at or theorizing about belief systems. In this chapter we shall look at both the structure and content of belief systems along three different, although similar and sometimes overlapping, dimensions: (1) open and closed, (2) scientific and prescientific, (3) experimental and nonexperimental.

OPEN AND CLOSED SYSTEMS

Some belief systems are loaded with isolated and compartmentalized beliefs. Such beliefs are thickly insulated against any chance of being short-circuited by other conflicting beliefs within the system and are tenaciously protected against threatening questions from without. When this is the case, we say the system is closed. Beliefs in open systems have not been enshrined, but allowed to grow out in the air and sunshine, to communicate freely, and to stand the test of logic and intelligent criticism. Closed systems hold their answers as absolutely conclusive, final, settled once and for all, whereas open systems hold their answers up to further questioning, testing, and possible revision which subsequent evidence may require.

Rokeach defines the extent to which a person's belief system is open or closed as being the extent to which the person, in any given situation in which he must act, "can receive, evaluate, and act on relevant information received from the outside on its own intrinsic merits, unencumbered by irrelevant factors in the situation arising from within the person or from the outside."[3] Rokeach offers such things as logically unrelated beliefs, habits, cues, motives, needs, anxieties, and so forth, as examples of irrelevant internal pressures that interfere with the free and open reception of information. By irrelevant external pressures he means those pressures of reward and punishment arising from external authority, such as may be exerted by parents, peers, teachers, and other authority figures, as well as group and institutional norms, or social and cultural norms.

The open-minded person is able to distinguish relevant and irrelevant information in any situation and react appropriately, correctly, in terms of what is relevant; the closed-minded person is not. The more open one's belief system or mind, the more one's evaluating and acting on information proceeds on its own merits, independently, in accord with requirements *inside* of the present situation. The more closed one's belief system or mind, the more one operates dependently, in accord with expectations about how some *outside* source wishes us to think and behave. An open-minded person more strongly resists externally imposed reinforcements, or rewards and punishments, than does a closed-minded person.

A person with a closed mind characteristically opposes far more than he supports. And he feels more strongly about what he believes and disbelieves than does an open-minded person. He is fiercely loyal to his own side and bitterly opposes everything and everyone else. He knows much more about what he accepts than what he rejects, tending to lump all his disbeliefs together in one package, tarring them all equally with the same brush. He accepts and respects information only from sources that agree with his point of view or that are approved by his authority figures, turning a blind eye and a deaf ear to all other sources of information. In effect, the person with a closed mind says, "Don't confuse me with the facts, my mind is already made up."

The mind which is already made up tends to view the outside world as a threatening place. The world of nature is an ominous jungle in which one can easily get lost, hurt, or eaten by bears. The world outside of his closed system is an evil, ugly, unpleasant

[3] *Ibid.,* p. 57.

place, and the people who live in it cannot be trusted to do the right and good thing. They are uncivilized beasts who are likely to invade your home, steal your food and other valuable possessions.

The person with a closed mind is filled with visions of doom and gloom. Lightning, fire, floods, and earthquakes are sure to get him if he doesn't watch out. He is leary of the future. He doesn't like risk, and bets only on sure things. The fear of failure and disappointment has him firmly in its grip.

The person with an open mind is characteristically more accepting than rejecting. He holds his beliefs and disbeliefs in relatively logical relationships, and is willing to question, analyze, and re-examine them from time to time. He avoids quick, unwarranted generalizations about what he does and doesn't believe. He views the world as being essentially friendly, trusts others, and is generally confident about the future. He regards authority figures as essentially helpful and loving. He sees himself as an adequate person, and is well adjusted to the realities of living in an uncertain-but-predictable world of nature. He demands a great deal of independence and autonomy for himself.

In an open society such as ours, it is widely assumed, at least on the surface, that open minds are good and closed minds are bad. In television westerns it seems that the good guys usually wear open minds under their white hats and the unshaven bad guys use their black hats to cover closed minds. In education the good teachers are usually pictured as attractive, pleasant, sympathetic, wise, and open-minded; the bad teachers are invariably closed-minded, heavy-handed, crabby, unreasonable, hateful, ugly old witches who delight in making the lives of little children miserable. We praise democracy as an open system and condemn dictatorships as closed systems. We glorify the objective, unprejudiced, open-mindedness of scientists and vilify the subjective, prejudiced, closed-mindedness of bigots and zealots.

We often hear broad-minded people called "liberals" and closed- or narrow-minded people called "conservatives." Freedom, flexibility, and egalitarianism are associated with the liberal "left," and restriction, rigidity, and dogmatism are associated with the conservative "right." This is a mistake. The liberal left can be just as rigidly dogmatic as the conservative right. And the conservative right-wing has frequently championed the cause of individual liberty. Today's conservatives were yesterday's liberals, just as to-day's liberals may become tomorrow's conservatives. In American politics the liberals are a left-wing party, but in many European countries the liberals are a right-wing party. To speak carelessly of liberals as open-minded and conservatives as closed-minded can lead only to confusion and misunderstanding.

The term *liberal* suggests an emancipation from convention, tradition, or dogma. However, liberalism may vary from belief that institutions and practices should be altered to fit changing conditions to belief in or preference for complete lawlessness. On one hand it suggests a commendable experimentalism, relativism, and open-mindedness and on the other a highly questionable un-orthodoxy, radicalism, or outright irresponsibility. The term *con-servative,* in a die-hard or closed sense, suggests a stubborn, trucu-lent desire to retain and maintain existing institutions, procedures, and ways, as well as to resist and suspect proposals for change. In a more positive or open sense, however, it suggests a strong sense of tradition and social stability, preferring gradual change and development with preservation of the best elements of the past to abrupt or revolutionary change.

One needs to be very careful in using such terms as liberal and conservative, left and right, egalitarian and authoritarian, particularly when talking about open and closed systems of belief. Open-mindedness or closed-mindedness is not so much a matter of *what* one believes as it is a matter of *how* one believes. In his studies of the organization of belief systems along the dimension of the open and closed mind, Rokeach is primarily concerned with the *structure* rather than the *content* of beliefs, while recognizing that a complete understanding of the nature of belief systems would include both the study of its structure and its content. His work is intended to give us insight into the general nature of all belief systems rather than solely their open and closed extremes. Comparison of extreme high dogmatic (closed) and low dogmatic (open) groups of people does not mean that people can be classi-fied simply into one or the other category. Nor should it imply a static condition for belief systems. There is no such thing as an absolutely open mind, or an absolutely closed mind.

A completely open mind would have to be an empty mind. A completely closed mind would have to be one that is entirely out of business. We would have to reject both extremes as desirable outcomes of education. We hope that youngsters will come out of school with minds that are alive and functioning—open*ing and* clos*ing*—discriminating in what is let in, what is kept, and what is let go. A mind or system of beliefs ought to be capable of opening in order to let out the old, the stale, the useless, and to let in the new, the fresh, and the useful. But it also ought to be capable of closing if it is to hold anything for more than a fleeting moment. A mind must close on an idea, at least tentatively, if any sort of decision is to be made or any sort of action is to be taken. A closed mind is dogmatic only if and when tentative working closures become final, fixed, frozen. Permanently frozen minds, whether frozen closed or frozen open, are incapable of intelligent thought and action.

PRESCIENTIFIC AND SCIENTIFIC PATTERNS OF THOUGHT

Although we may be reluctant to admit it, many of us have relatively closed belief systems. We are the products of closed patterns of thought. With all the individual liberty that is afforded American citizens we have inherited through our culture strongly enforced patterns of prescientific thinking and behaving from which we may not deviate without fear of severe punishment (more psychological or social than physical). The whole educational enterprise in America (which includes homes, churches, and information media such as newspapers, radio, and television, as well as the schools) is steeped in practices of propriety which stem from systems of belief over two thousand years old. Passing generations have known that their institutions, beliefs, and customs which they cherish can be preserved only by engendering them in the young. Throughout the history of mankind education has been used universally as a tool for the deliberate control and direction of the growth of the young into the mold of firmly established cultural systems and patterns.

Education has been the glue which has held together the old systems of the past, and which gums up all efforts to establish new and different systems. All this makes schools the stage for the conflict between opposing patterns of thought within our cultural heritage: the older or *prescientific* outlook, and the newer or *scientific* outlook. During the past three or four centuries the scientific mode of thought has been developing with rapidly increasing tempo, and quite probably within our lifetime or, at least, the lifetime of the children we teach, this comparatively open pattern of thought will predominate, and ours will become a thoroughly scientific culture. When this happens, our children will experience a way of life quite different from the one that has seemed right and natural to us and our fathers.

Right now, all of us are feeling the upheaval of the passing of the old prescientific era. As the scientific era gathers momentum we find ourselves caught in a tremendous and turbulent conflict which is shaking us loose from our foundations. New ideals and beliefs, new processes and practices, and new ways of life are challenging cherished old ideals and beliefs, familiar old processes and practices, and comfortable old ways of life. The confusion and frustration those of us concerned with teaching feel within ourselves during this overwhelming transition period can be made understandable by examining the fundamental distinctions between the prescientific and scientific patterns of thought.

One of the most interesting contrasts of the differences between prescientific and scientific modes of thought is made by Wendell Johnson, eminent semanticist, in his book called *People in Quandaries.*[4] Like John Dewey, his thesis is that science, clearly understood, can be used in everyday life as a sound basis for warmly human and efficient living. While many people think of science primarily as a body of knowledge, a subject in the school curriculum, or as information and gadgets resulting from the labors of laboratory men, Johnson views science as a generally practical *method* whereby ordinary human beings in their daily lives may forestall shock and disappointment, avoid or resolve serious conflicts, increase their efficiency and zest for living—in short, live sanely.

METHOD OF SOLVING PROBLEMS

On no other issue do the prescientific and scientific minds differ more significantly than on their methods of dealing with problems. Persons with a scientific frame of mind approach their problems

[4] Wendell Johnson, *People in Quandaries* (New York: Harper & Row, 1946).

by asking clear, well-defined questions. They inquire into the problem by making observations, in a calm and unprejudiced manner. Then they report and use these observations in such a way as to answer the questions that were asked to begin with. Any pertinent beliefs or assumptions that were held before they began their inquiry are revised in light of the observations made and the answers obtained. Then more questions are asked in accordance with the newly revised notions, further observations are made, new answers arrived at, beliefs and assumptions are again revised, after which the whole process starts over again. It never stops.

an untenable stereotype

Persons of a prescientific set of mind go about solving problems by an entirely different method. First of all, they avoid as much responsibility for dealing with problems as the law allows. They look to someone else to take care of their problems for them. When problems cannot be ignored or pushed aside, they depend on advice and detailed instructions from someone in authority such as a parent, teacher, priest, politician, or, in modern times, a scientist. This is the irresponsibly innocent, helplessly dependent approach we find to be a charming characteristic in children.

The prescientific method is authoritarian, and its distinctive characteristics are rules, rigidity, revolt, revolution, and re-establishment. Its authority resides not only in certain anointed persons but also in some book of rules. Its games are always played "according to Hoyle," without any question as to who Hoyle is or was. The source of his authority goes unquestioned, and no one dreams that these rules could possibly be revised to fit new circumstances or needs. The prescientific approach establishes beliefs, customs, and rules of conduct on authority, sanctifies them, and gives them the force of law now and forever after. They are set in cement, solidified in their original forms, to stand rigidly as something to rely on, to put one's faith in. Time goes on, and the conditions which gave rise to these standards of belief and practice pass, fade away, and are forgotten. While everybody talks about the old ideals, nobody does anything about them. They no longer bear any relation to the values and practices which function privately in everyday life, although they are included in all official ceremonies and public rituals. Since the old ideals were established as absolute, permanent truth, they cannot be changed gracefully. The source of their authority is usually remote, vague, and unattainable. They remain fixed until they become so intolerably out of line with fact that they incite bloody revolt. The old authoritarian establishment is overthrown violently. Then, still thinking prescientifically, a new authority is installed with a new revolutionary set of beliefs, customs, and rules of conduct—which are promptly proclaimed to be the gift of the Great Giver of Truth, and the process of solidification begins all over again, possessing within it the seeds of the next revolt against rigidity.

USE OF LANGUAGE

The language of a person with a scientific orientation, according to Wendell Johnson, is designed to be factually meaningful, clear, and valid. The scientific person differentiates sharply between assumptions and statements of fact, and asks two important questions: "What do you mean?" and "How do you know?" Scientific language emphasizes questions—answerable questions. On the principle that the clarity of the question determines the clarity of the answer, only clearly and precisely stated questions are tolerated; vague or meaningless questions are shunned as being a waste of time and energy. Every statement conveys information about the speaker as well as information about whatever the speaker is talking about. Thus, the person of scientific orientation is frequently heard to qualify his statements with such self-references as "It seems to me," "From my point of view," "Such and such appears to be the case." There is little or no tendency to speak through the voice of another, or, as Johnson puts it, to ventriloquize. Instead, the person of a scientific orientation recognizes the voice of the Law as the voice of the Judge himself, and realizes that what he says are his own judgments and evaluations even though he may be quoting another man's words.

The language of a person with a prescientific orientation, in contrast, is designed to control the behavior of those spoken to. The validity of pronouncements by properly appointed authority is not to be questioned. The prescientific person tends to regard assumptions and statements of fact as the same. Prescientific language emphasizes answers rather than questions. Its questions are usually vague and meaningless, and the answers to such questions cause misunderstandings and disagreements, and give rise to misinformation and misleading theories. In evaluating statements of factual significance, self-reference is ignored in favor of frequent and unqualified use of forms of the verb *to be* in flat-footed statements such as "It is so." "These are the facts." "You were wrong." "I am right." There is a marked tendency in the prescientific orientation to ventriloquize or to speak as though with the voice of another. They do not seem to realize that it is their own judgments and evaluations that they are pulling out of the mouths of the authorities and straw men they quote.

VIEW OF REALITY

The person of a scientific outlook tends to see a heterogeneous world rather than a homogeneous one. For him the world consists of dissimilar ingredients, and is made up of parts or elements that are not unified into a single, simple, master pattern. His world is complex, filled with endless variety and diversity, and he enjoys discerning, demarcating, and analyzing the differences he sees. Likewise, the scientific viewpoint welcomes disagreement, dissension, and controversy as natural and necessary in a world which gives rise to a never-ending series of differences. Exceptions to the rule are sought rather than ignored or buried. Differences are valued as much or more than similarities. As one important consequence, the individual is valued as an individual, and not discounted merely as an example of a type or class.

The person of a prescientific outlook has a better eye for similarities than for differences. He likes to see a world in which there are no discordant elements. In his world things of a type are expected to be always what they are supposed to be, to stay put, and to show no variation. He likes things to hold still, and when they don't, he may become quite ill and call out to "Stop the world, I want to get off!" His is a simple, static world in which everything goes according to some master plan. The prescientific viewpoint tries to homogenize reality by blending, grinding, or reducing it to particles of a uniform size, distributing them evenly to achieve unvarying uniformity. Rules are venerated, and strict conformity to them is demanded. As a result, the individual is not particularly important except as he represents a general type or classification.

Not all scientists, it should be noted, are necessarily of a scientific mind. One can, as many do, work in the field of science and hold a frame of mind which is essentially prescientific in the sense of the discussion here. Likewise, so-called humanists may be quite scientific in point of view. This is the difficulty in using loosely such terms as scientific and prescientific in discussions of belief systems. No apology is intended, however, as our purpose has been to dramatize in rather bold contrast the extremes of these well-known types of patterns of belief. The terms are useful if one recognizes their limitations.

SCIENTIFIC ATTITUDE AND DEMOCRACY

John Dewey, among others, made a long and concerted effort to wean people away from the prescientific or theological outlook. He tried to hitch the concept of democracy up to the scientific mode of thought. Dewey was concerned about the eclipse of faith in democracy, particularly just prior to World War II. At that time democracy was challenged by totalitarian dictators of the Fascist or extreme right-wing variety on the grounds that human nature is such that people cannot be trusted as the source of authority in government, just as it was challenged by communist dictators on the left on economic grounds. He noted that comparatively few people were influenced by the attitude of science. Instead of forming their beliefs on the basis of factual evidence, gained by intelligent inquiry, the great majority of persons seemingly form their beliefs by habit, accidents of circumstance, propaganda, personal and class bias. Dewey believed that the continued reliance on outmoded prescientific thought put the fate of democracy in danger, claiming that "The future of democracy is allied with the spread of the scientific attitude."[5]

Dewey saw the adoption of the scientific attitude as a democratic people's only protection against wholesale misleading propaganda, our own as well as that of the foreign enemy. It was his conviction that the extension of the use and influence of the scientific attitude was the sole guarantee that there could ever be masses of free citizens who are intelligent enough to meet the challenge of the problems they must deal with in a democratic society. Of

[5] John Dewey, *Freedom and Culture* (New York: G. P. Putnam's Sons, 1939), p. 148.

course, Dewey saw education as the chief means of spreading the scientific attitude, saying: "Until what shall be taught and how it shall be taught is settled on the basis of formation of the scientific attitude, the so-called educational work of the schools is a dangerously hit-or-miss affair as far as democracy is concerned."[6]

This close relationship which Dewey reasoned between science, democracy, and education is made clear throughout his philosophy of experimentalism, which is the third dimension of belief patterns to be dealt with in this chapter.

EXPERIMENTAL AND NON-EXPERIMENTAL BELIEFS

It was Dewey's observation that modern science provides the intellectual tools which make possible the reshaping and re-creating of the world through purposeful social action. He advocated the application of the scientific method, which was developed in the process of man's learning to understand the natural environment, to human affairs. This is the method of inquiry and discovery. It learns from its successes and failures, and is thereby self-correcting. As new, more effective procedures and products are discovered, older, less desirable ones can be discarded. Thus, by the same sort of continuous inquiry and experimentation, what is truthful or good in human conduct can be determined.

Inherent in the experimental approach is an opposition to fixed, unchanging principles of reality, morality, and conduct. Likewise, experimentalism rejects a dualism between intellect and action. Instead, it stands for the utilization of unfettered intelligence, the development of working hypotheses, and deliberate introduction of change or reconstruction. Experimentalism is predicated on the belief that programs of action in social affairs should be regarded as theories to be supported or rejected, as they are in the natural sciences, by the consequences they bring about.

Let us look at a synopsis of the characteristic beliefs of the experimental mind in contrast with the characteristic beliefs of the non-experimental mind. The lists below are by no means complete. Our purpose at this point in the discussion is not precision, but simply to provide an overview to help the reader to grasp the general picture.

[6] *Ibid.,* p. 150.

Characteristic Beliefs of the NON-EXPERIMENTAL MIND	*Characteristic Beliefs of the* EXPERIMENTAL MIND
1. Supernatural orientation. Holds a dualistic theory of reality which claims the universe is divided into two distinct and separate entities, the inner world of the mind and the outer world of matter. The spiritual and physical worlds are two independent realms of existence having only certain and limited points of contact with each other. Man has a soul which is apart, above, or beyond his physical organism.	1. Natural orientation. Believes in the continuity of nature, and rejects all forms of supernaturalism stemming from the dualistic beliefs of classical philosophy and theology that there is a spiritual realm which lies beyond experience. Mind and body are continuous, inseparable. Man doesn't really have a "spirit" which is separable from his body and the natural world.
2. There is some one final, ultimate end or purpose to which mankind aspires. Man's destiny is either determined by circumstances beyond his control or, if not, man can help mold his own destiny by bringing supernaturally inspired ideals and moral purposes to bear upon the course of natural events. Ends or goals are fixed, enduring, universal, absolute, having been decided upon from "on high" prior to and apart from passing situations of the moment.	2. Ends are never final. Every means is a temporary end until it is attained; every end becomes a means of carrying activity further as soon as it is achieved. Rejects externally supplied ends imposed by some authority which limit intelligence and permit nothing but a mechanical choice of means. Ends, or goals are flexible, experimental, subject to revision based on consideration of changing circumstance.
3. Absolutism. In quest of certainty, looking for the absolute reality, essence, or inner	3. Relativism. Nothing is or can be absolutely certain. Change is the basic characteristic of

nature of things. There is nothing new under the sun. Man can do nothing to alter the course of nature because all events have been predetermined by immutable natural and supernatural laws. Likes situations closed, settled, nailed down, fixed with as much certainty as possible. Reaching a condition in which there were no more problems would be the perfect life. Believes a statement of fact must be *either* true *or* untrue from all standpoints and conditions.

4. Man is basically a passive spectator in events which he is powerless to influence. Man gains knowledge by having things impressed upon his mind. He cannot know the world as it really is but only the impressions made on the mind. The mind is formed from without, as one molds or shapes a piece of clay. Knowledge is the sum total of what is known, as that is handed down by books and learned men. True knowledge is primarily mental; the more passive the mind the easier it is to impress knowledge upon it.

nature, and man has some degree of control over this change. Man is capable of managing his own destiny in an understandable and predictable world. What something is, totally independent of any observer or frame of reference, is a scientifically meaningless question. Likes situations kept open and flexible, relative to changing conditions. Welcomes the excitement and challenge of problems. Believes a statement of fact may be *both* true *and* untrue, depending on the standpoints and conditions of the observations.

4. Man is basically an active participator in the affairs of his world. Knowledge is gained by actively responding to things and by putting things to use and discovering the consequences that result. Man acts upon as well as reacts to his environment. He is not entirely shaped from without, but also shapes himself from within to a considerable extent. Man doesn't learn from books alone. Knowledge is not something one absorbs, as a sponge absorbs water; it is produced by purposeful activity.

5. Emotions are antithetical to the intellect. The intellect is pure light; the emotions are a disturbing heat. The mind turns outward to truth; the emotions turn inward to considerations of personal advantage and loss. In the absence of a moral code supported by absolute authority, bodily appetite and passion overpowers intelligence. Man's natural impulses are intrinsically depraved and must be controlled by a higher, external force. The ends and laws which regulate human conduct have been determined by the superior intelligence of an ultimate being.

6. Theoretical knowledge is derived from a higher source than practical experience. Practice is subordinate to knowledge, merely a means to it. The crudest kind of knowing is connected with everyday affairs and serves the purposes of ordinary individuals who have no intellectual interests. True knowledge is the result of purely theoretical insight on the part of scholars. Knowledge exists for its own sake free from practical considerations. The worth of a theory has nothing

5. Emotions and the intellect are closely connected, not opposed to each other. Knowledge separated from the emotional concerns of the knower simply is not possible. Man's primitive impulses are neither good nor evil, but become one or the other according to the objects for which they are employed. The use of the scientific method can be extended to solve the problems of men in the area of values and moral judgments. Questions of values and morals ought to be open to experimentation and intelligent inquiry. The source of moral authority is inside nature rather than outside of it.

6. Theory has to do with reorganizing practice instead of being complete on its own account in isolation from practice. Practical activities are intellectually narrow only insofar as they are routine or carried on under the dictates of authority for some disconnected purpose. Intellectual studies, instead of being opposed to the active pursuits of everyday affairs, stem from practical problems and seek to discover useful generalizations about them. Practice carried on in the

to do with how it works in practice.

7. Learning is the sum of impressions made on the mind as a result of the presentation of material to be known. Learning is the acquisition of knowledge by the minds of individuals. Truth exists ready-made somewhere; the task of the scholar is to find it. Inquiry into the accumulated body of knowledge must necessarily precede inquiry into practical, personal, or social problems. One must possess knowledge before he can put it to intelligent use.

absence of a sound theory is unintelligent, irresponsible, pointless.

7. Learning is an act of intelligent inquiry, not merely the acquisition and possession of knowledge. *Ac*quiring is always secondary and instrumental to *in*quiring. Knowledge is artificial and ineffective in the degree in which it is merely presented as truth to be accepted, held, and treasured for its own sake. When knowledge is cut off from use it loses all meaning or else becomes an object of aesthetic contemplation. The value of knowledge lies in its use in the future, in what it can be made to do.

pARt II

The Theory and Measurement of the Experimental Mind

U NDERSTANDING the relationship of teaching practices to philosophic beliefs is much too complex a problem to give adequate consideration to all of the possible patterns involved. Therefore, this book will focus sharply on a single dimension, namely, that of the "experimental mind." The choice of this dimension, based on John Dewey's philosophy of experimentalism, was made for two reasons: First, experimentalism is relevant to the problem. It is generally assumed that American education has been influenced, if not dominated, by Dewey's philosophy for much of the last half century. Whether one agrees with Dewey or not, it must be agreed that his philosophy has been a factor which cannot be overlooked in the development of American education. Second, experimentalism provides an available and useful theoretical framework for relating beliefs and practices in education. To a greater extent than any other major philosopher, John Dewey explicitly connects educational practices to philosophic beliefs. He conveniently describes specific teaching practices he believes are compatible with the fundamental assumptions of his general philosophy. Furthermore, he describes in detail those practices which are not compatible with his philosophy because they are grounded in fundamental assumptions he considers false.

Dewey's philosophy of experimentalism is a vast and complex system of thought. One might catch hold of it from many different approaches. In developing the theoretical framework for the study presented here, we have chosen to concentrate on Dewey's theory of the relation of knowledge and action. Dewey underscored the importance of this particular theory in his philosophy by using "A Study of the Relation of Knowledge and Action" as the subtitle to his book, *The Quest for Certainty*.[1] It is very interesting that in Dewey's own rejoinder to the critical analysis and evaluation of his philosophy by a group of eminent contemporaries[2] he chose to cite and reaffirm his statements in that particular book more frequently than and almost to the exclusion of all his many other works. Previously, Dewey had identified his central concern with this same sort of theory in *Democracy and Education*,[3] particularly in those chapters dealing with the topics of Method, Subject-matter and Theories of Knowing.

In *Democracy and Education*, Dewey was talking about teaching practices. At that stage of the game he was dealing with what might be called the theory of the relation of subject matter and method. This is never quite so clear until after one reads *The Quest for Certainty*, in which Dewey develops this notion into a more highly sophisticated theory at the level of knowledge and action. It then becomes clear that if we equate *knowledge* with *subject matter* and *action* with *method*, Dewey used the same basic framework in developing both theories.

It seems reasonable for us to borrow this framework from Dewey and use it to explore the relationship of philosophy and practice. It is this framework, as we have dug it out of Dewey and interpreted it, that is herein called "experimentalism" or the "experimental mind." The reader should be warned that it represents only one specialized interpretation of Dewey's philosophy of experimentalism, and does not pretend to embrace or exhaust the whole of it.

According to our analysis of Dewey's philosophy, the teacher whose beliefs about educational practices are in agreement with experimentalism will believe: (1) that subject matter and method are continuous or unified, and (2) that the characteristics of the teacher's classroom practices should be identical, insofar as possible,

[1] John Dewey, *The Quest for Certainty* (New York: G. P. Putnam's Sons, 1929).

[2] Paul A. Schilpp, ed., *The Philosophy of John Dewey* (New York: Tudor Publishing Company, 1939).

[3] John Dewey, *Democracy and Education* (New York: The Macmillan Company, 1916).

with the essentials of reflective thinking. On the other hand, the teacher whose beliefs about educational practices are in conflict or disagreement with experimentalism will believe: (1) that subject matter is something separated from method, that method is merely a means to the acquisition and possession of subject matter, and (2) that the characteristics of the teacher's classroom practices need not be identical with the features of reflective thinking, and that the value of any given classroom practice lies not in the methods used in learning, but, rather, in the amount and kind of subject matter presented to and retained by the students.

At the level of fundamental philosophic beliefs, the teacher whose beliefs are in agreement with experimentalism will believe in the natural continuity of such things as mind and body, emotions and intellect, empirical knowing and rational knowing, objective knowing and subjective knowing, activity and passivity in knowing, theory and practice, ends and means, knowing and doing. In contrast, the teacher whose fundamental philosophic beliefs are in conflict or disagreement with experimentalism will believe that all the above mentioned pairs of things are separated. For example, they may believe that mind is superior to matter, that practice is inferior to theory, that subjective knowing is much less valuable than objective or "pure" knowing, that certain ends justify questionable means, and so forth. Dewey calls such beliefs *dualisms*.

In Part II, we will look more closely at John Dewey's philosophy of experimentalism as a theoretical dimension for relating beliefs and practices in education.

4

A PHILOSOPHY OF
EXPERIMENTALISM

"PRAGMATISM," "instrumentalism," and "experimentalism" are terms frequently used interchangeably in connection with a system of thought which is identified by critics, sympathetic and hostile alike, as *the* American philosophy. "Pragmatism" is the original term, and was first used by Charles Sanders Peirce, recognized as the first of the Peirce-James-Dewey line of modern pragmatists. William James was chiefly responsible for popularizing pragmatism, both as a word and as a philosophy, even though he thought it an "oddly named thing." Dewey developed a comprehensive system of philosophy of pragmatism, and made an effort to change its name, first calling it "instrumentalism," and finally "experimentalism." Experimentalism, then, is a form of pragmatism; more specifically, it is John Dewey's brand of pragmatism.

WHAT IS PRAGMATISM?

In common usage, the word pragmatism has come to indicate the testing of the truth of ideas or theories by their practical consequences. Pragmatists share the characteristic American distrust for purely theoretical or intellectual activity, and demand to know, as James put it, the "cash value" of theoretical claims to truth, knowledge, or virtue. According to pragmatic philosophy, our intellectualizing and our theorizing must have as its purpose the attempt to deal with difficulties and solve problems that arise in the course of everyday events in the natural world of experience. The cash value of our ideas is to be found in the use to which ideas can be put. Of any claim to truth the pragmatist bluntly asks, what difference would it make if I believed it, and what consequences would follow if I act on it? If it would not make the slightest difference whether one believed it true or false and if it would in no way affect one's actions, then the theory has no cash value and is rejected as "idle" or false.

According to William James, theories are instruments. They are instruments that we use to enable us to understand and solve problems in our daily lives. The truth of ideas or theories, therefore, ought to be judged in terms of their success in performing this "instrumental" function. From judging that the function of theory is to deal with experience, James concludes that a theory is true if it works. This criterion for judging the "truth" or usefulness of theories, the pragmatists claim, is essentially the criterion of evaluation used in science.

For the pragmatist, then, truth is something that happens to an idea, rather than a fixed or static property of an idea. An idea can be neither true nor false until one discovers whether it works by testing it in terms of its consequences and its compatibility with other working ideas. Truth is relative. At various times in history certain theories and ideas may work satisfactorily, but with the passage of time, additional experience, and emerging problems, what is "true" changes, expands, and grows to meet developing conditions.

Pragmatists determine what is good or bad, or right or wrong, in much the same way they determine if an idea is true or false. Likewise, James developed a conception of the universe which closely corresponds to his theory of truth and goodness. For James there is no fixed world to be uncovered through experience, but rather a continuous quest for workable solutions to difficulties. He saw a pluralistic universe, with many diverse features and possibilities which cannot be known all at once, or once and for all. Instead the universe can be examined only tentatively, as it emerges and develops. Truth (like goodness, nature, and knowledge) grows and develops to meet new situations and new needs. This evolutionary quality of truth is the central characteristic of the pragmatic outlook.

Now that we have given a brief explanation of what pragmatism is—the thing which Dewey's philosophy is a special version of—let us next turn to a more detailed discussion of what his experimentalism is about.

EXPERIMENTAL METHOD

Experimentalists, along with all pragmatists, are not so much adherents to a doctrine as they are advocates of a method. They are generally committed to the belief that human beings, living together in societies, can learn to transfer the experimental method used in the natural sciences to the areas of the human and social sciences. Dewey constructed his theory of knowledge squarely upon the experimental method which he described as "the method of getting knowledge and making sure it is knowledge, and not mere opinion—the method of both discovery and proof."[1] It is upon this same method that Dewey also based his theories of value, and, of course, education. According to Dewey, the essentials of the experimental method are identical with the essentials of an educative experience.[2]

NATURALISM

Although method is central in the philosophy of experimentalism, the experimentalist is committed to something more than method. A naturalistic outlook is as essential to Dewey's philosophy as the experimental method of inquiry. One might go so far as to say that Dewey's entire philosophy should be designated as naturalism, or, at least, that the naturalistic spirit is fundamental to a clear understanding of it.

Naturalism is expressed positively in experimentalism as a belief in what is called the "continuity" of nature. Dewey's naturalistic outlook involves an unqualified acceptance of Darwin's principle of biological evolution, which shows clearly through his postulation of the continuity of all forms of nature—human, organic, and physical. The influence of Darwin's *The Origin of Species,* which incidentally was first published in the year of Dewey's birth, 1859, is revealed in Dewey's conviction that there is no breach of continuity between operations of inquiry and biological operations and

[1] John Dewey, *Democracy and Education* (New York: The Macmillan Company, 1916), p. 393.
[2] *Ibid.,* p. 192.

physical operations. By "continuity" he means that intellectual or rational operations grow out of organic activities, without being identical with that form from which they emerge.[3]

In what is perhaps Dewey's clearest summation of his philosophy of experimentalism, Chapter XXV of *Democracy and Education,* he opposes *continuity* to *dualism,* using the term "dualism" to represent the traditional theories about reality and knowledge which are dependent upon the presupposition of a split between the physical world and the mental world. He says:

A number of theories of knowing have been criticized in the previous pages. In spite of their differences from one another, they all agree in one fundamental respect which contrasts with the theory which has been positively advanced. The latter assumes *continuity;* the former state or imply certain division, separation, or antitheses, technically called dualisms.[4]

Dewey frequently emphasizes the organic and functional relation between parts and wholes, and embraces the belief that the evolution of nature is the record of the activity and making of wholes or organisms which cannot be analyzed into discrete elements or reduced to the sum of their parts. This position gives experimentalism much in common with Gestalt psychology. This bent can best be seen in Dewey's characteristic style of philosophizing. His favorite tactic in argumentation is to interpret problems as stemming from some philosophic dualism and to show the fallacy of the two extreme and separate sides of this dualism (as thesis and antithesis) and then to show the natural continuity or relation which reunites both within some inclusive framework (synthesis).

Using this mode of argument, Dewey rejects the theories of knowledge of both idealism and realism, saying that "knowing is not the act of an outside spectator but of a participator inside the natural and social scene."[5] He also sees a relationship between this unnatural split between matter and mind and the artificial barriers which have separated the rich from the poor, noblemen from the

---

[3] John Dewey, *Logic, The Theory of Inquiry* (New York: Holt, Rinehart, and Winston, Inc., 1938), pp. 18–19.

[4] Dewey, *Democracy and Education, op. cit.,* p. 388.

[5] John Dewey, *The Quest for Certainty* (New York: G. P. Putnam's Sons, 1929), p. 196.

baseborn, and rulers from the ruled. These barriers or dualisms create all kinds of unnecessary difficulties, largely because they interfere with "fluent and free intercourse." He also associates dualisms with the setting up of different social groups and classes, "each with isolated subject matter, aim, and standard of values."[6] Indeed, Dewey's foremost philosophic purpose, running through his many writings, is committed to the overcoming of the dualisms between science and morals, means and ends, mind and body, theory and practice, thought and action, which pervade our cultural heritage.

Following Dewey's example, experimentalists find it easier to express their naturalism negatively through colorful and vigorous attacks upon dualisms, such as Geiger's criticism of the theories of knowledge which stem from nonexperimental philosophies:

If indeed there are two worlds, an inner and an outer, one of mind and one of matter, of appearances and of reality; and if man is but a passive spectator viewing one world through the peep-hole of another, then perhaps all he can do is to attempt feebly and imperfectly to secure a copy of what he sees. His mind becomes a duplicating machine, directed to making more or less faithful reproductions. These are called ideas. Knowing is, in consequence, not an integral part of the world but an outside and alien intruder which, for some reason or another, is bound to keep turning out facsimiles. Except for this practice . . . knowing is passive and inoperative, it does not *do* anything to the world.[7]

The dualistic theory of reality and knowledge, which to Dewey was implied in the idealist and realist resolutions regarding the problem of knowledge, results in a curious dilemma. With two separate worlds on his hands, or, more accurately, in his thinking, the dualist must conjure up some sort of mystical connection between these two worlds—or lose one of them. If he gives up the physical world (as some idealists try to do), the mental world within which he is confined consists of nothing more than meaningless symbols which have no reality outside his own mind. If he gives up the mental world (as some realists try to do), he denies to himself any possible means of having any knowledge whatsoever

[6] Dewey, *Democracy and Education, op. cit.*, p. 388.
[7] George R. Geiger, *John Dewey in Perspective* (New York: Oxford University Press, 1958), p. 231.

of the world with which he is left.[8] In support, Lovejoy adds, "both the idealist and the realist must admit that there is an absurdity in the very idea of knowledge."[9]

RELATIVISM

The experimentalist, following Dewey's lead, tries to avoid the knowledge dilemma of the idealist and realist by denying the split or dualism, or discontinuity, in the first place. He firmly believes in the "continuity" of nature and vigorously rejects its "bifurcation" and all forms of supernaturalism stemming from the dualistic presupposition of classical philosophy and theology that there is a spiritual realm which lies beyond experience. He does this by adopting a relativistic theory of reality and knowledge, assuming a "both-and," rather than an "either-or" outlook. He believes that a statement of fact may be *both* true *and* untrue, depending upon the consequences as seen from the standpoint of the observer and what he assumes the fact to include or what he assumes it to mean. He believes that a statement of fact can never be accepted as absolutely and irrevocably *either* true *or* untrue, from all standpoints, under all circumstances and conditions, for all purposes.[10]

Being a relativist, the experimentalist believes the nature of a thing is determined by what it does, or can be used for. A thing becomes a chair by being sat upon. The same object becomes firewood for a man freezing to death in the Klondike. Who is to say what it *really* is? The relativist-experimentalist is content to let it really be a chair under some circumstances, and really firewood under other conditions, and really something else under still other conditions. It is what it becomes.

Instead of seeking absolute reality behind the appearances presented to us in experience, the experimentalist takes what is given to him in experience, and goes forward with it. Armed with his method, his freedom, and his confidence in his ability to cope with

[8] Albert G. Ramsperger, *Philosophies of Science* (New York: Appleton-Century-Crofts, Inc., 1942), chap. IX.

[9] A. C. Lovejoy, *The Revolt Against Dualism* (La Salle, Ill.: Open Court Publishing Company, 1930), p. 379.

[10] Ernest E. Bayles, *Democratic Educational Theory* (New York: Harper & Row, 1960), p. 75.

the future, the experimentalist has abandoned the "quest for certainty." Instead, the experimentalist is engaged in the search for a modicum of security through active control of the changing course of events in his life. He believes that "intelligence in operation," another name for the experimental method, is the key to gaining control of, and security in, nature.[11]

The experimentalist, then, believes it is possible to find security in a hazardous world of change *without absolute certainty*. He does not share the dualist's fear that the world would fall apart at the seams without some sort of eternal and unchanging reality to give it permanence and stability. In response to the dualist's fear that a relativistic world can only be one of confusion, chaos, and doubt, the experimentalist replies that there can be recognizably similar objects in nature. Nature contains things that remain relatively unchanged while others change. Not everything changes at once, or at the same rate. A given element of nature is significantly conditioned only by a limited part of the total context of nature. We can single out and identify objects in nature, such as snow storms in Wisconsin and the coming of seventeen-year locusts in Illinois, and determine the conditions of their occurrence with a high degree of accuracy. Every new experience is not a complete surprise: Our world becomes a familiar one and we act in it with some confidence that it will fulfill our needs.[12]

For the experimentalist, change is a basic characteristic of nature, and nature is capable of being understood by man, and man is charged with the responsibility for the control of change in nature. He does not have to accept passively the world as he finds it, to play the helpless victim of some mysterious pattern of predetermined fate. He can grow, progress, and make a better life for himself—if he uses his intelligence. Man, so to speak, is in the saddle, capable of managing his own destiny in an understandable and predictable natural world. This view requires a great deal of faith in the worth and intelligence of human beings, a faith which is one of the strongest characteristics of the experimental mind.[13]

[11] Dewey, *The Quest for Certainty, op. cit.,* p. 204.
[12] Ramsperger, *op. cit.,* p. 136.
[13] Dewey, *The Quest for Certainty, op. cit.,* chap. VIII.

SCIENCE, MORALS, AND VALUES

Perhaps the most revolutionary characteristic of experimentalism is its belief that the use of the scientific method can be extended to solve the problems of men in the area of values and moral judgments—to open these traditionally "closed" regions of human experience to experimental inquiry.

Believing in the continuity of nature as he did, Dewey made a long and concerted effort to take the question of values out of its traditional supernatural setting and put it in a naturalistic setting. He tried to do away with the segregation of "fact" and "value," and felt that "the problem of restoring integration and cooperation between man's beliefs about the world in which he lives and his beliefs about the values and purposes that should direct his conduct is the deepest problem of modern life."[14]

For Dewey the term "value" has two different meanings. First, to value means to prize, to esteem: It is the act or attitude of finding something worthwhile, cherishing it, and holding it dear. On the other hand, to value means to apprize, to estimate; it is an act of intelligence, an operation of passing judgment upon the nature and amount of the value of something as compared with something else. It is the second meaning which is essential to Dewey's theory of value and distinguishes it from what he called "empirical theories" which "do everything possible to emphasize the purely subjective character of value." Dewey objected that such theories restrict the term value to objects *antecedently* enjoyed, apart from any reference to the method by which they come into existence. He thought it was a mistake to take casual experiences of liking and enjoyment to be values in and of themselves. For him, enjoyments become values only when regulated by intelligent operations. In his words, "Operational thinking needs to be applied to the judgment of values just as it has now finally been applied in conceptions of physical objects."[15]

Experimentalists hold that man's beliefs about value are interwoven (constitute a continuity) with all other aspects of his past, present, and future experience. Beliefs about value arise out of experience and are concerned with possible future experience—

[14] *Ibid.*, p. 255.
[15] *Ibid.*, p. 258.

exactly as are all other beliefs. Value judgments can be controlled, grounded in, and warranted by empirical evidence developed through experimental inquiry in much the same way that statements of fact are developed in science. Saying that "X is worthy of being valued" is much the same as saying that "such and such is the case."[16] This can be so, however, only if one looks to experience as the basis for forming grounded value assertions rather than to the exhortation, preaching, and emotional persuasion of some external authority.

To declare that something has value, according to Dewey, is to assert that it meets specifiable conditions. "It is, in effect, a judgment that the thing 'will do.' It involves a prediction; it contemplates a future in which the thing will continue to serve; it *will* do. It asserts a consequence the thing will actively institute; it will *do*."[17] To say that something is enjoyable or satisfying is a proposition of fact; to say that it is satisfactory or has value is an estimate, an appraisal, a judgment denoting an attitude *to be* taken. It is in the latter sense that values are related to making choices about what ends, goals, or purposes to strive for. *"Judgments about values are judgments about the conditions and the results of experienced objects; judgments about that which should regulate the formulation of our desires, affections and enjoyments.* For whatever decides their formation will determine the main course of our conduct, personal and social."[18]

For Dewey, of course, what it is that should decide the formation of value judgments is warranted evidence—the findings of the natural sciences. He says, "A moral that frames its judgments of value on the basis of consequences must depend in a most intimate manner upon the conclusions of science. For the knowledge of the relations between changes which enable us to connect things as antecedents and consequences *is* science."[19]

In order to understand Dewey's approach to values, the bases he uses for making choices, it is helpful to understand his thinking with regard to desirable aims or ends. Dewey holds that values

---

[16] H. Gordon Hullfish and Philip G. Smith, *Reflective Thinking* (New York: Dodd, Mead & Company, Inc., 1961), chap. VII.

[17] Dewey, *The Quest for Certainty, op. cit.,* pp. 260–261.

[18] *Ibid.,* p. 265.

[19] *Ibid.,* p. 274.

"coincide" with aims or ends. Just as there is no eternal, unchanging reality for Dewey, there is no final, absolute end to which he aspires. As he says, "Every means is a temporary end until we have attained it. Every end becomes a means of carrying activity further as soon as it is achieved."[20] He rejects aims which are imposed on a process of action from without, externally dictated orders to do this and not to do that, aims which are fixed and rigid, divorced from the means by which they are to be reached. He proposes, instead, the following criteria of good aims: (1) aims must be an outgrowth of existing conditions; (2) aims must be flexible, capable of alteration to meet new circumstances; and (3) aims must stimulate intelligence and a "freeing of activities." He suggests that we think in terms of "ends in view" or "active aims" rather than final or absolute ends, and explains what he means by these terms in the following illustration:

The only way in which we can define an activity is by putting before ourselves the object in which it terminates—as one's aim in shooting is the target. But we must remember that the *object* is only a mark or sign by which the mind specifies the *activity* one desires to carry out. Strictly speaking, not the target but *hitting* the target is the end in view; one *takes* aim by means of the target, but also by the sight on the gun. The different objects which are thought of are means of *directing* the activity . . . The doing with the thing, not the thing in isolation, is his end. The object is but a phase of the active end—continuing the activity successfully. This is what is meant by the phrase . . . "freeing activity."[21]

Ends which do not grow up within an activity as a plan for its direction, ends which are not *both* ends *and* means, inhibit rather than free intelligent activity. According to Dewey, they "limit intelligence because, given ready-made, they must be imposed by some authority external to intelligence, leaving to the latter nothing but a mechanical choice of means."[22] It is this point that is at the heart of experimentalism's rejection of sanctioned ends, moral laws, commandments for human conduct, and transcendental values which are absolute and justify any means necessary to attain them.

[20] Dewey, *Democracy and Education, op. cit.,* p. 124.
[21] *Ibid.,* p. 123.
[22] *Ibid.,* p. 122.

Dewey noted that prior to the scientific revolution, concepts derived from "pure reason" and "divine revelations" were readily superimposed upon beliefs about natural phenomena. He also noted that science has been painstakingly restricted to a tightly closed world of phenomena, and that the world of higher "realities" understood without the aid of the senses has been appropriated by ideals and spiritual values, each having a "complete jurisdiction and undisputed sovereignty in its own realm."[23] This neat little arrangement leaves beliefs about values pretty much in the position in which beliefs about nature were before the scientific revolution. Dewey and his experimentalist followers, of course, would like to extend the scientific revolution to reunite beliefs about value and beliefs about nature.

CONTINUITY VERSUS DUALISM

If there is one word which can represent the basic notion underlying experimentalism, that word is *continuity*. Likewise, if there is one word which can represent what experimentalism opposes, that word is *dualism*. Within the context of the above discussion, these two terms, *continuity* and *dualism,* serve as the focal points around which the theoretical framework of the instruments for measuring agreement-disagreement with experimentalism, presented in Chapter 6, are organized.

Dewey believed that the limitations of the actual realization of his philosophy "spring from the notion that experience consists of a variety of segregated domains, or interests, each having its own independent value, material, and method, each checking every other." He located the cause of such limitations in the division of society into rigidly marked-off classes and groups. He saw that these "social ruptures of continuity" have their formulation in such dualisms or antitheses as labor and leisure, individuality and association, culture and vocation. Analyzing further, he found that such social issues have their counterparts in the formulations of classic philosophic systems, and involve such fundamental problems of philosophy as mind (or spirit) and matter, body and mind, the mind and the world, the individual and his relationships to others. Underlying all of these dualisms he found "the fundamental assump-

[23] Dewey, *The Quest for Certainty, op. cit.,* p. 59.

tion to be an isolation of mind from activity involving physical conditions."[24]

In Dewey's discussion of theories of knowledge, he identifies other antithetical conceptions—such as the opposition of empirical and higher rational knowing, external and internal knowing, objective and subjective knowing, activity and passivity in knowing, as well as the opposition between the intellect and the emotions. "All of these separations," he says, "culminate in one between knowing and doing, theory and practice, between mind as an end and spirit of action and the body as its organ and means."[25] In still another discussion he identifies the separation of knowledge from action or practical activities and traces it to the fundamental assumption of traditional (nonexperimental) philosophy that true knowledge must be immutable, absolutely certain.[26]

In contrast to such dualisms, and in consequence of his having analyzed them as dualisms, Dewey puts forward a philosophy "which recognizes the origin, place, and function of mind *in* an activity which controls the environment." His philosophy involves such conceptions as: (1) the biological continuity of human impulses and instincts with natural energies; (2) the dependence of growth of mind upon participation in purposeful activity; (3) the influence of physical environment through the social uses made of it; (4) the utilization of individual variations in desire and thinking for a progressively developing society; (5) the unity of subject matter and method; (6) the continuity of ends and means; (7) the recognition of mind as thinking which perceives and tests the meaning of behavior.[27]

In this chapter we have discussed the fundamental philosophic beliefs which characterize Dewey's philosophy of experimentalism. These beliefs are the bases for the development of the *Personal Beliefs Inventory* which is presented in Chapter 6.

[24] Dewey, *Democracy and Education, op. cit.*, pp. 376–377.
[25] *Ibid.*, pp. 389–391.
[26] Dewey, *The Quest for Certainty, op. cit.*,
[27] Dewey, *Democracy and Education, op. cit.*, p. 377.

5

EDUCATIONAL PHILOSOPHY
OF JOHN DEWEY

BOTH FRIENDS and enemies have confused Dewey's philosophy of experimentalism with "progressive education" and the "soft-subject" of "child-centered" curriculum. Although Dewey did not flatly repudiate the progressive education movement, he reacted critically to many of the practices and misconceptions popularly associated with it.[1]

DEWEY AND THE PROGRESSIVES

Boyd Bode, an eminent experimentalist, was an early and severe critic of progressivism. He pointed out that progressive education was decidedly not an expression of experimentalism, and that, in fact, it had failed to develop a clear basic philosophy of any kind:

The fact that the progressive movement has never come across with an adequate philosophy of education warrants the assumption that it does not have any. . . . To the casual observer, American education is a confusing and not altogether edifying spectacle. It is productive of endless fads and panaceas; it is pretentiously scientific and at the same time pathetically conventional; it is scornful of the past, yet painfully inarticulate when it speaks of the future. The tremendous activity now going on in education is evidence of far-reaching social changes, but we do not seem to know what these changes signify or how they are to be directed.[2]

[1] John Dewey, *Experience and Education* (New York: The Macmillan Company, 1938).
[2] Boyd H. Bode, *Progressive Education at the Crossroads* (New York: Newson and Company, 1938), pp. 85–86.

Teachers in America never really caught on to what Dewey was talking about. One should read Ernest Bayles' "John Dewey and Progressivism"[3] for documentation of his contention that the educational practices which are laid at the door of progressivism are not justifiably attributable either to Dewey or to his philosophy, but, instead, primarily to the writings of William Heard Kilpatrick of Columbia's Teachers College. It was Kilpatrick who introduced the "project method" and "pupil purposing, pupil planning, pupil executing, and pupil judging." Kilpatrick, as the "Trail Blazer" of Progressivism, was strongly influenced by the romanticism of Rousseau and by the psychology of Thorndike, whose views were clearly incompatible with Dewey's. Thorndike spearheaded the mechanistic-behavioristic movement in educational psychology. Rousseau and his follower Froebel were the forces behind the child-centered point of view. Twentieth-century progressives took up many of the educational practices advocated by Dewey, but they did not take up the beliefs basic to his general philosophy of experimentalism. They could not sever themselves clearly from the old moorings of realistic and idealistic philosophies. They attacked the absolutism of subject matter and in its place made the child an absolute with which there was to be no tampering.

In a similar analysis, Woodring identifies Dewey's philosophy as a major influence on American education throughout the first half of the twentieth century, but he adds that far from every educational proposal or innovation made during this time is traceable to Dewey's doorstep. He agrees with Bayles that the form taken by the "new education" during the thirties and forties was based more on the complex and confused assumptions of Thorndike, Rousseau, Freud, and the social reconstructionists than on Dewey's experimentalism.[4]

SUBJECT MATTER VS. THE CHILD: AN IRRELEVANT DUALISM

The controversy over the "subject-centered" versus "child-centered" approach to curriculum planning and organization gen-

---

[3] Ernest E. Bayles, *Democratic Educational Theory* (New York: Harper & Row, 1960), chap. XV.

[4] Paul Woodring, *A Fourth of a Nation* (New York: McGraw-Hill Book Company, Inc., 1957), chap. III.

erally assumes the specter of John Dewey to be behind the child-centered position. To assume this, however, is to misunderstand the nature of Dewey's philosophy. Dewey, of course, did oppose the classic thesis that schools should be exclusively concerned with the development of the mind, and was a party to the pragmatic antitheses that schools should provide for the growth of the whole child. His objection to the unnatural "bifurcation" of the child into a mind divisible from a body (the former to be dealt with by the school and the latter to be ignored or restricted by the school insofar as possible) is consistent with his rejection of all discontinuities and dualisms. Advocating that the curriculum consider the whole child rather than only one aspect of the child is by no means equivalent to advocating a child-centered curriculum. Although it was Dewey's predisposition to dismiss this whole controversy as an irrelevant dualism, if he were to advocate any kind of a "centered" curriculum, it would surely have been an "inquiry-centered" curriculum. Dewey indicates as much when he says, "Processes of instruction are unified in the degree in which they center in the production of good habits of thinking. While we may speak, without error, of the method of thought, the important thing is that thinking is the method of an educative experience."[5]

THE UNITY OF SUBJECT MATTER AND METHOD

Dewey's educational recommendations have been assumed to favor method at the expense of subject matter, which is true only if one insists upon pitting subject matter against method in an "either . . . or" dichotomy. It was Dewey's intention to repair the split between subject matter and method, not to widen it. If the "new education" watered down the content of the curriculum or neglected subject matter in favor of method, this was done in spite of Dewey's educational philosophy of experimentalism, not because of it.

Dewey's position regarding the relationship of subject matter and method should be unmistakable. As early as 1902 in *The Child and the Curriculum* he identified "three typical evils" which result

[5] John Dewey, *Democracy and Education* (New York: The Macmillan Company, 1916), p. 192.

from treating subject matter as something "cut off and fixed."[6] In his *Democracy and Education,* immediately beneath the heading of Chapter XIII, the words, "The Unity of Subject Matter and Method," appear in bold, black letters as his first major subheading. Following this, Dewey again attacks the idea that mind and the world of things are two separate and independent realms, saying that this theory is a philosophic dualism which carries with it the conclusion that method and subject matter of instruction are separate affairs. Thus separated, subject matter becomes a body of ready-made facts and principles, and method is limited to a consideration of ways in which subject matter may be best presented to and impressed upon the minds of students, or a consideration of the ways in which their minds may be brought to bear upon the matter in order to facilitate its acquisition and possession. This familiar dualism makes it possible, Dewey suggests, for a teacher to develop a complete kit of teaching methods with no knowledge of the subjects to which these methods are to be applied, and *vice versa.* He ridicules the notion of any such split between subject matter and method as "radically false."[7]

In contrast, Dewey views method (a word he uses synonymously with *thinking*) as the directed movement or employment of subject matter toward desired results. For Dewey, method is not antithetical to subject matter. Although method is a *way* of acting, and we can discuss it by itself, it is nothing in and of itself. Method has no existence outside of material; it *exists* only as a way-of-dealing-with-material. As he says:

When a man is eating, he is eating *food.* He does not divide his act into eating *and* food. But if he makes a scientific investigation of the act, such discrimination is the first thing he would effect. He would examine on the one hand the properties of the nutritive material, and on the other hand the acts of the organism in appropriating and digesting. Such reflection upon experience gives rise to a distinction of *what* we experience (the experienc*ed*) and the experienc*ing*—the *how.* When we give names to this distinction we have subject matter and method as our terms. . . . This distinction is so natural and so im-

---

[6] John Dewey, "The Child and the Curriculum," from *Dewey on Education* (New York: Bureau of Publications, Teachers College, Columbia University, 1959), pp. 91–112.

[7] *Ibid.,* p. 194.

portant for certain purposes, that we are only too apt to regard it as a separation in existence and not as a distinction in thought.[8]

THE ROLE OF SUBJECT MATTER

For Dewey, the organized subject matter of the various fields of study represents "working capital," the "ripe fruitage of experience," which is available to further new and future experiences. He points out that subject matter as it has been logically organized and crystallized by adult experts is remote from the experience of the immature learner. He identifies three stages in the growth of subject matter in the experience of the learner:

1. The learner's initial subject matter is always a matter of active doing, or, as the famous-but-meaningless slogan goes, "learning by doing."[9] This is only the beginning, although there may be good reason to believe that some Deweyites have regarded it as the end, too. Dewey, however, devotes much more time and space to the second stage.

2. The material encountered in purposeful doing is "surcharged and deepened through communicated knowledge and information."[10] This is a vague statement, and may have contributed to teachers' misunderstanding and oversight of this crucial aspect of Dewey's educational philosophy. The troublesome word here is "communicated." Dewey denies that any idea can possibly be communicated *as an idea* from one person to another. At best, "communication may stimulate the other person to realize the question for himself and think out a like idea."[11] Dewey, of course, clearly rejects the popular concept that knowledge is most effectively acquired by the appropriation of facts and information from teachers and books. He says, "Knowledge which is mainly second-hand, other men's knowledge, tends to become merely verbal." Communication which cannot be organized into the existing experiences of the learner "becomes *mere* words; that is, pure sense-stimuli, lacking in any meaning" which serve only to call out mechanical reactions and regurgitations. At this stage, informational knowledge has the office of an "intellectual middleman" which

---

[8] *Ibid.*
[9] *Ibid.*, p. 217.
[10] *Ibid.*, p. 216.
[11] *Ibid.*, p. 188.

should serve as a kind of "bridge for the mind in its passage from doubt to discovery."[12] Such bridging-type "communication" of subject matter is an integral part of the process of inquiry and discovery, the experimental method.

3. Through repetitions of the process of inquiry and discovery, subject matter is "enlarged and worked over into rationally or logically organized material—that of the one who, relatively speaking, is expert in the subject."[13]

Dewey's map analogy may be useful in clarifying the distinction he makes between "subject matter in itself" and "subject matter in relation to the child." He compares this difference "to the difference between the notes which an explorer makes in a new country, blazing a trail, and the finished map that is constructed after the country has been thoroughly explored. The two are mutually dependent." The map becomes a "formulated statement of experience," or, in other words, subject matter. "The map is not a substitute for a personal experience" and "does not take the place of an actual journey." The map (subject matter) is "a summary, an arranged and orderly view of previous experiences, (which) serves as a guide to future experience; it gives direction; it facilitates control; it economizes effort, preventing useless wandering, and pointing out the paths which lead most quickly and most certainly to a desired result. Through the map every new traveler may get for his own journey the benefits of the results of others' explorations without the waste of energy and loss of time involved in their wanderings—wanderings which he himself would be obliged to repeat were it not for just the assistance of the objective and generalized record of their performances."[14]

The problem for the teacher, Dewey says, is to keep the experience of the student moving in the direction of what the expert already knows. Thus, the teacher must know both subject matter and the characteristic needs and capacities of the student. The teacher must also recognize that his part in the educational process is to furnish an environment which stimulates and directs the student's course, and to recognize that when he has "provided the conditions which stimulate thinking and has taken a sympathetic

[12] *Ibid.*, p. 221.
[13] *Ibid.*, pp. 216–217.
[14] *Ibid.*, pp. 102–103.

attitude toward the activities of the learner by entering into a common or conjoint experience, all has been done which a second party can do to instigate learning."[15]

Although Dewey makes *ac*quiring secondary to *in*quiring, it should be quite clear that he sees the process of inquiry cutting into and eating up unlimited amounts and kinds of subject matter. He views subject matter not as the end of education but as an essential ingredient in keeping the educative process alive and growing. The difference is subtle, but vital.

Uninformed opinion and widespread teaching practice to the contrary, Dewey's is an extremely "hard-nosed" philosophy which demands that students encounter substantial, challenging problems sufficiently tough and troublesome to cause them to "stop and think." Anyone with the idea that John Dewey advocated watering down the subject matter content of the curriculum either hasn't read him first-hand, or failed to understand him when they did.

THE NATURE OF EXPERIENCE

Dewey views experience as having both an active and a passive aspect. The active part of experience is *trying* and the passive part of experience is *undergoing* the consequences of that trying. He makes a point of distinguishing mere activity from experience. He calls "experience" only what involves (1) acting, (2) consequences, and (3) the noting of the *connection* between the acting and its consequences. Activity isn't an experience unless we learn something from it. Dewey says:

To "learn from experience" is to make a backward and forward connection between what we do to things and what we enjoy or suffer from things in consequence. Under such conditions, doing becomes a trying; an experiment with the world to find out what it is like; the undergoing becomes instruction—discovery of the connection of things.[16]

REFLECTION IN EXPERIENCE

The discernment of the connection between what we try to do and what happens in consequence always involves some element of thought or reflection. So, in this sense, all experience is reflective.

[15] *Ibid.*, p. 188.
[16] *Ibid.*, p. 164.

However, some types of experience require more reflection than do others. Simple trial and error experiences, for example, require only that we hunt and pick until we find something which works, and we continue with whatever it is until it fails, and then we look for something else to do. This method proves satisfactory only in relatively routine or unimportant matters which do not require much precision, sophistication, or intelligence. When the quality of an experience moves up the value scale, however, it demands an increasing amount of care, deliberation, and thought. We bring to bear on an experience only that amount of our intelligence which the significance of the experience demands. When an experience is of such a quality that it causes us to hesitate, or stop, and *intentionally* try to discover the *specific* connection of its elements, Dewey calls this a reflective experience *par excellence,* or thinking.[17]

Dewey has a great deal to say about thinking—what it is and what it is not. He equates thinking with what makes experience intelligent—what alters experience by discovering connections. He contrasts thinking with routine and capricious behavior. Thoughtful behavior is acting with an end in view; routine behavior simply lets things go on as they always have, and capricious behavior makes the momentary act a measure of value and ignores the connections of present action with past and future results. Reflective action accepts responsibility for the consequences which flow from present action; both routine and capricious behavior refuse such responsibility.

Thinking is equated by Dewey with the process of inquiry. Thinking is a matter of looking into things, or investigating. In reflective thinking, "*ac*quiring is always secondary, and instrumental to the act of *in*quiring."[18] Assured and already acquired knowledge is the raw material of thinking, and, therefore, plays an important role in it. Thinking, however, springs only from situations which are incomplete or uncertain or problematic, and it is an act of seeking, or a quest, for something that is not now certain or known or already at hand.

Thinking, Dewey reminds us, always involves risk. Its conclusions cannot be guaranteed in advance. Thinking is always tentative or hypothetical until confirmed by empirical evidence. Even

[17] *Ibid.,* pp. 169–171.
[18] *Ibid.,* p. 175.

then, the results are never held dogmatically as final. Thinking is a rhythmic, pulsating, but *continuous* process.

THE ESSENTIALS OF AN EDUCATIVE EXPERIENCE

Dewey, as we have noted, indicates that the general features of a quality experience are the same as the general features of reflective thinking. He then goes on to show that the characteristics of the method of reflective thinking are identical with the essentials of an educative experience. In the process of drawing his connections between *experience, thinking,* and *education* in Chapters XI, XII, and XIII of *Democracy and Education,* Dewey makes six different listings of the general features of "method."[19] These lists are, curiously, not identical. Some lists contain elements omitted in others, and he varies the order in which elements are listed. He refers to these elements as "general features," "steps," "stages," "characteristics," and "essentials." This diversity in his description may represent an aversion to solidifying the characteristics of reflective thinking into one rigid formula or a single set of principles and procedures.

A summary of Dewey's description of "the essentials of method" in connection with "thinking in education" can be made as follows:

1. *Situation of experience.* The initial stage of thinking is *experience.* A pupil experiences something by acting upon it, doing something with it. He does something and has something done to him in return. He undergoes the consequences of his actions. Then he notes the interaction of his actions, the material acted upon, and the resulting consequence. "Hence," according to Dewey, "the first approach to any subject in school, if thought is to be aroused and not words acquired, should be as unscholastic as possible." He concludes that methods which are permanently successful in formal education "give the pupils something to do, not something to learn; and the doing is of such a nature as to demand thinking, or the intentional noting of connections; learning naturally results."[20]

2. *Problem.* The situation suggests something to do which is new, uncertain, or problematic. Dewey points out the importance

[19] See the Appendix for a composite list of Dewey's statements regarding the features of the method of reflective thinking.

[20] Dewey, *Democracy and Education, op. cit.,* p. 181.

of discriminating between genuine and mock problems and asks the following questions regarding the nature of the problem:

(a) Is there anything *but* a problem? Does the question naturally suggest itself within some situation of personal experience? Or is it an aloof thing, a problem only for the purposes of conveying instruction in some school topic? Is it the sort of trying that would arouse observation and engage experimentation outside of school?

(b) Is it the pupil's own problem, or is it the teacher's or textbook's problem, made a problem for the pupil only because he cannot get the required mark or be promoted or win the teacher's approval, unless he deals with it.[21]

3. *Generation of ideas.* An important element in thinking is the rough idea, the guess, the initial hypothesis. This is the creative or idea stage of thinking. As Dewey puts it, "Ideas . . . whether they be humble guesses or dignified theories, are anticipations of possible solutions. They are anticipations of some continuity or connection of an activity and a consequence which has not yet shown itself."[22] At this stage of thinking in education "suggestions run beyond what is, as yet, actually *given* in experience. They forecast possible results, things *to* do, not facts (things already done). Inference is always an invasion of the unknown, a leap from the known. . . . In this sense, a thought (what a thing suggests but is not as it is presented) is creative—an incursion into the novel. It involves some inventiveness."[23]

4. *Observation and collection of data.* Dewey believed strongly in the necessity of having data available to deal with difficulties which arise, saying "The material of thinking is not thoughts, but actions, facts, events, and the relations of things." He wanted subject matter provided, and was not so choosey as one might suppose as to the means by which it was gotten. He approved of memory, observation, reading, and communication as "avenues" for supplying data. He thought the relative proportion to be obtained from these various avenues could be decided only in light of a particular prob-

21 *Ibid.,* p. 182.
22 *Ibid.,* pp. 188–189.
23 *Ibid.,* p. 186.

lem in hand. He cautioned against developing a "crippling dependence" upon first-hand observations as well as an "excessive reliance upon others for data (whether got from reading or listening)," adding that the most objectionable of all subject-matter supply routes is "the probability that others, the book or the teacher, will supply solutions ready-made, instead of giving material that the student has to adapt and apply to the question in hand for himself." Dewey argued that "the accumulation and acquisition of information for purposes of reproduction in recitation and examination is made too much of," and preferred having information or knowledge made "the working capital, the indispensable resources, of further inquiry; of finding out, or learning, more things."[24]

5. *Reasoned hypothesis or ideas.* Having made observations and a collection of data, there ought to be an elaboration of initial or rough hypotheses, making them more precise and more consistent by squaring them with a wider range of facts, developing out of them clearly answerable questions or testable hypotheses. What is given, what is already there and assured, can be helpful in defining, clarifying, and locating the question but cannot supply the answer. Projection, invention, ingenuity, devising—*ideas,* in short, come in for that purpose. "Data *arouse* suggestions, and only by reference to the specific data can we pass upon the appropriateness of the suggestions."[25]

6. *Experimental application and testing.* A stand is taken on one or more of the projected hypotheses as a plan of action. Something is done to bring about the anticipated result. The anticipations, hypotheses, or ideas are "tested by the operation of acting upon them."[26] Dewey believed that the pupil ought to have "opportunity to test his ideas by application, to make their meaning clear and to discover for himself their validity."[27]

7. *Conclusion, evaluation, report of results.* If the tested hypothesis "brings about certain consequences, certain determinate changes, in the world, it is accepted as valid. Otherwise it is modi-

[24] *Ibid.,* pp. 184–186.
[25] *Ibid.,* p. 186.
[26] *Ibid.,* p. 189.
[27] *Ibid.,* p. 192.

fied, and another trial is made."[28] Results of experimental testing are faithfully reported, whether the experimenter likes them or not. The results, or tested consequences, are used "to guide and organize further observations, recollections, and experiments."[29]

Dewey states that the extent and accuracy of getting a rough idea, guess, or hypothesis (feature 3) and making careful inquiry into all available data related to it (feature 4), and using the collected data to develop a more elaborate and more precise idea or hypothesis (feature 5) are what mark off a quality or reflective experience from an experience on the trial and error level. Rather than acting upon the first thoughts which pop into their heads, pupils stop and think, consider the facts of the case, and come up with a plan of action warranted by the use of intelligence. Thus, features 3, 4, and 5 combine to constitute "thinking" in a reflective experience.[30]

SOME EDUCATIONAL EVILS

In contrast to the educational practices stemming from the continuity of subject matter and method implied in the features of reflective thinking, Dewey points out "some evils in education that flow from the isolation of method from subject matter," which are as follows:

1. *The neglect of concrete situations of experience.* Dewey complains about teachers who treat subject matter as a ready-made systematized classification of facts and principles and then treat method as a separate consideration of the ways in which the mind may be externally brought to bear upon the subject matter in order to facilitate its acquisition and possession.[31] This leads teachers to rely upon methods authoritatively recommended to them, rather than to discover and use methods which are an expression of their own intelligent observations. Under such circumstances, Dewey contends a teacher's methods have a mechanical uniformity, assumed to be alike for all minds. He would prefer that teaching

[28] *Ibid.,* p. 177.
[29] *Ibid.,* p. 189.
[30] *Ibid.,* p. 176.
[31] *Ibid.,* p. 193.

method be derived from observation of what actually happens in the classroom with a view to seeing that it happens better next time. But it was Dewey's opinion that "in instruction and discipline, there is rarely sufficient opportunity for children and youth to have the direct normal experiences from which educators might derive an idea of method or order of best development. Experiences are had under conditions of such restraint that they throw little or no light upon the normal course of an experience to its fruition."[32]

2. *Reliance upon extrinsic motivation.* When material is treated as something ready-made apart from method, Dewey says there are just three ways in which to motivate concern with the alien subject matter: "One is to utilize excitement, shock of pleasure, tickling the palate. Another is to make the consequences of not attending painful; we may use the menace of harm. . . . Or a direct appeal may be made to the person to put forth effort without any reason . . . however, the latter method is effectual only when instigated by fear of unpleasant results."[33]

3. *Learning is made a direct and conscious end in itself.* It was Dewey's observation that "children do not set out, consciously, to learn walking or talking." Instead, they set out to exercise and display their "impulses for communication and for fuller intercourse with others." Dewey believed that methods of teaching children to read or to deal with number "or whatever" should "follow the same road." Teaching methods should engage the child's activities, "and in the process of engagement he learns." They should not "fix his attention upon the fact that he has to learn something and so make his attitude self-conscious and constrained." Dewey added that "when the subject matter is not used in carrying forward impulses and habits to significant results, it is just something to be learned. The pupil's attitude to it is just that of having to learn it. Conditions more unfavorable to an alert and concentrated response would be hard to devise." Even though Dewey advised that "Frontal attacks are even more wasteful in learning than in war," he cautioned that "this does not mean, however, that students are to be seduced unaware into preoccupation

[32] *Ibid.*, pp. 197–198.
[33] *Ibid.*, p. 198.

with lessons. It means that they shall be occupied with them for real reasons or ends, and not just as something to be learned."[34]

4. *Following mechanically prescribed steps.* Dewey connected "rigid woodenness" and "cut and dried" teaching methods to the influence of the conception of the separation of mind and matter. He condemned teaching which compels children to recite or to go through "certain preordained verbal formulae," a practice he saw based on the assumption "that there is one fixed method to be followed." He stated flatly that "Nothing has brought pedagogical theory into greater disrepute than the belief that it is identified with handing out to teachers recipes and models to be followed in teaching."[35]

5. *Imposing a general method upon all alike.* Supplying students with "models of method to be followed in acquiring and expounding a subject," according to Dewey, "is to fall into a self-deception that has lamentable consequences." "Imposing an alleged uniform general method upon everybody breeds mediocrity,"[36] he said. "The teacher who does not permit and encourage diversity of operation in dealing with questions is imposing intellectual blinders upon pupils—restricting their vision to the one path the teacher's mind happens to approve," he added. The chief cause of teachers' devotion to uniformity and rigidity of procedure is that it promises prompt, correct results. It is the zeal for "answers" that Dewey saw as the explanation of teachers' zeal for rigid and mechanical methods.[37]

SUMMARY

In his philosophy of education, John Dewey stressed the importance of the continuity or unity of subject matter and method. It was his belief that such a unity could best be achieved by making the features of a reflective experience (the experimental method) and the features of an educative experience identical. For him, education *is* thinking, a process of intelligent inquiry and experimentation in which there is a continuous interaction of subject

[34] *Ibid.,* pp. 198–199.
[35] *Ibid.,* pp. 199–200.
[36] *Ibid.,* pp. 202–203.
[37] *Ibid.,* p. 206.

matter and method. He depreciates school practices which fail to permit or stimulate thinking, and traces their origins to false assumptions that subject matter is something existing by itself apart from method; or that method is a method of acting, by itself, rather than a method that has meaning only as a way-of-dealing-with-matter.

The centrality of the method of reflective thinking to Dewey's educational philosophy can best be summed up in his own words:

The experimental method is new as a scientific resource—as a systematized means of making knowledge, though as old as life as a practical device. Hence it is not surprising that men have not recognized its full scope. For the most part, its significance is regarded as belonging to certain technical and merely physical matters. It will doubtless take a long time to secure the perception that it holds equally as to the forming and testing of ideas in social and moral matters. Men still want the crutch of dogma, of beliefs fixed by authority, to relieve them of the trouble of thinking and the responsibility of directing their activity by thought . . . but every advance in the influence of the experimental method is sure to aid in outlawing the literary, dialectic, and authoritative methods of forming beliefs which have governed the schools of the past. . . . In time the theory of knowing must be derived from the practice which is most successful in making knowledge; and then that theory will be employed to improve the methods which are less successful.[38]

[38] *Ibid.*, pp. 394–395.

6

THE MEASUREMENT
OF EXPERIMENTALISM

FROM OUR ANALYSIS of Dewey's theories regarding (1) knowledge and action, and (2) subject matter and method, plus the description of the characteristics of his philosophy of experimentalism presented in Chapters 4 and 5, we have developed a theoretical framework for the measurement of the experimental mind.

THE EXPERIMENTAL MIND

A. *Fundamental philosophic beliefs.* The experimental mind believes in the continuity of each of the pairs of things listed below, and rejects the beliefs that they can or should be divided and separated into dualisms: Disagreement with the experimental mind implies belief in discontinuity or dualism of the six pairs of items below, replacing the connective "and" with a disjunctive "versus" in each case.

1. Mind and Body
2. Permanence and Change
3. Science and Morals
4. Emotions and Intellect
5. Freedom and Authority
6. Knowing and Doing

B. *Educational beliefs.* The experimental mind believes in the continuity of subject matter and method, which is expressed in the essential features of reflective thinking[1].

[1] John Dewey, *Democracy and Education* (New York: The Macmillan Company, 1916), pp. 176–177, 180–192, and 203.

1. There is a situation of experience.
2. A problem develops.
3. Ideas are generated.
4. Observations are made, data is collected.
5. Hypotheses are reasoned out.
6. Experimental applications and tests are made.
7. Conclusions are evaluated and reported.

Disagreement with the experimental mind implies belief in the dualism of subject matter vs. method, which is expressed in Dewey's list of "some evils in education that flow from the isolation of method from subject matter,"[2] such as:

1. Neglect of direct experience.
2. Reliance upon extrinsic motivation.
3. Making learning a direct and conscious end in itself.
4. Following the prescribed steps of an established method.
5. Imposing a general method for all alike.

The only way we can tell whether the theoretical framework outlined above is worth anything is to test it experimentally and to evaluate its consequences. This is precisely the procedure advocated by Dewey. Such a test cannot be expected to prove or disprove conclusively Dewey's theory, or, more correctly, the theoretical framework extracted from Dewey, but the findings which result can raise or lower confidence in its validity.

Research on the relationship of philosophy and practice in education depends upon the availability of instruments which can be used to measure both beliefs and behavior along a single, explicitly defined dimension. Dewey's experimentalism represents a pertinent and well-known dimension which accommodates both theory and practice. It represents a comprehensive system of thought which connects specific educational theories and practices to basic philosophic theories, such as theories of knowledge, being, reality, value, and so forth. Quite apart from any use they may have in measuring agreement—disagreement with Dewey's philosophy and the extent to which Dewey influences teachers' beliefs and practices, such instruments will have value if they permit *comparable* measurement of both theory and practice in terms of a common referent.

[2] *Ibid.*, pp. 197–200.

The Experimentalism Scale

This scale was developed for the primary purpose of measuring individual differences in agreement or disagreement with John Dewey's philosophy. In constructing the scale Dewey's writings, principally *Democracy and Education* and *The Quest for Certainty,* were gleaned for clear-cut statements of what he was *for* and what he was *against*. In many cases the language used by Dewey seemed remote from the experiences of present-day teachers and was thought likely to have little meaning for them. An attempt was made to find up-to-date equivalents of some of the statements. Altogether, more than 1200 statements were developed.

At this point, the massive collection of statements seemed like a gigantic jigsaw puzzle which defied classification and organization. Early attempts to organize all these items into a single theoretical framework were frustrating, indeed. The framework of Dewey's theory of the relationship of knowledge and action described earlier was then hit upon as the organizational dimension of this scale because of its capacity to hold logically all of the major kinds of statements that had been gathered.

In fitting the statements within the categories of the framework, items which were obvious duplicates were eliminated. Some items were combined. Others were modified or restated for added clarity and simplification. By this process, the number of statements was reduced to 272.

So far, the development of the statements had been based primarily upon editorial judgment. The statements had been evaluated only informally, on a hit-and-miss basis, with colleagues in education and philosophy. Obviously, there had been many opportunities to distort Dewey's meaning by quoting out of context and by tampering with his original language. In order to establish greater confidence in the statements, it was necessary to submit them to judges competent to decide the positive or negative connotation of each item with respect to Dewey's experimentalism.

Six judges were selected who were familiar with the general and educational philosophy of John Dewey and with teaching-learning situations in school classrooms. Three of the judges were professors of philosophy or philosophy of education, and three of the judges were professors of education, all on the faculty of the University of Wisconsin, Madison. The special competencies and interests of the judges complemented each other ideally. Subsequent revisions and additions of statements were cleared with this panel of judges, with additional consultation from a noted Dewey scholar in the Philosophy Department.

The judges were asked to make judgments of each of the 272 statements which were incorporated into two questionnaires. One hundred twenty-two statements of basic philosophic beliefs concerning the relation of knowledge and action were listed randomly on a *Personal Beliefs Questionnaire.* One hundred fifty statements describing teacher practices concerned with the relation of subject matter and method were listed randomly on a *Teacher Practices Questionnaire.* The judges were told that the statements had been derived from Dewey's writings; that approximately half were taken to represent *continuity,* the theory Dewey advanced positively; and that the other half were taken to represent *dualisms,* the theories criticized by Dewey. The judges were asked to indicate which items on the questionnaires they believed to be compatible with Dewey's philosophy, which items they believed to be incompatible with Dewey's philosophy, and which items they believed did not represent, for any reason, either of these points of view.

A statement was accepted as compatible with experimentalism if rated positively by five or more judges. Likewise, a statement was accepted as incompatible with experimentalism if rated negatively by five or more judges. All other statements were rejected, or revised and resubmitted to the judges. It was felt that such requirements were more than sufficient to establish confidence that the statements do represent what is claimed for them to represent. Upon this procedure rests our assumption that if a person strongly agrees with the positive statements it indicates that his beliefs are highly compatible with Dewey's, and if he strongly disagrees it indicates that his beliefs are at the opposite extreme from Dewey's.

The Experimentalism ("X") Scale is composed of three parts: The *Personal Beliefs Inventory,* the *Teacher Practices Inventory,* and the *Teacher Practices Observation Record.* We shall discuss each of these inventories separately before looking at how they can be used in combination for the measurement of experimentalism in the study of the relationship of theory and practice in education.

THE PERSONAL BELIEFS INVENTORY

The Personal Beliefs Inventory is preceded by the following instructions, which are similar to those used with the D Scale[3] and the F Scale[4]:

This is a study of what people believe about a number of philosophic questions. The best answer to each statement is your personal belief. Many different and opposing points of view are presented here. You will find yourself believing some of the statements, not believing some, and uncertain about others. Whether you believe or do not believe any statement, you can be sure that many people feel the same as you do.

Mark each statement in the left margin according to how much you agree or disagree with it. Please mark every one.

Write 1, 2, 3, or 4, 5, 6, depending on how you feel in each case.

1: I agree very much.   4: I disagree a little.
2: I agree on the whole.   5: I disagree on the whole.
3: I agree a little.   6: I disagree very much.

The Personal Beliefs Inventory has evolved through five revisions in order to make refinements in line with the development of the theoretical framework, to increase reliability, to find the most discriminating items, and to arrive at the optimum number of items needed to test subjects while adequately representing the categories of the framework, and to facilitate administration and scoring with as much ease as possible.

Presented here are the combined A and B forms of the fifth revision. An (A) or (B) following the item numbers below indicates the form from which each statement has been taken. Plus-items are compatible with experimentalism and minus-items are incompatible with experimentalism. This inventory contains an

[3] Milton Rokeach, *The Open and Closed Mind* (New York: Basic Books, Inc., 1960).

[4] T. W. Adorno *et al., The Authoritarian Personality* (New York: Harper & Row, 1950).

equal number of plus- and minus-items. The ratings which persons filling out the inventory give the *plus-items are reversed,* e.g., a "1" is counted as "6," a "2" is counted as "5," a "3" is counted as "4," a "4" is counted as "3," a "5" is counted as "2," and a "6" is counted as "1." With the reversals of the plus items made in the margin to the left, all the individual item scores, including those for the unchanged minus items, are added up to provide a total score. The higher the total score, the higher the agreement with experimentalism, and the lower the total score, the less the agreement with experimentalism.

As they are presented below the items are listed in plus and minus groups within the categories of the framework. In preparing the inventory for use the items should, of course, be listed randomly, and a master scoring sheet prepared on which the "plus" or "minus" value of items is indicated.

I. ITEMS INVOLVING MIND AND BODY

Dewey believed in the continuity of mind and body and rejected the dualistic notion that there is something which is called "mind" or "consciousness" or "soul" which is severed from "matter" or "body" or the "physical organs of activity." The items reflecting this problem concerning the conception of mind are as follows:

(a) *Plus-items compatible with Dewey*

1. Man doesn't have a "spirit" which is separable from his body and the material world. (A)
2. There is no spiritual realm which lies beyond man's experience in the natural world. (B)

(b) *Minus-items in conflict with Dewey*

3. The mind is a group of "contents" which come from having certain material presented to it. (A)
4. The mind possesses faculties for remembering, imagining, reasoning, willing, and so forth, which are developed by exercise and discipline. (B)
5. The mind is formed from without, as one molds and shapes a piece of clay. (A)
6. "Mind" is purely intellectual and cognitive; bodily activity is an irrelevant and intruding physical factor. (B)

II. ITEMS INVOLVING PERMANENCE AND CHANGE

Man's quest for absolute certainty in a relative and changing world of nature, according to Dewey, is a principal factor in a breakdown in the relation of knowledge and action. Dewey would give up traditional philosophy's search for immutable truth. The following items deal with beliefs regarding change and certainty:

(a) *Plus-items compatible with Dewey*

   7. What is right and good at one time and place may not be right and good for all times and places. (A)

   8. All "truths" are relative. (A)

   9. Nothing is or can be unchanging, absolutely certain. (A)

   10. A statement of fact can be *both* true *and* untrue depending on the standpoints and conditions of the observations. (B)

   11. Man's choices are good only if they prove successful in helping him live with some degree of security and equilibrium in the world of nature. (B)

   12. You can never prove that any fact is unconditionally true. (A)

   13. There can be no final, absolute ends to which all men aspire. (B)

   14. What something may be when totally independent of any observer or frame of reference is a scientifically meaningless question. (B)

   15. The nature of a thing is determined by what it does, or can be used for; it is what it becomes with intelligent use. (B)

(b) *Minus-items in conflict with Dewey*

   16. Reaching a condition in which there were no more problems would be the ideal life. (B)

   17. To know something is to know the inner nature of things, i.e., as they really are prior to investigation. (A)

III. ITEMS INVOLVING SCIENCE AND MORALS

Characteristic throughout Dewey's philosophy is his contention that the experimental method—the method of science, broadly conceived—ought to be extended to deal with all of the personal and social problems confronting man, and not restricted just to the problems involving the physical or natural sciences. Beliefs concerning this issue are represented by the following items:

(a) *Plus-items compatible with Dewey*

    18. What is morally right and wrong should be decided on the basis of scientific inquiry. (A)

    19. Questions of value and moral judgment ought to be open to experimentation. (A)

    20. Questions of values and morals should be taken out of their traditional supernatural setting and put in a naturalistic setting. (A)

    21. The use of the scientific method can be extended to solve the problems of men in the area of values and moral judgments. (B)

    22. What is morally right and wrong ought to be decided on warranted evidence—the findings of empirical science. (B)

(b) *Minus-items in conflict with Dewey*

    23. The ends and laws which should regulate human conduct have been determined by the superior intelligence of an ultimate Being. (B)

IV. ITEMS INVOLVING EMOTIONS AND INTELLECT

    The notion that natural human feelings are something inferior to be depreciated and overcome in the pursuit of higher intellectual activities of the mind is attacked by Dewey. He points out the difficulty this unnatural separation causes in dealing with problems of authority and discipline in morals and education. His belief, of course, is that reliance upon the method of intelligence is a preferable alternative to depending upon external control or giving way to caprice and anarchy.

(a) *Plus-items compatible with Dewey*

    24. Man's primitive impulses are neither good nor evil, but become one or the other according to the objects for which they are employed. (A)

(b) *Minus-items in conflict with Dewey*

    25. The mind turns outward to truth; the emotions turn inward to considerations of personal advantage and loss. (A)

26. The senses and muscles are merely external inlets and outlets of the mind. (B)

27. In the absence of a moral code supported by absolute authority, bodily appetite and passion overpowers intelligence. (B)

V. ITEMS INVOLVING FREEDOM AND AUTHORITY

With respect to the problem of Free Will and Determinism, Dewey rejects both extremes. For him, man is not completely a free agent, nor are his activities and thoughts determined completely by the many influencing factors that impinge upon them. The person who believes that everything that happens in this world is determined by forces beyond his control is relieved of the trouble of thinking and the responsibility for directing his own activity by thought. Man can be free, according to Dewey, only if he lives in a world which is not "completely tight and exact in all its constituents"—a world which is to some degree indeterminate, uncertain, subject to chance. Contingency is a necessary condition of freedom, but "we are free only in the degree in which we act knowing what we are about." Man is capable of intentionally bringing about probable consequence if he uses foresight and intelligence.[5] The following items relate to beliefs of this sort:

(a) *Plus-items compatible with Dewey.*

28. Change is a basic characteristic of nature, and man has some measure of control over this change by using his intelligence. (A)

29. Man is capable of managing his own destiny in an understandable and predictable natural world. (B)

(b) *Minus-items in conflict with Dewey*

30. Man's destiny is in the hands of a supernatural power. (A)

31. Man's destiny is determined by circumstances of nature which are beyond his control. (B)

VI. ITEMS INVOLVING KNOWING AND DOING

The essential feature of the theory of knowing which Dewey advanced is to maintain the continuity of knowing with doing something to things, altering conditions. The value of knowledge

[5] John Dewey, *The Quest for Certainty* (New York: G. P. Putnam's Sons, 1929), pp. 249–250.

lies in the future, in what it can be made to do. When knowledge is cut off from use in giving meaning to what is blind and baffling, it loses all meaning and becomes nothing more than "an object of aesthetic contemplation." The separation of knowing and doing, which Dewey condemns, stems from what he called the false notion that knowledge is derived from a higher source than practical experience, and possesses a higher and more spiritual worth. Dewey rejected theories in which inquiry is seen as a means to the acquisition of knowledge, and, instead, favored the theory of knowledge in which *ac*quiring is always secondary and instrumental to *in*quiring.

(a) *Plus-items compatible with Dewey*

32. Knowledge is artificial and ineffective in the degree in which it is merely presented as truth to be acquired and possessed for its own sake. (B)

(b) *Minus-items in conflict with Dewey*

33. Practice is subordinate to knowledge, merely a means to it. (A)

34. Learning is an application of mental powers to things to be known. (A)

35. Truth exists ready-made somewhere; the task of the scholar is to find it. (A)

36. Knowledge is truth to be accepted, held, and treasured for its own sake. (A)

37. Learning is the sum of impressions made on the mind as a result of presentation of the material to be known. (A)

38. Knowledge is the result of theoretical insight on the part of scholars. (B)

39. Knowledge is the sum total of what is known, as that is handed down by books and learned men. (B)

40. Man gains knowledge by having things impressed upon his mind. (B)

THE TEACHER PRACTICES INVENTORY

The Teacher Practices Inventory is preceded by the following instructions, which are similar to those used with the *Personal Beliefs Inventory*.

This is a study of what people believe is good teaching. Each statement below describes teacher behavior—something a teacher might do in a elassroom. Many different and opposing kinds of teacher practices are presented here. As you read these statements, you will find yourself agreeing with some, disagreeing with some, and uncertain about others. The best answer to each statement is your personal belief or opinion.

Mark each statement in the left margin according to how much you agree or disagree with it. Please mark every one.

Write 1, 2, 3, or 4, 5, 6, depending on how you feel in each case.

1: I agree very much.   4: I disagree a little.
2: I agree on the whole.   5: I disagree on the whole.
3: I agree a little.   6: I disagree very much.

Combined A and B forms of the fifth revision are presented below. As with the *Personal Beliefs Inventory*, plus-items are compatible with experimentalism and minus-items are in conflict. *The Teacher Practices Inventory* contains an equal number of plus- and minus-items. For our purposes here the items have been clustered in plus or minus groups within the categories. In using the inventory the items should be listed randomly and their "plus" or "minus" value indicated on a master scoring sheet. *All ratings given the plus-items are to be reversed,* exactly as is done in scoring the *Personal Beliefs Inventory* (P.B.I.). When these reversals have been marked in red pencil in the left margin they are added up with the unchanged ratings of the minus-items to provide a total score. High scores indicate high compatibility with Dewey's educational beliefs and low scores indicate lack of agreement or conflict.

All of the plus-items appear in the first seven categories. This is because these categories represent the seven steps or features of the educative experience advocated by Dewey. All of the minus-items appear in categories VIII to XII, as these represent the "evils in education" which Dewey opposed.

I. ITEMS INVOLVING SITUATIONS OF EXPERIENCE

This category represents the first stage of Dewey's method of reflective thinking, which he equates with an educative experience —a process which is begun by giving pupils something to do which calls for the noting of connections between their doing and its consequences.

Plus-items compatible with Dewey

1. Teacher focuses attention on what the students do or say, rather than on what the teacher does or says. (A)
2. Teacher allows students to move freely about the room while engaged in purposeful activity. (B)
3. Teacher gives students a number of starting places and a number of different ways of getting at what is to be done. (B)
4. Teacher engages students in dramatizations, music, art, and other creative activities. (B)
5. Teacher makes "doing something" with a thing, rather than the *thing* itself, the center of students' attention. (B)

II. ITEMS INVOLVING THE DEVELOPMENT OF CHALLENGING PROBLEMS

There can be no stimulus to thought unless some difficulty, problem, or trouble develops to prevent the completion of the pupil's activity and the realization of his purpose. Dewey would have the teacher deliberately confront pupils with problematic situations which require them to make choices, ask questions which "stump" pupils—the sort they cannot answer without taking time to think and to investigate. Although he wanted to make problems large enough and tough enough to challenge thought, he thought they should be small enough and familiar enough so that the student is not overwhelmed. In addition, he was concerned that the problem be what the pupil sees as a genuine problem, rather than the teacher's or textbook's problem.

Plus-items which agree with Dewey's philosophy of education

6. Teacher asks students to work on their own problems, rather than something made a problem only for the purpose of conveying instruction in some school subject. (A)
7. Teacher lets students become involved in ugly or distressing aspects of subjects. (A)
8. Teacher insists that students face up to the realities of unpleasant predicaments and plights they get themselves into. (B)
9. Teacher encourages students to adventure into "deep water," to tackle problems that appear to be "over their heads." (B)

III. ITEMS INVOLVING THE GENERATION OF IDEAS

This is the creative stage of thinking, where pupils are encouraged to catch hold of ideas and "run with them" beyond what is, as yet, known for sure. They wrestle with the conditions of the problem at first hand, offer tentative explanations and interpretations of their difficulty, and seek strategies for finding their own way out. The following items tap the teacher's beliefs regarding the value of having pupils formulate tentative hypotheses.

Plus-items compatible with Dewey

10. Teacher encourages students to suggest what might be done—to make "hypothetical leaps" into the unknown or untested. (A)

11. Teacher gives students a wide choice in how they answer questions. (A)

12. Teacher gives students a free rein in devising and inventing proposals for what might be done to clear up troublesome situations. (B)

13. Teacher urges students to put everyday things to uses which have not occurred to others. (B)

IV. ITEMS INVOLVING THE OBSERVATION AND COLLECTION OF DATA

This category might be called "The Use of Subject Matter." Of the large number of items originally occupying this category, only one was found to have any power to discriminate experimentalists from nonexperimentalists. It was difficult to find anyone who did not agree with Dewey that the pupil should look for detailed facts and information needed to deal with the problem he faces, or that the best kind of subject matter is that which the student has to adapt and apply to the question for himself. Neither could we get anyone to quarrel with the belief that a child should compare his present problem with other problems he has faced before, that he find accounts of the experiences of other people in circumstances similar to his own, and to contrast their findings with his own. Apparently, there is an almost universal belief that subject matter, of any shape or form whatever, is invaluable to the process of education.

Plus-items which agree with Dewey's philosophy of education

14. Teacher gives students opportunity to select facts and information which they consider appropriate to the question. (A)

V. ITEMS INVOLVING THE DEVELOPMENT OF REASONED HYPOTHESES

Again, there is far more to this category than we could get discriminating items for. Apparently everyone is for reason, like God, mother, and country. There was little or no opposition to Dewey's recommendations to the effect that teachers, if they accept pupils' guesses at possible answers, should insist that they follow up their guesses by checking them against all available evidence; that teachers should lead pupils to develop their tentative suggestions in an orderly way, to make their ideas more precise and more consistent; that pupils should square their ideas with a wider range of facts or support their beliefs and opinions with factual evidence. The statements dealing with the development of precise ideas or refined hypotheses are as follows:

Plus-items compatible with Dewey

15. Teacher has students compare the value of alternative courses of action and pass judgment on their relative desirability. (A)

16. Teacher frequently asks students to choose among several alternatives. (B)

VI. ITEMS INVOLVING EXPERIMENTAL APPLICATION AND TESTING

This step is the "proof of the pudding." The educational practices recommended by Dewey would have the pupil take a stand upon one hypothesis or proposal and carry through with it to see what happens. Guesses are tested by acting upon them. The pupils do something to bring about the results anticipated from their study. Items pertaining to such beliefs are as follows:

Plus-items compatible with Dewey

17. Teacher permits students to go ahead with plans based on foresight, observation, and consideration of several alternatives—even when sure their judgment is mistaken. (A)

18. Teacher gives students a chance to discover by experiencing actual effects whether their choice of this rather than that idea was a judicious one. (A)

19. Teacher encourages students to put their suggestions to a test with such remarks as "You'll never know unless you try it." (B)

VII. ITEMS INVOLVING THE EVALUATION AND JUDGMENT OF RESULTS

In the "spirit of science" children are encouraged to view the results of their experiments dispassionately, to accept failure as one of the calculated risks of trying. This requires a shift in emphasis in the evaluative climate of the classroom. Pupils need to be freed from constant external judgments by the teacher and to be made responsible for making self-evaluations. They will participate in the evaluation of their own efforts, and will be given an opportunity to make revisions and corrections in their work accordingly. Teachers should, in this view, encourage answers to be treated as intermediate in learning, not final. This category either involved distinctions so subtle they escaped the grasp of teachers or the items were badly composed and confusing, for only one survived the rigors of the item analyses.

Plus-items compatible with Dewey

20. Teacher asks the students to help decide when questions have been satisfactorily answered. (A)

VIII. ITEMS INVOLVING NEGLECT OF DIRECT EXPERIENCES

The items which follow represent the opposite side of the coin to the items in category I. Obviously, if a pupil is expected to sit quietly for long stretches at a time, listening, watching, or waiting his turn in a situation in which the teacher is the principal actor, he cannot be engaged in the kind of experiences Dewey would like him to have. Signs that direct experience is neglected show up in the classroom in the form of restrictive control of bodily movement and permission to talk, and are often based on the assumption that children cannot be trusted to "behave themselves," requiring rules and procedures to limit their opportunities for misbehavior.

Minus-items in conflict with Dewey

21. Once work has begun, teacher insists that students remain in their places and concentrate on the task at hand. (A)

22. Teacher calls for the undivided attention of the group and scolds those who do not respond. (A)

23. Teacher limits physical activity to the gym or playground. (B)

IX. ITEMS INVOLVING RELIANCE UPON EXTRINSIC MOTIVATION

It was Dewey's belief that the teacher should organize learning around the sort of things that would arouse the child's interest and attention outside of school. Such things "in the raw," just as they "come down the pike" in the everyday world, require nothing added, no sugar-coating or external pressure, to make them appealing to children. Only when the subject matter of school lessons is taken out of its natural state and ground up into easily digested bits and pieces with all of the juice squeezed out of it, does it become such dry tasteless stuff that children must be bribed, beaten, or bamboozled into swallowing it. Natural interest in subject matter is killed by practices which discourage arguments and disagreements among pupils, and which put a damper on instances of spontaneous enjoyment or excitement of pupils. Extrinsic motivation is necessary when the objective is to capture answers apart from the enjoyment of the chase—or the sport of inquiring and questioning. It will take the form of using competition between pupils as a means of stimulating them to their best efforts, appealing to pupils to "try harder," punishing failure to pay attention and get interested. Motivation of this sort is a sure indication that subject matter has been reduced to routine *stuff*, cut and dried, and separated from the method of its making. Beliefs related to the treatment of subject matter which requires extrinsic motivation are as follows:

Minus-items in conflict with Dewey

24. Teacher motivates students to greater intellectual effort by rewarding them with grades, marks, prizes, or privileges. (A)

25. Teacher organizes learning around questions posed by the teacher or textbook. (B)

26. Teacher sticks to questions which can be answered by

looking in the textbook or other references readily available in the school. (B)

27. Teacher accepts material in the approved textbook as a reliable measure for the appropriateness of information brought in by students from other sources. (B)

28. Teacher asks the kind of questions that students should be able to answer if they have studied the lesson. (A)

X. ITEMS INVOLVING THE MAKING OF LEARNING
   A DIRECT AND CONSCIOUS END IN ITSELF

Dewey rejected the notion that the purpose of education is to acquire and possess knowledge. He saw learning not as an end in itself, but as a means to the useful purposes to which it can be put in the future. Disagreement with Dewey on this issue is indicated in practices which make it urgent to get problems solved. Questions are answered as if confusion and puzzlement on the part of pupils were some sort of intolerable disease which must be prevented or, when it occurs, cured as quickly and correctly as possible. The characteristic climate in which such practice thrives is direct, businesslike, controlled. There is no dillydallying, no wasting of time with roundabout, indirect approaches. The teacher assigns the work to be accomplished. Youngsters are in school to study and learn, not to play games or go on wild goose chases. Students are to stick to facts, what is known for sure, and their suggestions are considered appropriate only when closely related to the subject being studied. Much time and effort is devoted to correcting pupils' mistakes and analyzing the causes of their failure.

Minus-items in conflict with Dewey

29. Teacher makes the acquisition of knowledge and skills the center of students' attention and effort. (A)

30. Teacher makes a direct presentation of the subject matter to be covered. (A)

31. Teacher makes students emphatically aware that they are here to study and learn. (B)

32. When one student fails to answer a question, asks another student to supply the correct answer. (A)

33. Teacher quickly tells students whether their answers are "right" or "wrong." (B)

XI. ITEMS INVOLVING THE MECHANICAL FOLLOWING
OF AN ESTABLISHED METHOD

Even though Dewey was an advocate of a method, he saw dangers in following that or any other method routinely—as if its steps had been prescribed and fixed by some unquestionable authority. He condemned teacher practices which follow "proven methods" worked out by "experts" and given ready-made in manuals and courses of study. Dualistic thinking is evident when teachers arrange a "developmental" series of lessons designed or "programmed" to direct the children's learning "systematically"; in short, sure steps. The teacher who assigns and clearly defines the study problem for students so they will have no doubts as to exactly what they are to do obviously sees the educational process as merely a means to the achievement of some external end imposed upon the pupils by the school, a notion which leads to lock-step rigidity in teaching methods.

Minus-items in conflict with Dewey

34. Teacher faithfully follows a planned schedule in order to get in the number of minutes each week allotted to each subject in the curriculum. (B)

35. Teacher shows students the most economical and efficient way to get a job done, and expects them to do it pretty much that way. (B)

36. Teacher tells students where to start and what to do to accomplish the task at hand. (B)

XII. ITEMS INVOLVING THE IMPOSITION OF
A GENERAL METHOD ON ALL ALIKE

Items in this category get at the teacher's beliefs concerning the individualization of instruction. Dewey objected to methods which drive students in a group, as if they were a herd of cattle, down the same path in order to reach the same goals at the same time. Indications that such is the case when teachers hold all students equally responsible for answering certain questions and for finishing a given assignment within a definitely fixed time limit. Another tip-off is the so-called democratic procedure of having pupils vote and abide by the will of the majority whenever there is disagreement about what is the good, right, or desirable thing to do.

Minus-items in conflict with Dewey

37. Teacher uses a set standard to judge the work of all students in the class. (A)

38. Teacher provides a model to show students exactly what their work should be like when it is finished. (A)

39. Teacher usually has all students working on the same page of the same book at the same time. (A)

40. Teacher provides approximately the same materials for each student in the class. (B)

PROCEDURES, SUBJECTS, AND ANALYSES

The *Personal Beliefs Inventory* and *Teacher Practices Inventory* are usually administered to persons in groups. They take both inventories in a single setting, the *Personal Beliefs Inventory* first, followed immediately by the *Teacher Practices Inventory*. Our usual practice has been to ask those filling out the inventories to put their names on them. We need to know the names of the subjects in order to obtain other data on them or to retest them at another time. If one feels that having the subjects give their names discourages frank and honest responses, they can be identified by having them give only their birth date, city and state of birth, sex, and other similar general information about themselves. When such information is matched with available institutional records the subjects can be identified by name. However, in the development of the inventories we have been concerned with learning what beliefs the subjects are *willing to admit to* rather than to seek to uncover what they *really* believe (whatever that means!).

Ordinarily, all 40 statements from both A and B Forms are combined into a single form of the *Personal Beliefs Inventory* and the *Teacher Practices Inventory*. When conservation of time is imperative or frequent retesting over an extended period is desired, each of the inventories may be divided into two forms. Form A of one inventory is always administered with Form A of the other, just as Form B of both inventories are given together. Forms A and B are approximately equivalent tests, or, more correctly, comparable-but-different forms of the same test.

The inventories of the Experimentalism Scale were administered to various groups during the years 1961–1965. The populations for whom reliability data have been obtained came from four different states: Wisconsin, Illinois, California, and New York. In Wisconsin, the largest number of subjects were persons involved with the teacher education programs at the University of Wisconsin, Madison. Included were undergraduate and graduate students preparing to be teachers in elementary and secondary schools; graduate students taking advanced work in education, educational administration and educational psychology; professors and supervisors of student teachers and interns; and cooperating teachers and administrators in public schools which participate in the student teaching and internship programs at the University of Wisconsin. In addition, data was obtained from the faculty of a small northern Wisconsin public school, including elementary and secondary teachers, the principals, and superintendent. Prior to 1965, data had been obtained only on subjects in Wisconsin. In order to extend the collection of reliability data to areas differing educationally and socially, Form 5 (combined A and B sub-forms) was administered in 1965 to senior college students in elementary and secondary education, and a selected group of both academic and education professors and supervisors of student teaching at Northwestern University in Evanston, Illinois, Sacramento State College in California, and the State University of New York, College of Education, at Albany.

RELIABILITY OF THE EXPERIMENTALISM SCALE

The inventories of the Experimentalism Scale, as we have already indicated, have gone through a number of revisions. These revisions were made to reflect the changing development, elaboration, and refinement of our thinking about the relationship of the items and the theoretical framework. Particularly, the revisions were efforts to increase or maintain reliability while searching for items with the strongest power for discrimination, and to reduce the number of items needed to adequately test the subjects.

The reliability coefficients for all forms of the *Personal Beliefs Inventory* and the *Teacher Practices Inventories* are shown in Tables 6A and 6B. Included are the number of items in each form, the groups to which they were given, number of cases, the mean score of the group, and the standard deviations.

Form 1 was composed of a 122-item Personal Beliefs Questionnaire with an internal consistency reliability of .78, and a 150-item Teacher Practices Questionnaire with a reliability of .94. As a result of an item analysis, we developed Form 2, a 36-item Personal Beliefs Q-sort with a split-halves reliability of .60, and a 60-item Teacher Practices Q-sort with a split-halves reliability of .72. We then went back and put Form 1 through another item analysis and abandoned the Q-sort format in favor of a questionnaire. Form 3 resulted. It is a 44-item Personal Beliefs Questionnaire with reliabilities ranging from .55 to .73, and an 82-item Teacher Practices Questionnaire with reliabilities ranging from .77 to .91.

Following repeated item analyses of Form 3, both the Personal Beliefs and Teacher Practices Questionnaires, in 1963, were reduced to 30 items each, comprised of two 10-item parts in which all items were "plus," and one 10-item part in which all items were "minus." This form, number 4, was administered to two groups of summer-session graduate students at the University of Wisconsin; first in June and again in August, providing data which yielded test-retest reliabilities of .63 and .75 for the Personal Beliefs Questionnaire, and .56 and .62 for the Teacher Practices Questionnaire. Although reliabilities increased for Personal Beliefs they fell off for Teacher Practices. In addition, this form had an imbalance of plus items, including many introduced for the first time, and not all of these proved to have good discriminating power.

The item analysis procedure used with the results obtained from the Form 1 to produce the Form 2 Q-sorts and later the Form 3 questionnaires followed closely the simplified item-analysis procedure described by Stanley.[6] Subsequently, the data from Forms 1 and 3 for both inventories was subjected to RAVE analysis. The

[6] Julian C. Stanley and C. C. Ross, *Measurement in Today's Schools* (Englewood Cliffs, N.J.: Prentice Hall, Inc., 1954), pp. 436–453.

RAVE analysis is a scaling technique for quantitative data, and is an iterative procedure which yields a set of item response weights which maximize the internal consistency of the inventories.[7] These analyses of the discriminating power of the items strongly influenced the development of Forms 4 and 5 of both inventories.

As we have already pointed out, Form 4 was overstocked with plus or positive statements of experimentalism. This was due primarily to the fact that item analyses repeatedly eliminated positive items in favor of negative items. To avoid letting the inventories be reduced to nothing but negative items, we went back to the theoretical framework of Dewey's experimentalism for as many strong new items as could be found. Enough of these survived the analysis of Form 4 data with reasonably strong discriminating power to give us an equally balanced number of plus and minus items for Form 5. This enabled the inventories to remain measures of what experimentalism is *for* as well as what it is *against*. Even so, the negative or minus items are generally more discriminating than the positive or plus items.

Throughout, most of our "choicest" positive statements of Dewey's philosophy had to be tossed out because we could find almost no one who would disagree with them. This fact lends credence to the notion that Dewey did not invent his philosophy out of thin air, but, instead, built it on the basis of his observations of the American scene. Apparently, people disagree with Dewey only when he points out the logical inconsistency between experimentalism and institutionalized or traditional philosophies.

Since we selected items with the strongest ability to discriminate, the inventories tend to measure only the *controversial* aspects of experimentalism. For this reason, the casual reader may be misled by the scale items to believe that John Dewey was even more controversial than he really was.

Form 5 of both inventories was developed to include two subforms, A and B, of 20 items each. Form 5-A was administered to a cross section of undergraduate and graduate students in edu-

[7] Ronald Ragsdale and Frank B. Baker, *The Method of Reciprocal Averages for Scaling of Inventories and Questionnaires: A Computer Program for The CDC 1604 Computer* (Mimeographed, Laboratory of Experimental Design, Department of Educational Psychology, University of Wisconsin, Madison).

cation at the University of Wisconsin in March, 1964. In May of 1964, Form 5-B was administered to this same group of subjects, giving us data which yielded similar forms reliability of .58 for the *Personal Beliefs Inventory* and .69 for the *Teacher Practices Inventory*. Additional data obtained from populations in California, Illinois, and New York by administering combined A and B subforms of Form 5 showed reliabilities ranging from .55 to .78 for Personal Beliefs and from .56 to .94 for Teacher Practices.

There is, of course, no absolute standard for judging the adequacy of reliability. A reliability of .80 or higher may be demanded for tests of mental ability or achievement, but considerably more latitude is granted measures of attitudes, personality, and values. The Experimentalism Scale falls in the latter category. Such scales contain such a wide range of items which do not appear, on the surface, to be related. Perhaps lower reliability coefficients are tolerated out of sheer wonder that any relationship or consistency can be found at all.

TABLE 6A. *Reliabilities, Means, and Standard Deviations of Successive Forms of the Personal Beliefs Inventory*

Form	No. of items	Group	No. of cases	Relia-bility	Mean	S.D.
1	122	El. Ed. Students, U.W.	102	.78	488	25.1
2 (Q-sort)	36	El. Ed. Student Tchrs., U.W.	36	.60[a]	....	....
3	44	Sec. Ed. Student Tchrs., U.W.	102	.72	79.4	11.1
3	44	Sec. Ed. Student Tchrs., U.W.	102	.64	81.1	12.0
3	44	Educ. Prof.-Supv., U.W.	22	.72	83.1	15.0
3	44	Co-op. Teachers, Wis. P.S.	58	.62	81.5	11.0
3	44	Supts., Principals, Wis. P.S.	122	.60	77.6	11.3
3	44	El. Ed. Students – I, U.W.	68	.55	82.7	27.4
3	44	El. Ed. Students – II, U.W.	68	.73	88.8	11.3
4	30	Grad. Students – I, U.W.	44	.63[b]	83.4	12.4
4	30	Grad. Students – II, U.W.	43	.75[b]	78.2	17.6
5 (A)	20	U.G. and Grad. Students, U.W.	154	....	70.8	9.9
5 (B)	20	U.G. and Grad. Students, U.W.	154	....	73.2	8.7
5 (A & B)	40	U.G. and Grad. Students, U.W.	154	.58[c]	....	....

[a] Split-halves reliability.

[b] Test-retest reliability.

[c] Reliability of comparable forms.

All other reliability figures represent Hoyt Internal Consistency Reliability Coefficients.

TABLE 6B. *Reliabilities, Means, and Standard Deviations of Successive Forms of the Teacher Practices Inventory*

Form	No. of items	Group	No. of cases	Reliability	Mean	S.D.
1	150	El. Ed. Students, U.W.	102	.94	553	40.0
2 (Q-sort)	60	El. Ed. Student Tchrs., U.W.	36	.72[a]	....	....
3	82	Sec. Ed. Student Tchrs., U.W.	102	.71	166.9	15.8
3	82	Sec. Ed. Student Tchrs., U.W.	102	.64	164.2	18.1
3	82	Educ. Prof.-Supv., U.W.	22	.91	176.6	26.9
3	82	Co-op. Teachers, Wis. P.S.	58	.77	177.5	16.5
3	82	Supts., Principals, Wis. P.S.	122	.84	174.7	14.5
3	82	El. Ed. Students – I, U.W.	68	.80	166.5	6.6
3	82	El. Ed. Students – II, U.W.	68	.85	203.1	19.0
4	30	Grad. Students – I, U.W.	44	.56[b]	....	....
4	30	Grad. Students – II, U.W.	43	.62[b]	....	....
5 (A)	20	U.G. and Grad. Students, U.W.	154	....	86.1	10.0
5 (B)	20	U.G. and Grad. Students, U.W.	154	....	90.6	10.4
5 (A & B)	40	U.G. and Grad. Students, U.W.	154	.69[c]	....	....

[a] Split-halves reliability.
[b] Test-retest reliability.
[c] Reliability of comparable forms.
All other reliability figures represent Hoyt Internal Consistency Reliability Coefficients.

In any event, the reliabilities found for the inventories of the Experimentalism Scale should be considered quite satisfactory. They compare favorably with the reliability coefficients reported for other respected measures in this area. For example, the reliabilities reported for the Allport-Vernon Study of Values[8] ranged from .39 to .84, while the reliabilities for the Dogmatism Scale[9] ranged from .68 to .93, and for the Total Opinionation Scale[10] they ranged from .67 to .76.

Means and standard deviations are shown in Tables 6A and 6B for Forms 1, 3, and 5. The means listed for the different forms cannot be compared because the number of items varies. It is possible, of course, to compare means obtained with the same form. For example, there were eight different groups tested with

[8] Gordon W. Allport and P. E. Vernon, *A Study of Values* (Boston: Houghton Mifflin, 1931).
[9] Rokeach, *op. cit.*, p. 90.
[10] *Ibid.*, p. 92.

Form 3, with the means clustering around 175 for Personal Beliefs and approximately 315 for Teacher Practices. This similarity of means and standard deviations gives us additional confidence in the reliability of the measurements.

A study of the mean scores obtained by the various groups taking Form 3 is very interesting. It shows that the average score made by those persons "agreed a little" with experimentalism, both with respect to Personal Beliefs and Teacher Practices. A close examination of the distribution of scores obtained from Forms 3 and 5 showed that average experimentalism scores ranged from "I disagree a little" to "I agree on the whole." To date we have not found a teacher with an average score which indicates much more than "a little disagreement" with Dewey on either inventory. This finding lends further support to the contention of many Dewey scholars that experimentalism is the indigenous American philosophy.

TEACHER PRACTICES OBSERVATION RECORD

The directions for the use of the *Teacher Practices Observation Record* are as follows:

The Teacher Practices Observation Record provides a framework for observing and recording the classroom practices of the teacher. Your role as an observer is to watch and listen for signs of the sixty-two teacher practices listed and to record whether or not they were observed, WITHOUT MAKING JUDGMENTS AS TO THE RELATIVE IMPORTANCE OR RELEVANCE OF THOSE PRACTICES.

There are three (3) separate 10-minute observation and marking periods in each 30-minute visit to the teacher's classroom. These are indicated by the column headings I, II, and III. During period I, spend the first 5 minutes observing the behavior of the teacher. In the last 5 minutes go down the list and place a check (√) mark in Column I beside all practices you saw occur. Leave blank the space beside practices which did *not* occur or which did *not* seem to apply to this particular observation. Please consider every practice listed, mark it or leave it blank. A particular item is marked only once in a given column, no matter how many times that practice occurs within the 10-minute observation period. A practice which occurs a dozen times gets one check mark, the same as an item which occurs only once.

Repeat this process for the second 10-minute period, marking in Column II. Repeat again for the third 10-minute period, marking in Column III. Please add the total number of check marks recorded for each teacher practice and record in the column headed TOT. There may be from 0 to 3 total check marks for each item.

The revised form of the *Teacher Practices Observation Record* is presented below. It contains 62 items or "signs" of teacher practices. With respect to Dewey's philosophy of experimentalism, 31 of these are positive and 31 are negative. All even-numbered items are positive and all odd-numbered items are negative, making it easy to score the results.

The *Teacher Practices Observation Record* is usually scored by first totaling the number of check marks for each item, placing either a 0, 1, 2, or 3 in the column headed TOT. Next, the totals for all of the odd-numbered items are *reversed,* changing 0 to 3, 1 to 2, 2 to 1, and 3 to 0. Then by adding the totals for *all* items (both the totals for the untouched even or "positive" items and for the adjusted odd or "negative" items) we get a net score. A maximum score of 186 indicates complete experimentalism and a minimum score of 0 indicates complete non-experimentalism. A score of 94 or above indicates the observed teacher practices are more experimental than non-experimental, and a score of 93 or below indicates the opposite.

TEACHER PRACTICES OBSERVATION RECORD

TOT	I	II	III	Teacher practices
				A. *Nature of the situation*
				1. T makes self center of attention.
				2. T makes p center of attention.
				3. T makes some *thing itself* center of p's attention.
				4. T makes *doing something* center of p's attention.
				5. T has p spend time waiting, watching, listening.
				6. T has p participate actively.
				7. T remains aloof or detached from p's activities.
				8. T joins or participates in p's activities.
				9. T discourages or prevents p from expressing self freely.
				10. T encourages p to express self freely.
				B. *Nature of the problem*
				11. T organizes learning around Q posed by T.

TEACHERS PRACTICES OBSERVATION RECORD (*Continued*)

TOT	I	II	III	Teacher practices
				12. T organizes learning around p's own problem or Q.
				13. T prevents situation which causes p doubt or perplexity.
				14. T involves p in uncertain or incomplete situation.
				15. T steers p away from "hard" Q or problem.
				16. T leads p to Q or problem which "stumps" him.
				17. T emphasizes gentle or pretty aspects of topic.
				18. T emphasizes distressing or ugly aspects of topic.
				19. T asks Q that p can answer only if he studied the lesson.
				20. T asks Q that is *not* readily answerable by study of lesson.
				C. *Development of ideas*
				21. T accepts only one answer as being correct.
				22. T asks p to suggest additional or alternative answers.
				23. T expects p to come up with answer T has in mind.
				24. T asks p to judge comparative value of answers or suggestions.
				25. T expects p to "know" rather than to guess answer to Q.
				26. T encourages p to guess or hypothesize about the unknown or untested.
				27. T accepts only answers or suggestions closely related to topic.
				28. T entertains even "wild" or far-fetched suggestion of p.
				29. T lets p "get by" with opinionated or stereotyped answer.
				30. T asks p to support answer or opinion with evidence.
				D. *Use of subject matter*
				31. T collects and analyzes subject matter for p.
				32. T has p make his own collection and analysis of subject matter.
				33. T provides p with detailed facts and information.
				34. T has p find detailed facts and information on his own.
				35. T relies heavily on textbook as source of information.
				36. T makes a wide range of informative material available.
				37. T accepts and uses inaccurate information.
				38. T helps p discover and correct factual errors and inaccuracies.
				39. T permits formation of misconceptions and overgeneralizations.

TEACHERS PRACTICES OBSERVATION RECORD (*Continued*)

TOT	I	II	III	Teacher practices
				40. T questions misconceptions, faulty logic, unwarranted conclusions.
				E. *Evaluation*
				41. T passes judgment on p's behavior or work.
				42. T withholds judgment on p's behavior or work.
				43. T stops p from going ahead with plan which T knows will fail.
				44. T encourages p to put his ideas to a test.
				45. T immediately reinforces p's answer as "right" or "wrong."
				46. T has p decide when Q has been answered satisfactorily.
				47. T asks another p to give answer if one p fails to answer quickly.
				48. T asks p to evaluate his own work.
				49. T provides answer to p who seems confused or puzzled.
				50. T gives p time to sit and think, mull things over.
				F. *Differentiation*
				51. T has all p working at same task at same time.
				52. T has different p working at different tasks.
				53. T holds all p responsible for certain material to be learned.
				54. T has p work indepndently on what concerns p.
				55. T evaluates work of all p by a set standard.
				56. T evaluates work of different p by different standards.
				G. *Motivation, control*
				57. T motivates p with privileges, prizes, grades.
				58. T motivates p with intrinsic value of ideas or activity.
				59. T approaches subject matter in direct, business-like way.
				60. T approaches subject matter in indirect, informal way.
				61. T imposes external disciplinary control on p.
				62. T encourages self-discipline on part of p.

The T.P.O.R. items, of course, are identical to, or only slightly modified versions of, the items on the *Teacher Practices Inventory*. This permits us to compare T.P.O.R. scores with T.P.I. and P.B.I. scores within the same theoretical framework. Originally, we used the items in the T.P.I. as a Q-sort for measuring the observed behavior of teachers. Observers made distributions of the Teacher Practices Q-sort immediately following observations of classroom teaching. By sorting the statements describing teacher practices into a prescribed normal distribution, keeping in mind the practices used by the teacher just observed, measurements of experimentalism evidenced in the teacher's overt behavior in the classroom were obtained and converted into scores which could be correlated with the teacher's scores on the verbal measures of experimentalism.

There were several objections to the Q-sort technique. First, it represented a "recall" or "general impression" of what happened during an observation, rather than a record made *at the time* the behavior occurred. Second, Q-sorts are clumsy to handle and time-consuming to execute. Observers frequently took up to two hours to "throw" the 60-item Q-sort which constituted Form 2 of the T.P.I. Obviously, we had to find a simpler, quicker instrument.

T.P.O.R. FILM STUDIES

The T.P.O.R. was used in the spring of 1964 for recording observations of five filmed teaching episodes by a large number of observer-judges at four different teacher education institutions in California, Illinois, New York, and Wisconsin. A year later T.P.O.R. observations were repeated on two of these films by the same observer-judges. These data were used to give us information about the consistency-stability reliability of the T.P.O.R.

The teaching episodes observed in this study were originally filmed at Madison, Wisconsin, in the early 1960s. For the purpose of this study 30-minute continuous and uninterrupted segments were cut from unedited films which were 50 to 60 minutes in length. Selection of the films and the segments taken from them was made for purposes of achieving variety in teaching style, and in grade level and subject taught. Teachers in the film were equally well-trained (all had master's degrees) and had ben selected for filming at the University of Wisconsin as "showcase" teachers. Film 1 was of a ninth-grade French class; Film 2, a seventh-grade mathematics class; Film 3, a fourth-grade unit on "Weather'; Film 4, a ninth-grade speech class; and Film 5, a seventh-grade science class.

The observer-judges were drawn from the faculties of two large midwestern universities and two large state "teachers college-type" schools—one in the east and one in the far west. The observer-judges included student teaching supervisors, education professors, and professors of academic subjects who volunteered their participation in the project. None of them had seen the films or the T.P.O.R. prior to the viewing sessions, held separately at the four different campuses over a span of six weeks. Conditions of the viewing sessions were similar. All observer-judges received the same 10-minute explanation, by the same person, for recording their observations in the T.P.O.R. During the viewing of Film 1 time was called periodically for the observer-judges and lights were switched on and off to make it easier for them to become familiar with the observational procedures and instrumentation. This constituted the total of *training* the observers. *No attempt was made to bring them to any sort of agreement* with respect to their recorded observations, nor was any discussion to this effect permitted. Assistance with respect to time and lighting was discontinued after the first film observation, putting the observers "on their own" in every respect.

Table 6C shows the mean T.P.O.R. score given each of the five films by the observer-judges on the first viewing. The French teacher in Film 1 was seen as the least experimental and the fourth-grade teacher in Film 3 as the most in agreement with Dewey. The range of more than 40 points between the high and low T.P.O.R. means indicates the ability of the instrument to differentiate various styles of teaching.

We looked for differences in the T.P.O.R. scores given at the four participating institutions. The location variable was found to have little or no influence. Using Scheffé's comparisons, no statistically significant differences were found among the T.P.O.R. means given at the various locations for Films 1, 2, 4, and 5. The

TABLE 6C. *Mean T.P.O.R. Scores Given Five Films by All Observers*

Film	No. of Observers	Mean	S.D.
1	130	80.01	13.32
2	124	115.86	16.84
3	119	120.96	22.74
4	119	104.24	17.10
5	67	98.84	12.88

only statistically significant differences were found between California and each of the other three locations on Film 3.

We also looked for differences in the T.P.O.R. scores given by the three major occupational classifications of observer-judges—college supervisors of student teaching, education professors, and academic professors. No statistically significant differences were found between any of these groups for Films 1, 2, 4, and 5. The only statistically significant differences were found between supervisors of student teaching and both education and academic professors on Film 3.

Mass observations of films are expensive and administratively difficult to arrange. For these reasons repeated observations the second year could be obtained on only two of the five films. Film 1 was eliminated because it had been usd as the *training* film and the conditions of the first viewing could not be simulated. Film 3 yielded a wide discrepancy between the scores given it in California and those given it at the other three locations, which we thought might be due to the artificial conditions under which it was filmed. Film 5 had not been observed at all four institutions. This left Films 2 and 4 selected by elimination for the second viewing. It was possible to obtain repeated T.P.O.R. scores on these films by only a portion of those who observed the first viewings.

Table 6D shows a fairly substantial difference between T.P.O.R. means recorded for the first and second viewings of Film 2. While this difference raises some questions about stability, both means for this sub-group of 69 observers lie well within one standard deviation of the mean of 115.86 for 119 first-viewing observers which may simply demonstrate the normal variability of T.P.O.R. scores. The differences between T.P.O.R. scores for the first and second viewings of Film 4 are very small.

TABLE 6D. *Mean T.P.O.R. Scores Given Films on Repeated Observations One Year Apart*

Film	Viewing	No. Observers	Mean	S.D.
2	1st	69	122.22	20.52
2	2nd	69	109.81	18.31
4	1st	72	107.15	17.15
4	2nd	72	105.14	18.12

RELIABILITY OF THE T.P.O.R.

In order for anyone to place confidence in the scores obtained with the T.P.O.R., its reliability as a measuring instrument must be established. There are three major problems involved in doing this:

1. Selecting *types* (or definitions) of reliability appropriate to the instrument and the purposes for which it is designed.
2. Selecting a meaningful *measure* (or yardstick) of reliability once the type is specified.
3. Selecting a good *estimator* of a given measure to give an estimate of reliability based on experimental data.

Reliability can be a tricky concept. We know that reliability always refers to consistency throughout a series of measurements, and that it is usually expressed in terms of something called *reliability* coefficients. Rarely do we make clear what kind of consistency has been figured. Although everybody in educational research *reads* reliability coefficients, few seem to really understand (or care) what these mean or how they were obtained. All that matters is that they be high. Once the standard for *highness* has been debated and denoted, then surpassed or fallen short of, what more is there to say about reliability?

There are many different kinds of reliability to be considered. Thorndike speaks of approaching the study of reliability from two quite different viewpoints. One approach is to be concerned about the actual or absolute magnitude of errors of measurements. In this case, reliability is expressed in terms of the variability of scores obtained by repeated testing of the same individual, and is based on a statistic called *standard error of measurement.* Another approach can be made in terms of the consistency with which individuals maintain the same relative position in the total group on repetition of a measurement procedure. In this case, consistency is expressed in terms of the correlation between two sets of scores, called the *coefficient of reliability.*[11] As a further example, Cronbach points out that not all reliability coefficients reveal the same or even com-

[11] Robert L. Thorndike, "Reliability," Chapter 15 in *Educational Measurement,* E. F. Lindquist, Editor. (Washington, D.C.,: American Council on Education, 1950), pp. 560–561.

parable information. He refers to *comparable-forms, split-half,* and *test-retest* reliability coefficients as ways to get at different aspects of reliability. The first is a *coefficient of equivalence and stability,* the second a *coefficient of equivalence* only, and the third a *coefficient of stability.*[12] Furthermore, we have something called *internal consistency* or *item reliability* which assesses test homogeneity—the extent to which all items measure the same attribute. This, of course, is a horse of still another color. All of which makes the use of the term *reliability* meaningless without some further differentiation and definition.

Dealing adequately with already difficult concepts of reliability becomes even more complex when one turns from consideration of tests of achievement and intelligence, and the like, to the measurement of classroom behavior by systematic observation. The question of the reliability of the observers and the recording of their observations must be added to the problem. In the past, most observational studies have limited their study of reliability to computing the correlation between two sets of observations or to figuring the percent of agreement between observers.

Keeping this tradition, in part, we computed the correlations between the T.P.O.R. scores obtained from the repeated observations of Films 2 and 4. It is curious to note in Table 6E that the correlations of the columns (10-minute observation periods) within each film observation are very high, but the correlations between the 1964 and 1965 observations are very low. The first indicates that the observers tended to maintain the same relative position in the group throughout the viewing of a single film on a given day. The second indicates that sizeable shifts in these positions took place during the intervening year. In other words, we got good consistency *within* one occasion or viewing, and again within another, but poor stability *between* two widely separated occasions. One must keep in mind, however, that such reliability coefficients normally decline proportionately with the length of time between tests. Had the repeat observations been made only a month or so apart we might expect considerably higher correlations.

Even so, correlation of two sets of scores by a number of different observers is not likely to be a very accurate estimate of re-

[12] Lee J. Cronbach, *Essentials of Psychological Testing,* Second Edition, (New York: Harper & Row, 1960), pp. 136–142.

TABLE 6E. Correlation of T.P.O.R. Scores Obtained from Repeated Observations of Films

FILM 2

T.P.O.R. column	1964 observation T.P.O.R. column				1965 observation T.P.O.R. column			
	1	2	3	TOT	1	2	3	TOT
1964 observation 1	1.00	.79	.69	.89	.36	.25	.12	.27
1964 observation 2	....	1.00	.81	.95	....	.29	.16	.31
1964 observation 3	....	....	1.00	.92	....	....	.20	.29
1964 observation TOT	....	....	....	1.00	....	....	....	.32
1965 observation 1	....	....	....	....	1.00	.61	.55	.80
1965 observation 2	....	....	....	....	....	1.00	.81	.93
1965 observation 3	....	....	....	....	....	....	1.00	.90
1965 observation TOT	....	....	....	....	....	....	....	1.00

FILM 4

T.P.O.R. column	1964 observation T.P.O.R. column				1965 observation T.P.O.R. column			
	1	2	3	TOT	1	2	3	TOT
1964 observation 1	1.00	.75	.52	.86	.32	.36	.25	.34
1964 observation 2	....	1.00	.71	.93	....	.46	.52	.52
1964 observation 3	....	....	1.00	.85	....	....	.67	.57
1964 observation TOT	....	....	....	1.00	....	....	....	....
1965 observation 1	....	....	....	....	1.00	.79	.71	.90
1965 observation 2	....	....	....	....	....	1.00	.83	.95
1965 observation 3	....	....	....	....	....	....	1.00	.92
1965 observation TOT	....	....	....	....	....	....	....	1.00

liability. It is difficult to make arrangements for large numbers of observers to view the same classroom on two different occasions, or to control variations between those occasions. Likewise, the number of classrooms observed on two different occasions by two different observers is likely to be small. In either case, the size of the N determines the precision of the correlation coefficient, and since the N of even well-financed observational studies rarely exceeds 100 the confidence intervals for the cofficients are extremely wide. Furthermore, such correlations are usually based on total scores which ignore variations in scoring individual items or categories. It is possible to obtain a perfect correlation of total scores when the reliability for the items is zero. If on a 70-item *sign* system, for example, the 35 odd-numbered items are marked "+" and the 35 even-numbered items are marked "0" on the first observation, and then exactly reversed on the second observation, identical total scores will be obtained and used to produce a deceivingly perfect reliability correlation.

Percent of agreement between observers tells almost nothing about the accuracy of the scores obtained. It is entirely possible to find observers agreeing 99 percent in recording behaviors on an instrument whose item or category consistency is very poor. Reliability can be low even though observer agreement is high. For example, observers might be able to agree perfectly that a particular teaching practice occurred in a classroom, yet if that same practice occurs equally, or nearly so, in all classrooms, the reliability of that item as a measure of differences between teachers will be zero. Near-perfect agreement could also be reached about the percentage of time a number of teachers employed certain categories of behavior; but if every teacher sharply reversed these percentages from period to period or day to day, the reliability of these categories would be zero. Errors arising from variations in behavior from one situation or occasion to another can far outweigh errors arising from failure of two observers to agree exactly in their records of the same behavior.

Yet, the reliability of most instruments for systematically recording the behavior of teachers requires a high percent of observer agreement. *Between-observer* agreement has become almost a cardinal principle in planning observational studies. According to established procedures, a sample of classrooms from the population to be studied should be visited by trained recorders using the observational instrument in the same way it will be used in any subsequent study. In order to study the *objectivity* of the items, i.e., how closely observers agree in recording identical behaviors, at least two recorders should be present on each visit, sitting in different parts of the room and making independent records. In order to be able to estimate how the two records based on different visits will agree, each class should be visited at least twice.[13]

Training of the observers undoubtedly would bring them into agreement with respect to recording or scoring identical behaviors, which would be reflected in a higher reliability coefficient. However, in the previously described film study in which the T.P.O.R. was tried out, *no attempt* was made to train the observers. To the contrary, we deliberately tried to *preserve the differences* among observers by selecting them from varying occupational groups, from varying sizes of institutions with varying orientations to teacher education, and from varying parts of the country. We wanted to test the reliability of the T.P.O.R. under uncontrolled field conditions to see what value it might have in the hands of the differing kinds of people who carry out the everyday responsibilities for teacher education in America. Hence, the component of variance due to the observers' variability in our study would be large, resulting in a small reliability coefficient. We did not get as much observer variability as might have been expected, however. When the Medley-Mitzel model[14] was adapted to fit our film study data the T.P.O.R. observations were found to have a modest but substantial reliability coefficient of 57.

The Medley-Mitzel model, however, stresses *between-observer* variability rather than *within-observer* variability. This raises a philosophical issue which goes beyond statistical consideration. Reliability coefficients which reward high agreement between observers imply that we should seek a single, uniform, *objective* system for

---

[13] Donald M. Medley and Harold E. Mitzel "Measuring Classroom Behavior by Systematic Observation," Chapter 6 in *Handbook of Research on Teaching,* N. L. Gage, Editor (Chicago: Rand McNally & Company, 1963), p. 309.

[14] *Ibid.,* p. 316.

observing and classifying teaching behavior. From the point of view of the framework underlying the development of the T.P.O.R., objectivity in perceiving and quantifying such behavior is neither possible nor desirable. *Between-observer* agreement may not only encourage a false sense of confidence with respect to the accuracy of measurements, but give us a false sense of objectivity regarding the observations. A team of observers can be brainwashed to the point of near-perfect agreement, but this does not erase the possibility that instead of several differing *subjective* judgments, they now make only one. Therefore, we sought another mathematical definition of reliability, one which is concerned primarily with *within-observer* variability.[15]

Using the formulation developed by William Mendenhall, Chairman of the Department of Statistics, University of Florida, the *within-observer* reliability of T.P.O.R. scores was computed for the two filmed teaching situations on which repeated viewings were

TABLE 6F. *Within-Observer Reliability Coefficients for T.P.O.R. Scores on Repeated Viewings of Films*

T.P.O.R. Column	FILM 2 N = 69 Reliability	error
TOT	.48	.0255
1	.57	.0177
2	.51	.0194
3	.51	.0177

T.P.O.R. Column	FILM 4 N = 72 Reliability	error
TOT	.52	.0191
1	.56	.0182
2	.57	.0244
3	.62	.0171

[15] Bob Burton Brown, William Mendenhall, and Robert Beaver, "The Reliability of Observations of Teachers' Classroom Behavior," (Mimeographed) February, 1967.

made a year apart. Table 6F shows eight reliability coefficients ranging between .48 and .62.

These coefficients of reliability, as is the case with those obtained using the Medley-Mitzel model, reflect *observer* reliability rather than *instrument* reliability. Observer reliability is always subject to variations in the selection and training of people and the control of conditions under which they use an instrument. People and conditions can be "improved" in subsequent studies, but once they are published, instruments rarely are. It is important to know about the internal consistency of the instrument, its item reliability —which tells us something of its potential in the hands of reliable observers.

Table 6G shows the results of submitting the film study data to the Kuder-Richardson formulation for measuring item reliability. If each item is highly correlated with every other item on the instrument, then the instrument has good item reliability or internal consistency.

In summary, we wish to emphasize that the T.P.O.R. was developed for wide-scale field use by *untrained* observers in the study of teaching behavior in relation to philosophic and education beliefs. Instead of trying to "train out" the pluralistic biases in the perceptions of our observer-judges, we deliberately left them alone, took them as they came, and tried to include them and take them into account as we analyzed the results obtained. This analysis, of course, awaits reporting elsewhere. Here we are concerned only with reporting, in the context of a discussion of problems involved in defining and measures of reliability, the reliability data obtained

TABLE 6G. *T.P.O.R. Internal Consistency Reliability Coefficients*

| Film | Viewing | No. of observers | T.P.O.R. columns | | | |
			1	2	3	TOT
1	1st	158	......	......	......	.86
2	1st	69	.79	.81	.83	.93
2	2nd	69	.77	.81	.79	.91
3	1st	140	......	......	......	.93
4	1st	72	.76	.77	.78	.90
4	2nd	72	.76	.78	.77	.91
5	1st	84	......	......	......	.85

from experimental use of the T.P.O.R. Having submitted this instrument to the hazards of uncontrolled use by uncontrolled observers, and then submitted it to the severest statistical procedures we could find, it came out with the following score card: (1) Correlation of observers' total scores within a given film viewing—VERY GOOD; (2) correlation of observers' total scores between repeat film viewings one year apart—POOR to FAIR; (3) between-observer reliability—FAIR; (4) within-observer reliability—FAIR; (5) internal consistency reliability—VERY GOOD.

part III

Exploration of the Experimental Mind

T HUS FAR we have provided the detailed specification of a theory taken from Dewey's experimentalism and developed some reliable instruments for measuring agreement-disagreement with it. The next step is to try out these instruments and to test the theory. If the theory is correct and the instruments are valid measures of it, then we should be able to use these measures of experimentalism as a means for studying interrelationships between beliefs and practices in education.

We have already established the *content* validity of the instruments. As indicated in Chapter 6, this was done by having a panel of qualified judges check the items against Dewey's general and educational philosophy. This gives us assurance that the instruments represent the content which they purport to measure. As important as logical methods of validation may be, we are also concerned with empirical validation of the instruments.

In Part III we will present data regarding the extent to which the *Personal Beliefs Inventory,* the *Teacher Practices Inventory,* and the *Teacher Practices Observation Record* validly measure experimentalism. These studies demonstrate the value of both the theory and the instruments for contributing to the increase of our knowledge about patterns of teacher behavior in the classroom and some of the critical philosophic factors to which such behavior is related.

PART III

Replies from
the Experienced Mind

7

BELIEFS OF
WELL-KNOWN EDUCATORS

ONE WAY TO FIND OUT whether the Personal Beliefs and Teacher Practices Inventories actually measure what they claim to measure is to try them out on people whose beliefs are well-known. If the inventories can distinguish between people who are known to be in agreement with Dewey's experimentalism and people who are known to disagree with it, then we will have further validated the instruments.

The Personal Beliefs and *Teacher Practices Inventories* (Form 3) were sent to about two dozen prominent American educators. Responses were received from 19 of these including such illustrious figures as William M. Alexander, Morey Appell, Melvin C. Baker, Arthur Bestor, Harry S. Broudy, R. Creighton Buck, George Burchill, Arthur W. Combs, Robert L. Curran, Jack R. Frymier, Ira J. Gordon, Vynce A. Hines, Phillip Lambert, Joe Park, Thomas A. Ringness, Carl R. Rogers, John Rothney, B. F. Skinner, B. Othanel Smith. Although operating under the restraint to respect the confidential nature of their responses, we shall attempt to compare and discuss the measurement of the beliefs of these well-known personalities on the American educational scene.

The fact that persons of this calibre responded at all lends a certain amount of prestige to the instruments, particularly in view of the personal or emotionally-charged nature of many of the items and the general reluctance these days to submit to psychological tests of any kind. Obviously, those who responded would not have bothered to do so if they regarded the instruments as an inappropriate or irrelevant waste of their valuable time.

When testing persons of such widely varying opinions about education, judging from their published works and public statements, one should expect the results to show a wide range of scores. They did. On Personal Beliefs we were able to obtain a spread of 77 points on a maximum possible range of 132 points, with a high score of 130 and a low score of 53. On beliefs about Teacher Practices there was a spread of 98 points on a maximum possible range of 246 points, with a high score of 233 and a low score of 135. Since there were an equal number of positive and negative items on each of the two tests, a score of 50 percent (66 on Personal Beliefs and 123 on Teacher Practices) represents the midpoint between agreement and disagreement with experimentalism. This means that none of the well-known educators were in net disagreement with experimentalism on beliefs about teacher practices, although some (like Arthur Bestor and Creighton Buck) were in exceedingly low net agreement. Only one score (the low of 53) on the *Personal Beliefs Inventory* showed net disagreement with experimentalism. This is consistent with all previous and subsequent results obtained with the inventories, which regularly produce ranges from slight disagreement or low agreement to high agreement with experimentalism. We rarely find anyone in out-and-out or strong disagreement with experimentalism on either of the beliefs instruments.

Let us now look at some comparisons of scores made by persons whose views regarding experimentalism are known to be at variance. Among those tested were three professors of educational philosophy, Melvin C. Baker of the University of Florida, Harry S. Broudy of the University of Illinois, and Joe Park of Northwestern University. Both Baker and Park are known as being exceptionally well-informed about and highly sympathetic to the philosophy of John Dewey. If our instruments are valid measures of agreement-disagreement with experimentalism, we should expect both of these Dewey scholars to score high. To the contrary, Broudy refers to himself as a classical realist, a philosophic position opposed on many basic issues to Dewey's pragmatic views. He should be expected to hold beliefs which would make him a relatively low scorer on any valid measure of experimentalism.

Of the 18 famous educators responding to the *Personal Beliefs*

Inventory Professors Baker and Park obtained the highest scores, both with identical scores of 130, the maximum being 132. Professor Broudy recorded the next to the lowest score, more than 50 points lower than Baker and Park. It is clear, then, that the *Personal Beliefs Inventory* can detect the obvious differences and similarities between the basic philosophical views of these educators.

A similar comparison of the beliefs about teacher practices of Professors Baker, Park, and Broudy was not possible because both Baker and Broudy found much difficulty in responding to the *Teacher Practices Inventory*. However, Joe Park, who did complete both questionnaires, was also one of the top scorers on the *Teacher Practices Inventory*, further indicating his strong agreement with Dewey's experimentalism.

Professor Broudy returned the *Personal Beliefs Inventory* with certain notations to indicate qualifications and also to distinguish between parts of the same question which in his opinion called for different answers (and which were very useful to us in subsequent revisions of the items). However, he wrote: "I can do nothing with the Teacher Practices Questionnaire because it lists all the *vices* of one approach and all the *virtues* of the other. I can agree or disagree only in certain contexts which, of course, are not indicated on the document. For example, I am bitterly opposed to teaching as a police action but where no other approach is possible, I would have to favor it. Likewise the virtues in the activity approach I applaud, but only if the 'vices' can be avoided. Further my responses would depend on type of subject taught and the age of the pupils."[1] Professor Baker also declined to respond to the Teacher Practices items apart from what he termed a "larger context."

Those of us who have worked most closely with the development and administration of the instruments have debated long and often about the "context" problem presented by the *Teacher Practices Inventory*. The temptation to stipulate specific situational contexts, including subject taught and the age of the pupils, in the directions for this inventory has been great. However, we have

---

[1] Harry S. Broudy, personal correspondence dated January 10, 1963, included here with Dr. Broudy's permission.

resisted on the grounds that it would greatly complicate the administration of the questionnaire and would restrict our generalization of the results. Instead, we maintain that it has been more useful to our purposes to let each respondent supply his own unspecified context. We prefer that each subject should respond in terms of what he thinks a "good" or "ideal" teacher should do *generally,* hopefully revealing the subject's basic attitude, predisposition, or set of mind toward teacher practices. The "context" question seems to bother the philosophers or philosopher-types more than any other group we have studied. Elementary and secondary school teachers, and those who work closely with such teachers, seem to have no difficulty in supplying their own contexts. At least, they rarely raise questions about it.

It is also interesting to compare the score made by Harry Broudy with those of his two famous colleagues at Illinois: Arthur Bestor and B. Othanel Smith. Bestor, a historian, is perhaps best known for his stinging attacks upon progressive education and professors of education, which he derogatorily called "educationists." In two books, *Educational Wastelands* and *The Restoration of Learning,* he advocated the abandonment of the soft "life adjustment" curriculum and a return to hard "academic" subjects. On the other hand, B. Othanel Smith, an education professor, has a reputation as a champion of "democratic" education and the utilization of the schools to bring about social change and progress. On the face of it, Bestor and Smith would seem to be miles apart on both questions of fundamental philosophy and educational practice. One might assume that on a measure of experimentalism Arthur Bestor would score somewhere on the lower end of the scale with Harry Broudy, and that B. Othanel Smith would score somewhere near the top with Baker and Park. Such was not the case.

On personal beliefs, Arthur Bestor scored one point higher than Smith, both of them only a few rungs above Broudy. Either Bestor is less opposed to Dewey's basic philosophy, and Smith in less agreement with it, than is generally supposed or the *Personal Beliefs Inventory* is not so valid a measure of experimentalism as other evidence would lead us to believe. On the *Teacher Practices Inventory,* however, Smith scored nearly fifty points higher than Bestor, who ranked next to last in that distribution of scores.

Even so, Smith's score fell below the median of the group of educators tested.

In examining the item by item responses given by Smith it becomes clear that in the nineteen sixties he is clearly not the experimentalist he was reputed to be ten or twenty years earlier. In recent years he has joined the analytic philosophers who are concerned chiefly with the meaning of language, which contrasts sharply with certain aspects of Dewey's pragmatic philosophy. This trend in the development of Smith's personal beliefs is reflected not only in the work he has published over the last ten years but also in his helpful comments written in the margins of his questionnaire, including: "Some of these items are mere definitions; some are statements of factual claims; some are imperative claims. To state that one believes or disbelieves a definition makes no sense. He may agree or disagree with it, but he cannot believe it. Item No. 3 (Learning is a process of intelligent inquiry) is a definitional statement. I can neither believe nor disbelieve it; I might say it is okay for certain purposes, but not for others. The mixing of kinds of statements makes my responses invalid for your purposes, I suspect." This being the case, according to Professor Smith's own analysis, we should not take his responses as proper evidence with which to validate or invalidate the inventories. We should, however, seriously consider his advice about the language of the items and to regard his comments, among others, as insight to the fact that scholars on the frontier of educational theory may simply know too much to respond meaningfully to items on any psychological test.

If we can reclassify B. Othanel Smith as a logical positivist and compare his scores to those of Carl Rogers, of nondirective counseling fame, and Arthur W. Combs, one of the leading proponents of a phenomenological approach to education, we have an interesting contrast between representatives of the two predominating schools of philosophy in the western world today: "the logicians and the lotus-eaters." The logical positivists or analytic thinkers, according to Mortimer Adler, are no longer concerned with "first-order questions" about the nature of being, causation, or free will. They are convinced that experience contradicts the idealistic theory that material objects are not in themselves "real" and that philosophy should abandon the study of the real world to science, leaving to philosophy only the question "What does it mean?" The partisans of phenomenology and existentialism, among which Carl Rogers and Arthur Combs must surely be numbered, insist that there must be something more. They are the lotus-eaters who emphasize the role of man, alone among other beings, a decision-making creature blessed, or cursed, with the freedom to choose among a myriad of possibilities in an absurd and mysterious existence.

While Dewey's philosophy of experimentalism shares much in common with both the logicians and the lotus-eaters, particularly their revolt against Absolutism, it differs markedly from both. Dewey had no liking for the trap of radical empiricism in which the logicians caught themselves. Although he shared with the lotus-eaters the belief that man must accept his freedom, Dewey emphasized man's responsibility for making *intelligent* use of that freedom for survival in a perilous world of continuous change while the existentialists believe that man can conquer the anxiety and despair that threaten him by "commitment" to a way of life. This gives existentialism a mystical element, either in its religious version in which the commitment is directed toward a spiritual goal or in its atheistic version in which commitment is demanded for its own sake only, making it the nihilistic philosophy of despair. Although Dewey would have no stomach for either version of this element, lotus-eaters like Rogers and Combs are likely to be in much closer agreement with Dewey's experimentalism than logicians like Smith.

The results on Personal Beliefs show both Rogers and Combs to be in general agreement with experimentalism, with a score well above the median. On the *Teacher Practices Inventory* Rogers' score was the highest of all, indicating nearly complete agreement with Dewey on the desirable classroom behavior of teachers. Combs scored nearly as well on Teachers Practices. Contrasting the high scores made by Rogers and Combs with the relatively low scores made by Smith, the instruments would seem to hold some promise for distinguishing the logicians and the lotus-eaters.

Perhaps the most interesting contrast provided by our informal little study of the beliefs of famous educators is the one between Carl Rogers and B. F. Skinner. Rogers, representing the personal, humanistic, or perceptual branch of psychology, and Skinner, representing the behavioristic or mechanistic branch of psychology, offer a most dramatic contrast. In fact, these two men have frequently appeared on the same platform to define and defend their opposing views in a most enlightening series of public debates. Skinner, of course, is the famous Harvard psychologist, inventor of the Skinner Box for the training of infants, inventor of the modern teaching machines, and renowned for his theory of positive reinforcement and experiments with it in which pigeons were taught to play ping-pong. Rogers, whom we have already discussed, is perhaps the most revered human being on the current American educational scene, best known for his advocacy of the "nondirective" approach to counseling and education.

The contrast between Rogers and Skinner can be made only on Personal Beliefs, as Skinner, too, found himself unable to complete the Teacher Practices Questionnaire, saying: "I'm afraid I am a very poor respondent. One difficulty is that I am right in the midst of doing a book on the technology of teaching, a large part of which is concerned with the redefinition of terms. This makes it very hard for me to evaluate the kinds of sentences in your questionnaire. I have done my best on 'personal beliefs' but am really stuck on 'teacher practices.' Just to begin with page 1—what does it mean 'to organize learning,' 'to motivate students to greater intellectual effort,' and so on? I am not a specialist in classroom practice and could not decide among the more meaningful items on your list without conceiving of a single teacher in a single classroom. I am sorry not to be of more help."[2]

In spite of the well-advertised differences between Rogers and Skinner, our results show only a two-point difference between them on Personal Beliefs, with Rogers slightly the more experimental. To a colleague of ours, these results constitute a most damaging blow to the validation of the *Personal Beliefs Inventory* on the grounds that "If it cannot detect any greater difference than that between the beliefs of Rogers and Skinner it can't be a measure of anything very relevant." An alternative conclusion, of course, may be that the differences between Rogers and Skinner may have been overdramatized, or, if not, their differences fall outside the framework of Dewey's experimentalism.

[2] B. F. Skinner, personal correspondence dated January 22, 1963, included here with Dr. Skinner's permission.

One must look at their responses on specific items to appreciate the surprising and intriguing similarities and differences in the beliefs of these two men. On the third form of the Personal Beliefs instrument, there were only three possible responses for each item: a + mark if you believe it, a − mark if you do not believe it, or 0 if you are uncertain or have no belief one way or the other about it. Skinner added three others: An S meant "I do not believe terms here can be usefully defined," which he used three times, and which we scored as if he had marked it 0; an S+ which meant "I might accept point otherwise expressed," which he used only once, and which we scored as a − mark; an S— which meant "I might not accept point otherwise expressed," which he used five times, and which we scored as a + mark. Skinner used no zeros, giving us either a clear-cut + or − or one of his special S's. Rogers used seven zeros, giving us either a decisive + or − on all other items. Out of the 44 items on the Personal Beliefs Questionnaire Rogers and Skinner were in clear agreement with each other 29 times. On 10 items one or the other of them matched an uncertain 0 against the other's + or −. This left only 5 items on which their responses were in direct opposition to each other, which are listed below:

Rogers	Skinner	Dewey		Item
−	+	−	11.	Man's destiny is determined by circumstances of nature which are beyond his control.
−	+	+	15.	The value of knowledge lies in its use in the future, in what it can be made to do.
+	−	+	22.	Whatever is carried on under the dictates of authority for some disconnected purpose limits intelligence.
+	−	−	26.	Practice is subordinate to knowledge, merely
	S—			a means to it.
−	(+)	−	29.	The mind is a group of "contents" which come from having certain materials presented to it from without.

After all, B. F. Skinner is an experimental psychologist. It should not come as a shock that he is thoroughly familiar with and considerably sympathetic to the modes of thought and methods inherent to the field in which he labors. While he is, indeed, an experimentalist, Skinner lacks the faith of Rogers and Dewey in man's ability to survive the hazards of chance in an open, uncontrolled society. As he indicates in his thought-teasing novel, *Walden Two,* as much as he may *wish* that man could really be free in an accidental world, his better judgment forces him to the reality that he is not. It is Skinner's conclusion that experimentally-inclined, freedom-loving people ought to take advantage of positive reinforcement to deliberately establish a closed society in the pattern of his fictional *Walden Two* in which at least the *feeling* of freedom is preserved.[3] An important difference between Rogers and Skinner, then, is identified in their responses to item No. 11 regarding the control of man's destiny. Skinner believes that some men, using the techniques of behavioral science, can create circumstances beyond the control of other men to determine the destiny of those other men. Rogers, of course, vehemently opposes Skinner on this score, as would Dewey. While Rogers and Dewey might agree that it could be done, they would argue that it shouldn't be done and that we should take steps to insure ourselves against it. Freedom, according to Rogers and Dewey, depends upon an open society. Skinner differs only in that he has given up any hope of achieving a truly open or democratic society, dismissing it as a naive dream. Pessimistically, he calls democracy old-fashioned, claiming it has been out-flanked and made obsolete by the here-and-now techniques of behavioral science. However, if one will look closely at the specific details and surface accouterments included in the daily life at *Walden Two,* it looks and feels very much like a life Rogers or Dewey might build and enjoy—if only they could forget that it had all been externally programmed for them.

Disagreement on a few items, no matter how crucial, is not cause to drum someone out of camp, particularly the camp of experimentalism. As our analysis has shown, experimentalism is a broad system of thought which contains a number of subdimensions or subfactors. For example, relativism is one of its key factors. Both Rogers and Skinner are thorough-going relativists, consistently rejecting the quest for absolute certainty and immutable truths on item after item. Likewise, they are in general agreement with Dewey regarding the nature of knowledge, and on most items

[3] B. F. Skinner, *Walden Two* (New York: The Macmillan Company, 1948).

about the nature of man and the relationship of ends and means. They fall out primarily only on questions of freedom and authority.

In summary, the fact that most of the well-known educators who were asked to respond to the inventories did so was encouraging. The Personal Beliefs instrument seemed to meet with more approval than the *Teacher Practices Inventory* about which there were some objections because of the lack of stipulated context. Both instruments produced a reasonably wide spread of scores, from slight disagreement or low agreement to high agreement with experimentalism. Those known to be pro-Dewey scored near the top of the scale while those known to be in critical disagreement with Dewey scored low (near the theoretical mean) on the scale. There were some surprises in which some individuals scored higher or lower in comparison than might generally have been expected, but there seemed to be reasonable explanations for these. While in no sense did this constitute a controlled study in which statistically supported conclusions were sought, it provided a number of enlightening and entertaining comparisons of the beliefs of some of our leading educators, as well as additional evidence, however rough, to further support the claim that these are valid measures of experimentalism.

8

EXPERIMENTALISM IN THE ACADEMIC DISCIPLINES

CONTINUING THE INQUIRY into the validity of the inventories as measures of experimentalism, we compared the beliefs of groups of academic scholars tested in California, Illinois, New York, and Wisconsin. The groups included college professors in the fields of mathematics, English, and foreign languages, history and social studies, natural sciences, and education at Sacramento State College, Northwestern University, the State University of New York at Albany, and the University of Wisconsin. Scores were obtained from these professors on Form 5 (A and B) of the *Personal Beliefs* and *Teacher Practices Inventories,* and the Dogmatism Scale.

Before we look at the data, let us first consider the grounds for anticipating what might be found. Professors of education are supposed to have been captives of John Dewey's philosophy. Even if this may not be quite so, it is reasonable to expect that education professors should be substantially more in agreement with experimentalism than their colleagues in the academic disciplines across the campus. Since Dewey's experimentalism was based upon the general method of science it would seem that professors in the natural sciences should score relatively high on valid measures of experimentalism. If this rationale holds for the natural scientist, it should also hold for scholars in the social sciences. However, our inclusion of historians in the same group with professors of political science, psychology, and sociology may weaken any claim that experimentalism is the method of inquiry inherent in these disciplines.

Mathematics and the languages are quite another story. The

essentially deductive methods of the literary disciplines differ sharply from the inductive methods of experimentalism. Although mathematics has often been called the "Queen of the Sciences" because it plays an important part in the work of every science, there are really two kinds of mathematics. On one hand there is applied mathematics, which is mathematics applied to every problem of the world around us, including the problems of the other sciences. On the other hand, there is pure mathematics, which is interested only in mathematics itself and has no interest in practical problems. For the pure mathematician, mathematics is not only logical, but beautiful as well. For him mathematics is an absolute which exists apart from actual physical objects. Nothing could be more diametrically opposed to Dewey's philosophy of experimentalism. If college professors of mathematics are pure mathematicians, one should expect them to score relatively low on the measures of experimentalism, as should the "men of letters" in English and foreign languages.

There is no reason to believe, however, that any one of the academic disciplines should produce or harbor more dogmatism than any other. If Rokeach's[1] theoretical formulations are correct, we should expect to find relatively high-scoring authoritarians or dogmatists among both experimental and nonauthoritarian groups, just as he found that both authoritarian left-of-center groups and authoritarian right-of-center groups score relatively high on the Dogmatism Scale. We should expect to find no significant differences between the various academic disciplines on the Dogmatism Scale.

Table 8A shows the results obtained for the five different groups of academic scholars. To find out where the five groups stand with respect to experimentalism, let us first compare their mean scores on the *Personal Beliefs Inventory*. We see that professors of mathematics are the least experimental and professors of education are the most experimental. The mean score for mathematicians falls approximately midpoint between "I agree a little" (160) and "I disagree a little" (120) levels. The mean for English and foreign language scholars falls somewhat short of "I agree a little." Means for the history and social studies, natural

[1] Milton Rokeach, *The Open and Closed Mind* (New York: Basic Books, Inc., 1960), chap. 6.

TABLE 8A. *Comparison Among Various Groups of Academic Scholars on the Personal Beliefs and Teacher Practices Inventories and the Dogmatism Scale*

Group	Number	Personal beliefs		Beliefs about teachers practices		Dog-matism	
		Mean	S.D.	Mean	S.D.	Mean	S.D.
1. Mathematics	12	141.7	15.8	157.8	15.5	164.2	14.6
2. English and Foreign Language	27	152.7	20.7	162.0	15.3	161.1	13.4
3. History and Social Studies	11	166.1	15.8	166.2	15.8	169.9	11.0
4. Natural science	19	163.0	24.3	162.5	15.0	166.0	15.9
5. Education	58	167.2	22.5	179.1	19.7	169.9	18.0
	Differences between means[a]						
1 vs. 2		−9.0		−4.2		3.1	
1 vs. 3		−24.4		−8.4		−5.7	
1 vs. 4		−21.3		−4.7		−1.8	
1 vs. 5		−25.5[b]		−21.3[b]		−5.7	
2 vs. 3		−13.4		−4.2		−8.8	
2 vs. 4		−10.3		− .5		−4.9	
2 vs. 5		−14.5		−17.1[b]		−8.8	
3 vs. 4		3.1		3.7		3.9	
3 vs. 5		−1.1		−12.9		0	
4 vs. 5		−4.2		−16.6[b]		−3.9	

[a] Significance tested by Scheffé's method of judging all contrasts.
[b] Statistically significant at the .05 level.

science, and education groups all exceed the "I agree a little" point. The mean of the mathematics group differs significantly from the means of the history and social studies, natural science, and education groups, confirming our expectations. The mean for the English and foreign language group differs significantly from the means of the history and social studies group and the education group, as we expected.

Looking at the results for the *Teacher Practices Inventory* we see that the range of means for the five groups of professors falls somewhat higher on the scale than those for Personal Beliefs. Mathematicians still are the least experimental and educationists are far and away the most experimental. In fact, the only significant differences occur between the means for each of the first four groups and the education group. The means for the liberal arts professors in the first four groups cluster around the "I agree a little" point while the education group begins to approach the "I agree on the whole" level.

On the Dogmatism Scale, the differences were much smaller. The history and social studies group and the education group were the most open-minded (least dogmatic) with identical means. The English and foreign language group had the lowest mean of the five groups. Even so, all groups were shown to be substantially open-minded, as one might expect from academic scholars at key institutions of higher learning.

We put all of the liberal arts professors together in a single "academic professor" group to be compared with the group of 58 professors of education. Table 8B shows, as popular opinion would lead one to expect, that educationists are, indeed, more experimental than academicians. However, the academicians were still found to be in general agreement with experimentalism, even if somewhat less so than their brethren in the field of education. This indicates that either the value conflict (with respect to Dewey's philosophy) between academicians and educationists has been over exaggerated or the inventories fail to measure it in its proper proportion. The fact that the positive items (which comprise 50 percent of all items) on both inventories have relatively weak discriminating power causes the range of scores to be pushed up into the "agreement" half of the scale. This may very well produce

T A B L E 8B.   *Comparison of Academic Professors and Education Professors on the Personal Beliefs and Teacher Practices Inventories, and the Dogmatism Scale*

| | | MEAN SCORES | | |
| | | | Beliefs about | |
Group	Number	Personal beliefs	teacher practices	Dogmatism
Education Professors	58	167.2	179.1	169.9
Academic Professors	69	155.8	162.1	164.4
Difference		11.4[a]	17.0[b]	5.5

[a] Significant at .005 level.
[b] Significant at .0005 level.

deception which one should guard against in interpreting scores. On the other hand, the inclusion of the "punchless" positive scores may give an indigenous American pragmatism an opportunity to make itself felt in the results.

Obviously, the *Personal Beliefs Inventory* was the most successful in differentiating between the groups, both in the number of statistically significant differences it produced and in the magnitude of those differences. By the same criteria the Dogmatism Scale was able to detect the least differences. As we had hoped, the Personal Beliefs instrument apparently measures something different than the Dogmatism Scale. Experimentalism and open-mindedness are not identical, according to the empirical evidence as well as our logical analysis. Theoretically, open and closed-mindedness is but one of the factors involved with the experimentalism dimension. Clearly there are several additional factors embraced by the experimental mind. We will look more closely at the relationship of dogmatism and experimentalism in Chapter 9.

Our main purpose in this study was to try to validate the Personal Beliefs and Teacher Practices inventories by the method of known groups. We argued that what we know about the academic disciplines would lead us to predict that scholars in the natural sciences and the social sciences (particularly the field of education) would test out as holding more experimental beliefs than would scholars in the fields of mathematics, English and foreign language. The findings corroborated this theory. If the logic of this theory holds water, then the findings constitute good evidence that we have valid measures of experimentalism.

9

EXPERIMENTALISM
AND EDUCATIONISTS

IN THE LAST CHAPTER we compared the beliefs of scholars from the various academic disciplines, and academicians with educationists. In this chapter we will look more closely at the beliefs of several subgroups within the "professional education" establishment, including public school teachers, supervisors, and administrators; student teachers, college supervisors of student teaching; graduate students; and professors of education.

Our expectation is that all subgroups of educationists are not of the same mind with respect to Dewey's experimentalism. To the experienced educational worker, there is an obvious difference between the theoretically oriented educationist (college professors of education) and the practically oriented educationist (the practitioners in the field). We would expect that despite much effort to sell an experimental approach to them the everyday practitioners have bought less of it than their education professors might like, or their critics have assumed.

Using Form 3 of the Personal Beliefs and Teacher Practices inventories we tested 372 educationists in Wisconsin including 68 college students majoring in elementary education (tested prior to taking any courses in education), 102 college students majoring in secondary education (tested at the beginning of their senior student teaching experience), 22 university supervisors of secondary student teachers, 58 cooperating public school teachers, and 122 public school administrators. As the results show in Table 9A, we found surprisingly little difference between the various groups of educationists on Personal Beliefs. University supervisors of student teaching scored highest and public school superintendents and principals scored lowest. Although for this type of data we cannot validly use regular multiple comparison tests for statistical significance because of lack of homogeneity of variance, it is doubtful that a five-point difference constitutes enough of a spread to warrant any conclusive generalizations.

On beliefs about Teacher Practices it is interesting to note that college students preparing to become teachers scored significantly lower than did groups of more mature and experienced educationists. This would indicate that experimentalism may be acquired or increased by experience. Since all of the supervisors, superintendents, and principals, and most of the cooperating teachers held advanced degrees, it may be that graduate work in education produces higher agreement with experimentalism. Or, it could

TABLE 9A. *Comparison of Various Groups of Educationists on the Personal Beliefs and Teacher Practices Inventories (Form 3)*

Group	Number	Personal beliefs Mean	S.D.	Beliefs about teacher practices Mean	S.D.
1. Elementary Education Students	68	82.70	27.4	166.51	6.6
2. Secondary Education Student Teachers	102	79.44	11.1	166.89	15.8
3. University Supervisors of Student Teaching	22	83.13	15.0	176.55	26.9
4. Cooperating Teachers for Sec. Ed. St. Tchrs.	58	81.53	11.0	177.53	16.5
5. Public School Supts. and Principals	122	77.57	11.3	174.70	14.5
Differences between means					
1 vs. 2		3.26		−.38	
1 vs. 3		−.43		−10.04	
1 vs. 4		1.17		−11.02	
1 vs. 5		4.87		−8.19	
2 vs. 3		−3.69		−9.66	
2 vs. 4		−2.09		−10.64	
2 vs. 5		1.87		−7.81	
3 vs. 4		1.60		−.98	
3 vs. 5		5.56		1.85	
4 vs. 5		3.96		2.83	

mean that the up-coming generation of teachers-in-training simply does not quite share the enthusiasm of previous generations for experimental teacher practices.

In order to gain additional insight into the nature of the differences, if any, among the various groups of educationists tested, we examined the responses to specific items of belief. For this purpose, we selected the ten items on Personal Beliefs and the ten items on Teacher Practices which item analysis showed to be most powerful in discriminating between high and low scorers. Without exception each of the ten best items on both inventories were negative, i.e., they represented statements of belief in *dis*agreement with Dewey's experimentalism. As the reader interprets the results of the comparisons shown and discussed below, he must remember that the experimentalist should disagree with each of the items.

PERSONAL BELIEFS

Two of the ten strongest items on Form 3, the *Personal Beliefs Inventory,* involve obvious religious connotations. It is interesting to note that the small rural public school faculty is shown to be substantially more religious than those educationists closely affiliated with the teacher education program at the University of Wisconsin. Likewise, school administrators lean more heavily toward conventional or traditional religious beliefs than do their teachers and the university personnel to whom they open their schools.

To the statement, "The ends and laws which should regulate human conduct have been determined by the superior intelligence of an ultimate Being," the groups responded as follows:

	Agree	Disagree	Uncertain
Elementary Education Students	37%	37%	26%
Secondary Education Students	38	34	28
University Supervisors	41	41	18
Cooperating Teachers (Secondary)	33	41	26
Superintendents and Principals	46	29	25
Public School Faculty*	58	17	25

* Data obtained from testing the elementary and secondary faculty of a small public school in northern Wisconsin (N = 64).

Although pretty well divided on the basic question, all groups seem to believe a bit more strongly in God as a moral authority than as a controller of destiny. Responses to the statement "Man's destiny is in the hands of a supernatural power" were:

	Agree	Disagree	Uncertain
Elementary Education Students	31%	43%	26%
Secondary Education Students	27	42	31
University Supervisors	36	36	28
Cooperating Teachers (Secondary)	36	35	29
Superintendents and Principals	42	29	29
Public School Faculty	47	23	28

As shown below, all of the groups strongly reject the statement, "Man's destiny is determined by circumstances of nature which are beyond his control." Apparently these educationists have much less toleration for natural than for supernatural determinism. Or, perhaps, they have more confidence in man's ability to control natural circumstances than supernatural powers. In any event, limited to the world of nature they show much stronger agreement with experimentalism. Their responses to the "destiny is determined by circumstances of nature" item were:

	Agree	Disagree	Uncertain
Elementary Education Students	10%	81%	9%
Secondary Education Students	16	67	17
University Supervisors	14	68	18
Cooperating Teachers (Secondary)	5	85	10
Superintendents and Principals	9	76	15
Public School Faculty	13	67	20

To the belief that "The mind is formed from without, as one molds and shapes a piece of clay," we obtained the following responses:

	Agree	Disagree	Uncertain
Elementary Education Students	29%	47%	24%
Secondary Education Students	24	45	31
University Supervisors	13	64	23
Cooperating Teachers (Secondary)	14	65	21
Superintendents and Principals	18	59	23
Public School Faculty	22	53	25

It would seem that students are a bit more idealistic about the possibility of external control over the formation of the mind than their more experienced, and perhaps disillusioned, colleagues.

Two of the ten most discriminating items relate to the relationship of emotions and intellect. Only the university supervisors consistently rejected this classic dualism. On these items, there seems to be rather broad disagreement with Dewey's belief in the continuity of emotions and intellect. Responses to the statement "The mind turns outward to truth; the emotions turn inward to considerations of personal advantage and loss" were:

	Agree	Disagree	Uncertain
Elementary Education Students	40%	34%	26%
Secondary Education Students	25	49	26
University Supervisors	28	36	36
Cooperating Teachers (Secondary)	55	16	29
Superintendents and Principals	52	18	30
Public School Faculty	49	20	31

Along this same line, responses to the statement "The senses and muscles are merely external inlets and outlets of the mind" were:

	Agree	Disagree	Uncertain
Elementary Education Students	50%	25%	25%
Secondary Education Students	50	26	24
University Supervisors	28	36	36
Cooperating Teachers (Secondary)	50	21	29
Superintendents and Principals	50	22	28
Public School Faculty	50	23	27

Three of the ten strongest Personal Beliefs items dealt with beliefs about knowledge and learning. There was sharp division among educationists on the first two of these items. The practitioners tended to accept these nonexperimentalist beliefs while the students and their university supervisors tended to reject them. On the third item in this group, all groups except the university supervisors took rather strong positions in opposition to Dewey.

Responses to the item "Truth exists ready-made somewhere; the task of the scholar is to find it" were the following.

	Agree	Disagree	Uncertain
Elementary Education Students	31%	48%	21%
Secondary Education Students	28	49	23
University Supervisors	27	55	18
Cooperating Teachers (Secondary)	43	36	21
Superintendents and Principals	46	29	25
Public School Faculty	49	23	28

To the belief that "Knowledge is the sum total of what is known, as that is handed down by books and learned men," the following responses were obtained:

	Agree	Disagree	Uncertain
Elementary Education Students	19%	72%	9%
Secondary Education Students	42	48	10
University Supervisors	18	68	14
Cooperating Teachers (Secondary)	47	41	12
Superintendents and Principals	37	48	15
Public School Faculty	28	55	17

Responses to the statement "Learning is the sum of impressions made on the mind as a result of the presentation of material to be known" were:

	Agree	Disagree	Uncertain
Elementary Education Students	71%	20%	9%
Secondary Education Students	56	28	16
University Supervisors	36	36	28
Cooperating Teachers (Secondary)	57	22	21
Superintendents and Principals	61	21	18
Public School Faculty	64	20	16

Of the ten most discriminating items, educationists agreed most strongly with Dewey and each other on rejection of the belief that "Reaching a condition in which there were no more problems would be the ideal life," as shown in the figures below:

	Agree	Disagree	Uncertain
Elementary Education Students	7%	90%	3%
Secondary Education Students	3	88	9
University Supervisors	9	91	0
Cooperating Teachers (Secondary)	0	97	3
Superintendents and Principals	4	90	6
Public School Faculty	8	84	8

TABLE 9B. *Percentages of Agreement-Disagreement with Ten Most Discriminating "Positive" Items on the Teacher Practices Inventory (Form 3)*

Item	Elem. Ed. Students A[a]	Elem. Ed. Students D[b]	Sec. Ed. Students A	Sec. Ed. Students D	Univ. Supv. A	Univ. Supv. D	Coop. Teachers A	Coop. Teachers D	Supts. & Principals A	Supts. & Principals D	Pub. Sch. Faculty A	Pub. Sch. Faculty D
1. T puts focus on what students do or say, rather than on what T does or says.	60	9[c]	52	15	45	14	76	5	71	8	67	11
2. T expects students to work on what they see as their own problems, rather than something made a problem only for the purpose of conveying instruction in some school topic.												
3. T lets students become involved in ugly or distressing aspects of subjects.	47	22	67	20	73	4	53	19	56	19	53	19
4. T encourages students to suggest what might be done—to make "hypothetical leaps" into the unknown or untested.	37	20	44	28	50	9	40	13	34	34	30	37
5. T gives pupils a wide choice in how they answer questions.	91	3	89	3	95	0	90	2	88	2	86	2
6. T selects the kind of subject matter which the student has to adapt and apply to the question for himself.	69	13	65	16	73	4	76	5	72	7	69	9
7. T has students compare the value of al-	65	7	63	10	50	23	67	17	60	18	53	19

ternative courses of action and pass judgment upon their relative desirability.

	A	D	A	D	A	D	A	D	A	D	A	D
ternative courses of action and pass judgment upon their relative desirability.	82	7	92	3	91	4	95	3	89	3	84	2
8. T lets students go ahead with plans based upon foresight, observation, and consideration of several alternatives—even when sure their judgment is mistaken.	66	10	56	21	68	14	74	14	80	11	86	8
9. T gives students a chance to discover by experiencing actual effects whether their choice of this rather than that idea was a judicious one.	81	1	89	2	91	0	85	0	84	1	83	1
10. T asks students to help decide when questions have been satisfactorily answered.	93	4	84	6	91	4	86	4	88	4	89	5

[a] A = Agreement.
[b] D = Disagreement.
[c] Figures do not total 100%, as we have omitted figures for the "uncertain" or "noncommittal" for editorial convenience.

TABLE 9C. *Percentages of Agreement-Disagreement with Ten Most Discriminating "Negative" Items on the Teacher Practices Inventory (Form 3)*

Item	Elem. Ed. Students A[a]	Elem. Ed. Students D[b]	Sec. Ed. Students A	Sec. Ed. Students D	Univ. Supv. A	Univ. Supv. D	Coop. Teachers A	Coop. Teachers D	Supts. & Principals A	Supts. & Principals D	Pub. Sch. Faculty A	Pub. Sch. Faculty D
1. Once work has begun, T insists that students remain in their places and concentrate on the task at hand.	58	12	51	28	32	32	38	38	48	32	56	27
2. T motivates students to greater intellectual effort by rewarding them with grades, marks, prizes, or privileges.	47	28	39	37	18	55	21	53	25	51	30	48
3. T asks the kind of questions that students should be able to answer if they have studied the lesson.	80	6	82	3	68	9	54	24	54	25	55	25
4. If one student fails to answer a question, T asks another student to supply the correct answer.	68	12	75	6	50	23	73	17	66	17	61	16
5. T begins lesson with a direct presentation of the subject matter to be covered.	37	31	38	31	14	32	36	28	39	31	41	34
6. T makes the acquisition of required knowledge and skills the center of students' attention and effort.	39	30	39	30	46	27	48	31	48	27	47	23
7. T provides a model to show the students												

142

	A[a]	D[b]	A	D	A	D	A	D	A	D	A	D
exactly what their work should be like when it is finished.	10	78	12	68	18	50	9	64	12	63	16	62
8. T frequently has all students working on the same page of the same book at the same time.	10	66	21	56	14	68	14	74	11	80	8	86
9. T frequently calls for undivided attention of the group and scolds those who do not respond.	27	51	20	57	9	68	10	78	20	66	28	58
10. T uses a set standard to judge the work of all students in the class.	13	72	25	64	14	64	5	79	10	76	14	73

[a] A = Agreement.
[b] D = Disagreement.

TEACHER PRACTICES

Form 3 of the *Teacher Practices Inventory* contained 20 items, 10 positive and 10 negative. Repeated item analyses showed the 10 negative items to be much stronger in power to discriminate than the 10 positive items. This fact was made doubly clear when we looked at the results obtained from the testing of 372 Wisconsin educationists, as indicated in Tables 9B and 9C.

With the exception of item 3, all these groups of educationists tend to agree rather strongly with positive statements of Dewey's educational philosophy. This is not true, however, when we look at the results obtained from the 10 strongest negative items, shown in Table 9C. Obviously, while educationists agree pretty much with the teacher practices Dewey was *for,* they show a much greater tendency to part company with him on the teacher practices he was *against.* In other words, while they believe in employing experimentalist practices, they also believe in employing a number of nonexperimentalist practices—even though Dewey went to great pains to point out the logical inconsistencies in doing so. This would indicate that while these educationists bought much of the "stuff" of Dewey's experimentalism, they did not buy the logical framework in which he put it.

Using Form 5 of the inventories we tested 364 educationists, again in the state of Wisconsin. This second large-scale testing of professional educators included both elementary and secondary student teachers, their cooperating teachers and their college supervisors of student teaching, methods professors, and general professors of education. This study yielded somewhat different results than did the earlier study using Form 3, reported earlier in this chapter.

For example, Table 9D shows that the cooperating public school teachers in the second study were far and away the least experimental of the groups tested, particularly on Personal Beliefs. This was not so on the earlier study. Perhaps the inclusion of elementary school teachers in the cooperating teacher group in the second study accounts for the difference. In addition, the second study included elementary education students who were near the completion of their professional preparation rather than

T A B L E 9D. *Comparison of Various Groups of Educationists on the Personal Beliefs and Teacher Practices Inventories (Form 5, A and B), and the Dogmatism Scale*

Group	Number	Personal beliefs Mean	S.D.	Beliefs about teacher practices Mean	S.D.	Dog-matism Mean	S.D.
1. Student Teachers	185	147.7	17.22	173.5	21.31	162.7	16.26
2. Cooperating Teachers	89	138.6	16.45	169.4	19.73	157.3	19.74
3. Methods Professors	22	156.2	18.04	173.6	17.83	164.6	12.00
4. College Supervisors	16	159.7	32.24	187.9	22.46	164.0	25.59
5. Education Professors	52	166.8	22.54	178.7	19.66	170.2	18.04

Differences between means[a]			
1 vs. 2	9.1	4.1	5.4
1 vs. 3	−8.5	−.1	−1.9
1 vs. 4	−12.0	−14.4	−1.3
1 vs. 5	−19.5	−5.6	−7.2
2 vs. 3	−17.6	−4.2	−7.3
2 vs. 4	−21.1	−18.5[b]	−6.7
2 vs. 5	−28.2	−9.7	−12.6
3 vs. 4	−3.5	−14.3	.6
3 vs. 5	−11.0	−5.5	−5.3
4 vs. 5	−7.5	8.8	−5.9

[a] Lack of homogeneity of variance on Personal Beliefs and Dogmatism scores makes it impossible to make multiple comparisons of the means. Significance of the differences between means on the beliefs about teacher practices were tested by Scheffé's method.

[b] Statistically significant at .05 level.

just beginning it as in the earlier study. As reported in the next chapter, there is some evidence to support the argument that the training given prospective elementary teachers may move them toward increased agreement with experimentalism—at least temporarily. This could mean that public school elementary teachers cooperating in the University of Wisconsin teacher education program are much less experimental than are the secondary teachers in that program. Furthermore, it indicates that Wisconsin's program in elementary education does something to change the beliefs of students toward greater experimentalism while the secondary education program does not. Of course, these are only conjectures, but long personal experience with teacher education programs at Wisconsin leads me to believe that subsequent testing would substantiate such a hypothesis.

Another explanation may be found in the differences between the forms of the inventories used to collect the data. Form 5 is an improved and more sensitive instrument than the larger and rougher Form 3. Proportionate weights of certain factors were sharply increased or eliminated entirely in the revisions involved in the development of Form 5 so comparison of summary scores obtained from the different forms becomes hazardous.

If we can have greater confidence in the results obtained with Form 5, then Table 9D indicates a substantial difference in the Personal Beliefs of student teachers and their cooperating teachers and the beliefs of university professors and supervisors involved in the professional training of teachers. On this basis, one might conclude that educationists with doctoral degrees are more experimental on Personal Beliefs than those without doctorates. Whether such differences result from the processes of training or selection one cannot be sure.

While similar differences show up on Teacher Practices, they are not quite so great. Supervisors of student teaching, who work closer to the everyday practical front, score in very high agreement with experimentalism, outstripping all other educationists in this regard. The supervisory group at Wisconsin is made up primarily of top-rank doctoral students and young assistant professors. The wide difference between the personal and educational values of university supervisors of student teaching and the cooperating public school teachers who direct the daily experiences of the student teachers raises some sobering questions. Are the cooperating teachers and college supervisors working at cross purposes? If so, does this represent a serious flap in the university's control of its programs in teacher education? What implications does this have for the selection of cooperating teachers in the future? Or does this constitute a fortunate check on overenthusiastic brainwashing on the part of colleges of education?

10

CAN BELIEFS BE CHANGED?

CAN BELIEFS be changed? Or are they firmly set at an early age long before students come to college and enroll in programs for the preparation of teachers. If beliefs (and behavior) of adult college students can be changed—and this is a basic assumption underlying the very idea of the professional training of teachers—then who influences these changes and in which directions?

From the previous chapter we learned that university personnel are somewhat more experimental in both their personal and educational beliefs than are their students and the public school personnel who cooperate in the training of teachers. What kind of influence do the experimentalist beliefs of these educationists have on prospective teachers? Do students become more experimental as the result of their experiences in the teacher education program?

In light of the great emphasis placed on the importance of the student teaching experience in the education of teachers, one should expect this experience to have some effect on the kind of teacher practices valued by the students. Recalling that the mean scores reported in Table 9A in the preceding chapter for secondary education student teachers were obtained immediately prior to their going out into the field to work under the supervision of those supervisors, cooperating teachers, and school administrators whose scores were also reported in Table 9A, one might expect those student teachers to score in higher agreement with experimentalism at the end of that experience. Such was not the case. At the conclusion of their field experience (ranging from seven to eighteen weeks full time) we tested these same students again, obtaining

TABLE 10A. *Pre- and Post-Test Scores for a Group of 102 Secondary Education Student Teachers on the Personal Beliefs and Teacher Practices Inventories*

| | Personal beliefs | | Beliefs about teacher practices | |
	Mean	S.D.	Mean	S.D.
Pre-test	79.44	11.1	166.89	15.8
Post-test	81.10	12.0	164.21	18.1
Difference	1.66[a]		−2.68[a]	

[a] Not statistically significant.

the results shown in Table 10A above. As can be seen, the secondary student teachers showed a very small gain on Personal Beliefs and some decrease on Teacher Practices. Obviously, the beliefs of the other groups of educationists did not have much effect on the beliefs of the students during the course of their practical field experience.

Of course, our data for this comparison is not very complete, as can be seen in the discrepancies between the N reported for students and cooperating teachers. Responses for nearly half of the cooperating teachers were lost, due to a misunderstanding on the part of the investigator in sharing his data with us. Nevertheless, the accidental nature of this reduction of the cooperating teacher N may be treated as a crude form of "random sampling," permitting us to use the data to draw some "big picture" considerations of the relationships at play here, providing we refrain from conclusive pronouncements.

Another interesting comparison can be made between the secondary education student teachers and the elementary education students whose initial scores were also reported in Table 9A. Both groups were tested in the same semester at the same institution, the School of Education at the University of Wisconsin, Madison. The secondary student teachers were either undergraduate seniors or postgraduate teacher interns who had completed at least a minimum of 18 credit hours in professional education courses by the end of their student teaching experience. By contrast, the elementary education students were either undergraduate sophomores or juniors who were tested during the first week of their first course in professional education. According to Table 10B, there is

TABLE 10B. *Pre- and Post-Test Scores for a group of 68 Elementary Education Students on the Personal Beliefs and Teacher Practices Inventories*

| | Personal beliefs | | Beliefs about teacher practices | |
	Mean	S.D.	Mean	S.D.
Pre-test	82.70	27.4	166.51	6.6
Post-test	88.75	11.3	203.09	19.0
Difference	6.05[a]		36.58[b]	

[a] Not statistically significant.
[b] Statistically significant at the .001 level.

precious little difference on beliefs about Teacher Practices between secondary education students who have finished their professional preparation and elementary education students who have not yet begun theirs. If we could assume that there are no basic differences between elementary and secondary students before they enter programs of teacher education, we would be justified in concluding that education courses had little or no influence on these secondary education majors insofar as their beliefs about Dewey's experimentalism are concerned.

We were able to make a check on the influence of a single education course on the beliefs of elementary education majors, with startlingly different results. Table 10B shows that during their introductory professional education course the elementary education students made a substantial change toward greater agreement with experimentalism on Personal Beliefs and a whopping gain of over 36 points on Teacher Practices. This increase can be easily explained by confessing that I was the instructor for 35 of the 68 subjects in this group, and that my role in the development of the Experimentalism Scale thoroughly contaminated that half of the population. Undoubtedly, this accounts for part of the enormity of the gain. However, it does not account for all of it. The instructor in the other section of the course was not intimately acquainted with the framework of the inventories, nor was he aware that his group would be retested at the end of the semester. Furthermore, upon comparing the distributions of pre-test and post-test scores we found that the 33 students in the other section accounted for about as much of the gain as did this experimenter's students. A better explanation may be found in the fact that both professors made a deliberate effort to provide opportunity for the students to identify and relate their basic philosophic beliefs and their beliefs about teacher practices along a variety of theoretical dimensions. This undoubtedly sharpened the students' perceptions of the logical relationships, consistencies and inconsistencies built into the inventories. Whether the students actually changed their beliefs or had merely learned enough to catch onto the underlying dimension of the inventories in order to oblige their professor with what they thought he wanted is a matter of conjecture. In any event, this experience gave us confidence that deliberate consideration of the relationship of educational theory and practice holds potential for modifying the beliefs of the participants, if only temporarily.

To follow up this idea, we studied the results of pre- and posttest scores on the *Personal Beliefs Inventory* and *Teacher Practices Inventory* obtained from two groups of summer session graduate students at the University of Wisconsin. The groups were approximately equal in size, one with 44 subjects and the other with 43 subjects. Both groups contained mixtures of men and women, experienced and inexperienced teachers, and public school administrators and supervisors, with ages ranging from 22 to 54 years. The groups were all graduate students in elementary education, most of whom were completing work for the masters degree, with a small sprinkling of doctoral candidates.

Group I constituted the student enrollment in a course titled "Issues in Elementary Education." The purpose of this course was to identify the critical instructional, curricular, and administrative issues of the elementary school and to relate them to persistent underlying historical, philosophical, and sociological issues. This group was taught by me, and approximately one week out of the eight-week summer session was devoted to Dewey's experimentalism as a relevant dimension for relating practical issues to theoretical issues. Throughout the course students were exposed to a number of differing theoretical frameworks. No effort was made to persuade the students to adopt any particular point of view, although they were urged repeatedly to strive for logical consistency between their basic philosophic beliefs and their beliefs about educational practice. The general approach was simply to dig into the belief systems of the students, hold them open to critical analysis, and put them back together again with some sort of logical clarity in light of an increased number of alternatives. Meeting the criterion of logical consistency, it was as easy for the non-experimentalist to succeed in the course as for the experimentalist —a fact which the students were apprised of repeatedly.

Group II constituted the student enrollment in a course titled "The Teaching of Reading in the Elementary School." This was an advanced "methods" course, designed for specialists and supervisors of the teaching of elementary school reading. Its approach was technical, heavily oriented toward the findings of research in this much-studied area of the curriculum. Its theoretical base was primarily psychological rather than philosophical. Its emphasis was clearly more practical than that of the "Issues Course" in which group I was enrolled. The instructor of group II was almost totally unaware of the background and details of the Experimentalism Scale, and, when we discussed it briefly at the conclusion of the study, not particularly enamored with either the theory or practice of Dewey's experimentalism.

Table 10C shows that group I was a little more than 5 points higher in agreement with Dewey on Personal Beliefs than group II at the time of the pre-test. Table 10D shows that both groups were somewhat more equal with respect to experimentalism on the Teacher Practices pre-test. At the conclusion of the eight-week summer session, however, group I showed rather dramatic shifts in the direction of greater agreement with experimentalism on both Personal Beliefs and Teacher Practices, while group II stood still or lost a little ground.

T A B L E 10C. *Comparison of Pre- and Post-Test Scores for Two Groups of Graduate Students on the Personal Beliefs Inventory (Form 4)*

	Group I (Issues course)			Group II (Reading course)		
	N	Mean	S.D.	N	Mean	S.D.
Pre-test	44	83.41	12.42	43	78.19	17.59
Post-test	44	101.39	19.32	43	77.60	18.40
Difference		17.98[a]			−.59[b]	

[a] Statistically significant at .001 level.
[b] Not statistically significant.

TABLE 10D. *Comparison of Pre- and Post-Test Scores for Two Groups of Graduate Students of Teacher Practices Inventory (Form 4)*

| | Group I (Issues course) | | | Group II (Reading course) | | |
	N	Mean	S.D.	N	Mean	S.D.
Pre-test	44	106.25	13.92	43	104.41	18.09
Post-test	44	122.95	16.14	43	101.95	18.62
Difference		16.70[a]			−2.46[b]	

[a] Statistically significant at .001 level.
[b] Not statistically significant.

These results, coupled with those reported in Table 10B, clearly indicate that beliefs can be changed, and with relatively little effort over a short period of time. The question of whether we changed beliefs or merely scores, of course, remains. It would be interesting to retest these same groups at a later time under different conditions and circumstances. If this were possible, perhaps we could make a judgment as to how "real" or permanent such changes turn out to be. In the light of the data we have collected on large numbers of educationists, it is a safe guess that such changes in beliefs are somewhat less real than they appear to be, and not so lasting as Dewey enthusiasts might hope.

More interesting than change toward or away from agreement with experimentalism, is change with respect to logical consistency. The correlations between Personal Beliefs and Teacher Practices reported in Table 10E show that group I evidenced much greater consistency in their belief system than did group II. Over the summer, group II failed to improve their consistency while group I brought theirs up from a correlation of .328 to .669. This represents a much higher level of consistency between philosophical and practical beliefs than we normally find in the many groups we have tested to date.

TABLE 10E. *Correlations Between Scores on the Personal Beliefs Inventory and Teacher Practices Inventory (Form 4)*

	Group I (Issues course)	Group II (Reading course)
Pre-test	.328	.008
Post-test	.669	−.044

TABLE 10F. *Correlations Between Pre- and Post-Test Scores Obtained by Two Groups of Graduate Students on the Personal Beliefs Inventory and Teacher Practices Inventory (Form 4)*

	Group I (Issues course)	Group II (Reading course)
Personal Beliefs	.629	.749
Teacher Practices	.557	.685

Table 10F presents further evidence that group I changed their beliefs to a much greater extent than did group II. The lower the correlation between pre- and post-test scores the greater the change. These correlations were done to establish the test-retest reliability of the instruments. In spite of the deliberate effort to cause group I to achieve greater consistency between the two different kinds of beliefs (which was successful), the test-retest reliability coefficients of .629 and .557 for that group remained reasonably high. This means that the change toward experimentalism was rather general or widespread throughout the membership of group I.

There is some basis for believing that teacher education programs could become more effective influences on changing educational practices if they would concentrate more on the development of logically consistent relationships between theory and practice rather than by propagandizing for or against specific practices themselves. Preaching the cause of certain "do's and don'ts" in absence of theoretical considerations leads only to the collection of a meaningless bag of teaching tricks on the part of teachers. Even though they may perform such tricks well, teachers so trained never quite understand what they are doing or why. Given avenues on which to move intelligently back and forth from beliefs to logically connected practices, change is able to move in knowable directions rather than drift or skitter willy-nilly. The teachers and prospective teachers I have worked with seem reluctant to change for change's sake. They fear stumbling in the dark. But show them how to move toward the things *they* believe are important to achieve, and they change with breathtaking swiftness.

11

AUTHORITARIANISM, DOGMATISM, AND EXPERIMENTALISM

IT IS TOO OFTEN assumed that the experimental mind is roughly the equivalent of an open, flexible, democratic mind, and the antithesis of a closed, rigid, authoritarian mind. It is a mistake to use such terms in the same breath. Authoritarianism, dogmatism, and experimentalism are not identical entities, and perhaps (in the case of experimentalism) not even different aspects of the same general dimension along which beliefs may be measured.

One of the best-known measures of beliefs is the Fascism (F) Scale developed by Adorno and his colleagues in California. This scale grew out of a series of studies into the nature of prejudice and anti-Semitism. These studies were concerned with the rise of what the authors saw as an "anthropological" species, which they called the authoritarian type of man. Their conception of the modern authoritarian, in contrast to the old-fashioned bigot, combines the technology of a highly industrialized society with irrational or antirational beliefs (classic example: Hitler's Nazi Germany). The authoritarian man "is at the same time enlightened and superstitious, proud to be an individualist and in constant fear of not being like all the others, jealous of his independence and inclined to submit blindly to power and authority."[1]

The F-Scale was designed to identify the *potentially Fascistic* individual, one whose personality structure is such as to render him particularly susceptible to antidemocratic propaganda. At the time when this scale was developed, Fascism had just been defeated in

[1] T. W. Adorno *et al.*, *The Authoritarian Personality* (New York: Harper & Row, 1950), p. ix.

154

war. One would think that the Adorno group would have had a difficult time finding subjects who would openly identify themselves with it, but they didn't. Instead, with alarming ease they found subjects whose outlook indicated that they would readily accept Fascism if it should become a strong or respectable social movement. A strong motivating factor in the development of the F-Scale was the opinion of its authors that "no politico-social trend imposes a graver threat to our traditional values and institutions than does Fascism, and that knowledge of the personality forces that favor its acceptance may ultimately prove useful in combating it."[2]

The F-Scale, and the related studies of *The Authoritarian Personality,* has been severely criticized because of the strong ideological bias on the part of its developers against Fascist authoritarianism. According to the standards of research in psychology and the other social sciences, this is undesirable to the extent that it leads to blind spots and to unsurmountable value judgments, which detract from the scientific merit of the research. Clearly, and without apology, these studies set out to establish empirical evidence that, broadly speaking, prejudiced, anti-Semitic, authoritarian man is characterized by beliefs and predispositions which are both unscientific and undemocratic. Whether they succeeded or not is open to discussion, but the important thing at this point is to understand that this was their intent.

Early in the study of authoritarianism the question was raised as to how general or specific prejudice is. Are those who are anti-Semitic also likely to express hostility toward other minority groups? Subsequent investigations indicated that the answer was yes. Those who scored high on anti-Semitism also tended to score high on other scales measuring attitudes toward other minority groups. On this basis, investigations branched out from the study of anti-Semitism to the broader study of ethnocentrism. An ethnocentric man is one who over-glorifies his own ingroup and at the same time strongly vilifies outgroups.

Out of this came the F-Scale, which was supposed to be an indirect measure of prejudice without mentioning the names of any specific minority group. By such means the hope was to get

[2] *Ibid.,* p. 1.

at personality predispositions underlying a fascistic outlook on life. According to the results of the California studies, which have been confirmed many times since by others, those who score high on the F-Scale also tend to score high on measures of anti-Semitism, ethnocentrism, and anti-Negro feelings, and also tend to be politically conservative.

The next step in this progression, although it came ten years after the publication of the F-Scale, was the Dogmatism (D) Scale, developed by Rokeach and his colleagues at Michigan State. The Dogmatism Scale uses the authoritarian personality structure of the California group, with which Rokeach was formerly associated, as one of its major points of departure. While Rokeach seems to be satisfied that the F-Scale adequately measures "Fascist authoritarianism," he is skeptical of it as a measure of "general authoritarianism." In his opinion, the use of the F-Scale as an "authoritarian personality scale" gives rise to some conceptual confusion, "because in the shift from 'Fascism in the personality' to 'the authoritarian personality' there is an unwitting leap from the particular to the general."[3]

If we try to generalize from the main ideological findings about high F-Scale scorers, Rokeach suggests that "it becomes embarrassing to point to persons who seem to be authoritarian and intolerant but are not fascistic, or anti-Semitic, or politically conservative."[4] Authoritarianism, intolerance, and prejudice are not the monopoly of such "rightist" groups. All of us have observed such phenomena among persons holding positions all along the political continuum from left to right. The fact that the Adorno group studied only right authoritarians and neglected to study left authoritarians is a serious defect in the findings reported in *The Authoritarian Personality*.

However, Rokeach rejects the notion of creating the dichotomy of "left" and "right" authoritarianism on the grounds that it closes the door in advance to the possibility that there may be still other forms of authoritarianism, for example, in the political center or outside the realm of politics altogether. Instead, he believes we should move from the study of right authoritarianism to the study of the general characteristics held in common by all forms of

[3] Milton Rokeach, *The Open and Closed Mind* (New York: Basic Books, Inc., 1960), p. 13.

[4] *Ibid.*, p. 14.

authoritarianism. From this conception, he moved the focus of his concern from the content of beliefs to the structure of belief systems. This switch from *what* a person believes to *how* one believes led to the switch from the study of authoritarianism to the study of dogmatism, which more adequately embraced the evolving dimensions of flexibility and rigidity of belief systems, or, as he put it in the title of his book, *The Open and Closed Mind.*

Obviously, in the development of the measures of experimentalism we have leaned heavily on the pioneer efforts of the Adorno group in measuring authoritarianism and the refinements and new directions added by Rokeach. However, we have jumped completely clear of the socio-psychological string which stretches from the study of Fascist authoritarianism to dogmatism to an entirely different starting point—the philosophically oriented experimentalism of John Dewey. Except for the uninvestigated assumption of the Adorno group that the beliefs of the authoritarian type man are antidemocratic and the untestable consensus that Dewey's experimentalism is *the* philosophy of democracy, there is very little ground for believing that there *should* be a close connection (in the form of a negative correlation) between authoritarianism or dogmatism and experimentalism. We know of no case which has been drawn up to claim such a relationship, and would resist any temptation to try it. We have looked at these relationships in this chapter only out of curiosity—stimulated primarily by the questions asked over and over to the effect: "How does your stuff correlate with the D and F Scales?" "Don't you get about the same results?"

We have collected some data which permits us to look at the experimental mind in relation to the open and closed mind. Dogmatism scores were listed alongside Personal Beliefs and Teacher Practices scores for various groups of educationists and academicians on Tables 8A and 9D in Chapters 8 and 9. While we observed wide variances between groups on measures of experimentalism, comparatively little difference showed up on the dogmatism scores. These findings would indicate that the experimentalism inventories measure something that Rokeach's Dogmatism Scale does not, and *vice versa.*

This should not surprise the person who has examined the theoretical rationale behind the two different measures. They were not meant or designed to measure the same things. The Dogmatism

Scale is concerned primarily with the structure rather than the content of beliefs. It is a measure of *how* beliefs are held, rather than of *what* beliefs are held. The Experimentalism Scales (the P.B.I. and T.P.I.) are very much concerned with content. They seek to learn what beliefs are held rather than how rigid or flexible the structure of belief systems may be.

A person may be dogmatically in agreement with John Dewey or dogmatically in disagreement with him. Likewise, a person may be open-minded, reasonable, or flexible with either acceptance or rejection of such beliefs. Experimentalism, contrary to the hopes of some of its strongest advocates, has no corner on open-mindedness—so our data seem to indicate.

Rokeach's Dogmatism Scale and the California F-Scale, along with Forms 5A and 5B of the *Personal Beliefs Inventory* and the *Teacher Practices Inventory* were administered to a group of 154 educationists. This group included both undergraduate and graduate students at the University of Wisconsin, Madison. Results of this testing are shown in Table 11A. Form 5A of both Experimentalism Scales was administered in March of 1964 and Form 5B was given in May of that same year. Slight gains are shown for the means of both inventories over this short period. However, this is probably due to the differences between the A and B Forms rather than to anything that happened to the subjects during this interval.

As shown in Table 11B, the correlation between equivalent A and B versions of Form 5 of the P.B.I. is .58, and the correlation between equivalent forms of the T.P.I. is .69. These are considered adequate or reasonably high. Consistent with the pattern firmly established for all studies involving the inventories, we again obtained very low correlations between P.B.I. and T.P.I. Scores, rang-

T A B L E 11A. *Scores Obtained for 154 Subjects on F-Scale, D-Scale, Personal Beliefs Inventory and Teacher Practices Inventory*

Test	Means	S.D.
F-Scale	90.5	22.5
D-Scale	130.4	27.0
P.B.I. (A)	70.8	9.9
P.B.I. (B)	73.2	8.7
T.P.I. (A)	86.1	10.0
T.P.I. (B)	90.6	10.4

T A B L E 11B. *Correlation of Equivalent Forms of the Personal Beliefs Inventory and Teacher Practices Inventory*

	P.B.I. (A)	P.B.I. (B)	T.P.I. (A)	T.P.I. (B)
P.B.I. (A)	X	.58	.16	.20
P.B.I. (B)		X	.17	.15
T.P.I. (A)			X	.69
T.P.I. (B)				X

ing from .15 to .20. This is taken as further corroboration of the theory-practice dilemma in education, discussed in detail earlier.

More important to the discussion here is Table 11C, which shows the correlations between scores for Forms A and B of the P.B.I. and T.P.I. and scores for the D-Scale and F-Scale. While all of these correlation coefficients are significant beyond the .01 level, they show that there is very much less relationship between experimentalism and authoritarianism, and between experimentalism and dogmatism (r ranges from .26 to .38) than is indicated between authoritarianism and dogmatism ($r = .69$).

Rokeach's Dogmatism Scale is an improvement on the California F-Scale, and has escaped much of the criticism heaped upon the latter. There is good reason to believe that the California F-Scale measures rightist rather than general authoritarianism. The D-Scale measures how rigidly one holds beliefs regarding the acceptance of not only authority, but of people and ideas as well. Nevertheless, while authoritarianism and dogmatism are different entities, they belong to the same family. If not brothers, they are at least cousins. While experimentalism shows some positive relation to authoritarianism-dogmatism, at best, we could only call it a shirt-tail relationship.

T A B L E 11C. *Correlations between Scores for Forms A and B of the P.B.I. and T.P.I. and Scores for the D-Scale and F-Scale*

	D-Scale	F-Scale
P.B.I. (A)	.28	.38
P.B.I. (B)	.26	.37
T.P.I. (A)	.36	.38
T.P.I. (B)	.34	.30
D-Scale	X	.69
F-Scale	.69	X

12

THE RELATIONSHIP
OF BELIEFS AND
CLASSROOM PRACTICES

WE HAVE USED the inventories to examine and compare the beliefs of known individuals and groups. Another way to test the value of these instruments is to see if they enable us to establish some meaningful patterns of relationship between beliefs and teacher behavior. If beliefs and practices prove to be related in the ways our theoretical formulation says they should, then we will have confirmed, substantiated, or validated both the instruments and the theory.

Recalling the discussion in Parts One and Two, an empirical investigation into the validity of our instruments and the theory on which they are based ought to yield evidence which supports the following propositions:

1. What teachers believe about basic philosophic questions (as measured by the P.B.I.) makes a difference in how they teach in the classroom.

2. In many cases there is a discrepancy (theory-practice dilemma) between what teachers believe about educational practices (as measured by the T.P.I.), and how they teach or fail to teach in the classroom (as measured by the Teacher Practices Q-sort or the T.P.O.R).

3. Where there is a discrepancy between educational beliefs and classroom practices, there will also be a discrepancy between educational beliefs and basic philosophical beliefs.

4. Basic philosophic beliefs are more consistently related to teachers' classroom practices than are educational beliefs.

5. Beliefs and practices should intercorrelate in ways com-

patible to our theoretical framework. That is, plus items should intercorrelate positively with plus-items; minus-items should intercorrelate positively with minus-items; and plus-items should intercorrelate negatively with minus-items.

PROCEDURES OF THE STUDY

To test these propositions we studied 36 senior student teachers majoring in elementary education at The University of Wisconsin, Madison. These subjects spent 10 weeks during the first semester of 1961-62 teaching full time in public schools in the vicinity of Madison. They were observed five different times by supervisors from the regular University student teaching staff and two times by a team of two research psychologists. The subjects had previously completed substantially all requirements for graduation and teacher certification except the final student teaching experience. All of the subjects were women, ranging in age from 20 to 25, averaging 21.1 years.

The subjects were in no sense a random or representative sample. They constituted the total membership of the class enrolled in elementary student teaching that semester. This group was selected simply because it was available for study, and because the qualified persons already scheduled to observe the classroom practices of the subjects generously volunteered to cooperate in the collection of the data. Although the use of student teachers as subjects introduced the added and uncontrollable variable of the influence of the student's cooperating teacher, this group was more than adequate for testing the measuring instruments and dealing with the questions involved in the study.

Data regarding the subjects' beliefs were collected by having them respond to the Form 2 Personal Beliefs and Teacher Practices Q-sorts. Data on the classroom practices of the subjects were obtained by having observers make distributions of the Teacher Practices Q-sort on the basis of what they observed the subject doing and saying in the classroom. This evidence of agreement-disagreement with experimentalism in the subjects' overt behavior in the classroom was converted into scores which were correlated with their scores on the verbal measures of experimentalism.

CORRELATIONS BETWEEN MEASUREMENTS OF EXPERIMENTALISM

Using the gross or total scores obtained from the three measures of experimentalism, standard correlation coefficients were computed to analyze the relationship between beliefs and practices. These are reported below in Table 12A. What we call the "original" coefficients can be interpreted only in relationship to the reliabilities for the instruments with which the measurements were made (as reported in Chapter 6, reliabilities for Form 2 ranged from .60 to .72). These were lower than the correlations between completely reliable or "true" measures of experimentalism would be if such measures were possible. To enable the original correlations to be interpreted in comparison with the highest possible or "perfect" correlations of 1.00, they were corrected for attenuation. All of these coefficients, both original and corrected, were significant at the .01 level, and should be considered fairly strong for this type of data.

Examination of the range of scores obtained from these measurements of experimentalism showed that none of the scores on either the Personal Beliefs or Teacher Practices Q-sorts fell below the halfway mark between perfect agreement and perfect disagreement. This may be interpreted as meaning that all 36 subjects were in some degree of agreement with Dewey in both aspects of their beliefs, ranging from very low to very high agreement. In contrast, the range of the observed classroom practices scores was much greater. Approximately 25 percent of these fell below the

TABLE 12A. *Coefficients of Correlations Between Three Measures of Experimentalism*

Measures correlated	Original coefficients	Corrected coefficients
Personal Beliefs Q-sort and Teacher Practices Q-sort	.42	.64
Teacher Practices Q-sort and Observations of Classroom Practices	.62	.75
Personal Beliefs Q-sort and Observations of Classroom Practices	.37	.49

dividing line between agreement and disagreement, indicating that a substantial number of the subjects used practices which were in conflict with experimentalism despite their avowed beliefs to the contrary. This discrepancy, of course, is not surprising. It is verification of the existence of the theory-practice dilemma pointed out in Chapter 1.

PATTERNS OF RELATIONSHIP

In order to differentiate groups of teachers, the highest 27 percent of the scores in the rank-order distributions for each of the three measures of experimentalism were designated as "high" scores. The lowest 27 percent were designated as "low" scores. The remainder in the middle were designated as "medium" scores. This simplified inspection of scores permitted us to see the patterns of relationship between beliefs and practices summarized in Table 12B.

Subjects who scored high on philosophic beliefs also scored high on educational beliefs in 50 percent of the cases, and in no case scored lower than medium. Subjects who scored medium on philosophic beliefs scored at that same level on educational beliefs in 50 percent of the cases, and scored low more often than high in the other half of the cases. The low scorers on philosophic beliefs were less predictable. Although they scored low on educa-

TABLE 12B *Patterns of Relationship Between Beliefs and Practices*

Relationship of philosophic beliefs to educational beliefs			Relationship of educational beliefs to teacher practices			Relationship of philosophic beliefs to teacher practices		
P.B.	E.B.	Total	E.B.	T.P.	Total	P.B.	T.P.	Total
H	H	5	H	H	7	H	H	3
H	M	5	H	M	3	H	M	7
M	H	3	M	H	2	M	H	5
M	M	8	M	M	9	M	M	3
M	L	5	M	L	5	M	L	8
L	H	2	L	H	1	L	H.	2
L	M	3	L	M	4	L	M	6
L	L	5	L	L	5	L	L	2

tional beliefs in half of the cases, 30 percent scored medium and 20 percent scored high on educational beliefs. Even though high agreement with experimentalism on philosophic beliefs was accompanied in all cases by medium or high agreement on educational beliefs, low agreement on philosophic beliefs did not preclude high agreement with experimentalism on beliefs about educational practices.

The same patterns of relationship appear in each of the three sets of columns in Table 12B, although the number of subjects within the groups varies sharply. In comparing these numbers educational beliefs appear to be more closely related to teacher practices than are philosophic beliefs. For example, seven out of ten high scorers on educational beliefs also scored high on observed teacher practices while only three out of ten high scorers on philosophic beliefs did. Furthermore, low scorers on philosophic beliefs were more often medium or high scorers than low scorers on observed teacher practices. These findings, while offering support for the hypothesis that beliefs make a difference in how a teacher teaches, damages the case we have tried to make for the importance of basic philosophic beliefs.

Whenever results don't come out as expected, researchers have a desire and obligation to find out why. So we tried looking at the data from a variety of different angles in hopes of gaining additional insight, and possibly some modicum of salvation.

Table 12C shows that when both philosophic and educational beliefs were high, observed teacher practices were also high in three cases out of five and were no less than medium in any case. When both types of beliefs were low, teacher practices were no more than medium in any case. Medium scores on both types of

TABLE 12C. *Patterns of Inter-relationship when Philosophic Beliefs and Educational Beliefs are Alike*

High scorers				Medium scorers				Low scorers			
P.B.	E.B.	T.P.	No. of cases	P.B.	E.B.	T.P.	No. of cases	P.B.	E.B.	T.P.	No. of cases
H	H	H	3	M	M	H	1	L	L	M	3
H	H	M	2	M	M	M	2	L	L	L	2
				M	M	L	5				

TABLE 12D. *Patterns of Inter-relationship when Philosophic Beliefs are Higher than Educational Beliefs*

Practices reflect philosophic beliefs				Practices reflects educational beliefs			
P.B.	E.B.	T.P.	No. of cases	P.B.	E.B.	T.P.	No. of cases
M	L	M	1	H	M	M	5
M	L	M	1	M	L	L	3
		Total	2			Total	8

beliefs, while resulting in high teacher practices in one case, resulted in low teacher practices in the majority of cases. This information indicates that when scores from the two different measures of beliefs are alike or similar, together they permit more reliable predictions than does either one separately.

Tables 12D and 12E show that whenever there was a difference or contradiction between philosophic beliefs and educational beliefs the teacher practices score seemed to reflect the educational beliefs score in a far greater number of instances than philosophic beliefs. This, of course, simply corroborated the evidence provided by the correlations in Table 12A and the comparisons of patterns in Table 12B, leaving little doubt that this is the case *when dealing with gross or total scores.*

However, we uncover some of the hidden power of philosophic beliefs when we look at the patterns in Table 12F. Of the nine different patterns shown on this table, the only clean and clear

TABLE 12E. *Patterns of Inter-relationship when Educational Beliefs are Higher than Philosophic Beliefs*

Practices reflect philosophic beliefs				Practices reflect educational beliefs			
P.B.	E.B.	T.P.	No. of cases	P.B.	E.B.	T.P.	No. of cases
L	H	M	1	M	H	H	3
		Total	1	L	H	H	1
				L	M	H	1
				L	M	M	2
						Total	7

TABLE 12F. *Patterns of Inter-relationship Between Philosophical Beliefs, Educational Beliefs, and Teacher Practices*

High scorers on philosophical beliefs				High scorers on educational beliefs				High scorers on teacher practices			
P.B.	E.B.	T.P.	Total	P.B.	E.B.	T.P.	Total	P.B.	E.B.	T.P.	Total
H	H	H	3	H	H	H	3	H	H	H	3
H	H	M	2	M	H	H	3	M	H	H	3
H	M	M	5	L	H	H	1	L	H	H	1
				H	H	M	2	M	M	H	1
				L	H	M	1	L	M	H	1
								M	L	H	1

Medium scorers on philosophical beliefs				Medium scorers on educational beliefs				Medium scorers on teacher practices			
P.B.	E.B.	T.P.	Total	P.B.	E.B.	T.P.	Total	P.B.	E.B.	T.P.	Total
M	H	H	3	M	M	H	1	H	H	M	2
M	M	H	1	L	M	H	1	L	H	M	1
M	L	H	1	H	M	M	5	H	M	M	5
M	M	M	2	M	M	M	2	M	M	M	2
M	L	M	1	L	M	M	2	L	M	M	2
M	M	L	5	M	M	L	5	M	L	M	1
M	L	L	3					L	L	M	3

Low scorers on philosophical beliefs				Low scorers on educational beliefs				Low scorers on teacher practices			
P.B.	E.B.	T.P.	Total	P.B.	E.B.	T.P.	Total	P.B.	E.B.	T.P.	Total
L	H	H	1	M	L	H	1	M	M	L	5
L	M	H	1	M	L	M	1	M	L	L	3
L	H	M	1	L	L	M	3	L	L	L	2
L	M	M	2	M	L	L	3				
L	L	M	3	L	L	L	2				
L	L	L	2								

pictures can be seen in the extreme upper left-hand corner by the high scorers on philosophic beliefs and in the extreme lower right-hand corner by the low scorers on teacher practices. High scorers on philosophic beliefs were *in no case* low scorers on either of the other two measurements of experimentalism. Likewise, low scorers on teacher practices were *in no case* high scorers on either of the two measures of beliefs. All of the other groups of scorers had "triple-mixed" patterns. For example, although high scorers on educational beliefs were also high or medium scorers on the other measures of experimentalism in eight out of ten cases, in two cases they scored low on philosophic beliefs. And, looking across the entire table, although observed teacher practices were closely related in more cases to educational beliefs than to philosophic beliefs, in one case a high scorer on teacher practices was also a low scorer on educational beliefs. Such three-way mix-ups make generalization without contradiction about educational beliefs impossible.

The fact that high scorers on philosophic beliefs were consistently high or medium scorers on all other measurements of experimentalism provides some insight into the role played by philosophic beliefs in the relationship of beliefs to practices. Beliefs about practice and observed classroom practices were found to be in conflict with philosophic beliefs when the latter were low, i.e., wide discrepancy between experimental beliefs and practices occurred only in the absence of strong and positive belief in experimentalism at the level of basic philosophic assumptions. In all cases where there was high agreement with experimentalism on philosophic beliefs, there was no great discrepancy between educational beliefs and observed classroom practices.

This examination of the patterns of interrelationship among the three different measurements of experimentalism may be summarized as follows:

1. High scores on philosophic beliefs precluded low scores on observed teacher practices.

2. High scores on educational beliefs precluded low scores on observed teacher practices.

3. Low scores on philosophic beliefs did not preclude high scores on either educational beliefs or observed teacher practices.

4. Low scores on educational practices did not preclude high scores on observed teacher practices.

5. Educational beliefs were much more often closely related to observed teacher practices than were philosophic beliefs.

6. Although philosophic beliefs were less often related to observed teacher practices than were educational beliefs, this relationship was still an important one. There was evidence to suggest that wide discrepancies between educational beliefs and observed classroom practices occurred only when teachers did not strongly

believe in the philosophic assumptions basic to experimentalism, which gives support to proposition number three on page one. To put it another way, low agreement on philosophic beliefs was a predictive clue to discrepancy and inconsistency between educational beliefs and educational practices—which is what we interpret John Dewey was trying to tell us.

INTERCORRELATIONS OF BELIEFS AND PRACTICES

The sort of examination we have just made of patterns of relationship is, at best, a crude business. Much greater precision is required to make the most of the data. We need to find out precisely what beliefs are related to what practices, and what beliefs are related to what other beliefs. To accomplish this we computed intercorrelations of selected statements of beliefs and observed classroom practices.

The number of intercorrelation coefficients required was reduced to a workable size by selecting only those items which were found to discriminate between those subjects who were in high agreement and those who were in low agreement or disagreement with experimentalism. Such item analysis reduced the number of philosophic beliefs from 36 to 14, educational beliefs and classroom practices (identical items) from 60 to 30, giving us a 74 by 74 matrix. The intercorrelations for this entire matrix are available in the original report of the study.[1] Those intercorrelations which were found to be significant at the 1 and 5 percent levels are summarized in the Appendix of this book.

The results of these item by item intercorrelations bore out our theory, particularly proposition number five. Generally, beliefs items compatible with Dewey's experimentalism (plus-items) were positively correlated with observed classroom practices which were also compatible, and were negatively correlated with those which were not. Between philosophic beliefs and educational beliefs there were 30 intercorrelations which substantiated the theoretical frame-

---

[1] Bob Burton Brown, "The Relationship of Experimentalism to Classroom Practices," Unpublished Ph.D. dissertation, The University of Wisconsin, Madison, Wisc., 1962.

work of the inventories and 6 which contradicted it.[2] Between educational beliefs and observed teacher practices we found 53 confirming intercorrelations and 9 contradictory ones. Between philosophic beliefs and observed classroom practices we found 44 confirmations and only 1 contradiction. This seems to be additional evidence that beliefs about educational practices are more prone to contradiction or inconsistency than are fundamental philosophic beliefs. At least, contradictions appear in substantial numbers only in relationships involving educational beliefs.

When we considered overall scores obtained from the three measurements of experimentalism, educational beliefs appeared to be much more widely related to teacher practices than were philosophic beliefs. As we have seen, simple correlation of overall scores does not tell the whole story. When we looked for gross patterns of relationships between beliefs and practices, and again when we studied the intercorrelations of specific beliefs and specific practices, we found a disturbing discrepancy between what teachers believe should be done and what teachers actually do. Our examination of the intercorrelations among specific items on the three measurements of experimentalism gave us evidence that fundamental philosophic beliefs are more consistently related to teacher practices than are educational beliefs.

Philosophic beliefs that ours is a world of change without absolute certainty in which truth is conditional or relative and in the continuity of Knowing and Doing were most consistently effective in distinguishing teachers who were in agreement with experimentalism on both educational beliefs and classroom practices. Likewise, philosophic beliefs in absolute certainty and immutable truth in the dualism of Knowing vs. Doing, in the dualism of Mind vs. Body, and agreement with traditional religious beliefs regarding spiritual being and the source of moral authority were most effective in differentiating teachers who were in conflict with experimentalism on both educational beliefs and classroom practices.

Educational beliefs in encouraging students to generate ideas

[2] A contradiction was indicated whenever we found a negative correlation between two theoretically "plus" items, or a negative correlation between two theoretically "minus" items, or a positive correlation between a theoretically "minus" item and a theoretically "plus" item.

or initiate and develop hypotheses were most consistently effective in differentiating teachers who were compatible with experimentalism on both philosophic beliefs and classroom practices. Beliefs favoring teacher practices which make learning a direct and conscious end in itself and beliefs in following mechanically the prescribed steps of an established method were most effective in distinguishing teachers who were in disagreement with experimentalism on both philosophic beliefs and classroom practices.

The teacher who was observed to provide situations of experiences consistently held both philosophic and educational beliefs which were also in agreement with experimentalism. The teacher who neglected direct experience and imposed a general method on all alike was most likely to hold both philosophic and educational beliefs which conflict with Dewey's experimentalism.

The most persistent discrepancy found between educational beliefs and teacher practices concerned the kind of problems around which teaching-learning is organized in the classroom. Many teachers believed that students should work on what they saw as their own problems rather than something that was the teacher's or textbook's problem, but only the most determined experimentalists actually organized learning around students' problems. Although experimentalist teachers organized learning around problems of genuine concern to students, they showed a preference for problems short in scope and shallow in depth—and not likely to stimulate much reflective thought. In contrast, teachers in low agreement with experimentalism organized learning in their classrooms around problems remote from the concern and interest of students, yet they showed a preference for problems of greater scope and challenge to students. Dewey would have despaired at this serious fault in the thinking of teachers who were otherwise in general agreement with his views. However, wide discrepancies between experimental educational beliefs and experimental classroom practices occurred only in the absence of high agreement with experimentalism on basic philosophic beliefs. When beliefs about teacher practices were supported by similar or logically compatible philosophic beliefs, we could predict with a high degree of accuracy whether observed classroom practices would be experimental or nonexperimental. Like most other measuring instruments, ours does a better job of discriminating cases at the extreme high and low ends than it does those which get lost in the crowd in the middle.

In summary, we may say that both the theory and the instruments developed to put it into application survived this particular test. They proved useful in studying the relationship of beliefs and practices, giving us some insights into patterns of beliefs and practices which differentiate several types of teachers and helping us shed some light on what kinds of practices are related to what kinds of beliefs.

It should be remembered that the population of this study was not a representative sample of any larger population. Therefore, its findings and generalizations may be applied only to the population studied. Any extensions or applications of these findings and generalizations may be stated only as possibilities, hypotheses, and implications.

In succeeding chapters several of the major patterns of relationship disclosed by the intercorrelations of beliefs and practices will be discussed in greater depth and detail. The statistical procedures and analyses of the findings of this study are much too complex to present here; the interested reader who wishes to examine them is referred to the original report of the study.[3]

---

[3] Brown, *op. cit.*

part IV

Qualitative Analyses of Relationships Between Beliefs and Practices

IN CHAPTER 12 we analyzed the interrelationships among items of teacher beliefs and practices primarily in quantitative terms. Although all the facts and figures are presented there, by themselves they do not communicate the full meaning of the interrelationships found among the items on the three different measurements of experimentalism. Further and somewhat more qualitative interpretation is needed. Part Four offers a descriptive analysis based upon the findings of the quantitative analysis given in the study discussed in Chapter 12. Such analysis involves a return to and an elaboration of the underlying theoretical framework.

In this descriptive analysis the patterns of interrelationships among items will be examined by "typing" teacher-subjects according to the position they took on a particular item or set of items. Each teacher-type is "described" by listing those statements from other measures of experimentalism which were found to be significantly correlated with the item or items characterizing that particular teacher-type. Chapter 12 presents descriptions of teachers typed according to their observed classroom practices. Chapters 14, 15, and 16 deal with beliefs factors which our empirical data indicated are most relevant to understanding the relationship between beliefs and practices along the dimension of the experimental mind.

13

THE EXPERIMENTALIST
TEACHER

"BY YOUR DEEDS you shall be known" is a familiar old saying. If there is any truth in this which can be applied to the problem at hand, then we should expect to learn some important characteristics of teachers' belief patterns from observations of their classroom deeds. Beliefs can be inferred from practices. According to our theoretical framework, teachers who teach experimentally should also think or believe experimentally. And our data indicates that such is, indeed, the case.

In the study of the relationship of experimentalism to classroom practices reported in Chapter 12 we computed the intercorrelations of 30 items of observed teacher practices with 30 identical items of educational beliefs and 14 items of philosophic beliefs. These intercorrelations enable us to describe the beliefs characteristics of teachers typed according to patterns of observed classroom practices.

The 30 items of observed classroom practices selected for this part of the study belong theoretically to the categories given in the first few pages of Chapter 6, comprised of Dewey's "essential features of reflective thinking" and "some evils in education." Insofar as they apply, these same categories will be used as designations of the different teacher-types in the examination of what practices are related to what beliefs, which follows.

In the charts below we give the title of each category and immediately below list the items of observed classroom practices which comprise it. This "describes" the characteristic behavior of the given teacher-type. Then we "describe" the beliefs of this teacher-type by listing the statements of philosophic and educational beliefs which were found to be significantly correlated with these items of observed behavior. (See Table A3 in the Appendix for exact correlation figures.)

Theoretically, the categories "Provided a Situation of Experience" and "Neglected Direct Experience" are opposite sides of the same coin. The intercorrelations involving items of observed classroom practices from these two categories were considered together in arriving at the descriptions of the teacher-types in Tables 13A and 13B.

TABLE 13A. *Teachers Who Provided Situations of Experience*

Observed Classroom Practices:

24+   Provides children a number of starting places and a number of different ways of getting at a task.

31+   Makes "doing something" with a thing, rather than the *thing* itself, the center of children's attention.

45+   Focuses attention on what the children do or say, rather than on what the teacher does or says.

Positive Correlations

Philosophic Beliefs:

1+   All "truths" are relative.

25+   Knowledge cannot be attained purely mentally—just inside the head.

29+   You can never prove that any fact is unconditionally true.

Educational Beliefs:

14+   Encourages children to suggest what might be done—to make "hypothetical leaps" into the unknown.

43+   Has pupils compare the value of alternative courses of action and pass judgment upon their relative desirability.

47+   Provides pupils a chance to discover by experiencing actual effects whether their choice of this rather than that idea was a judicious one.

Negative Correlations

Philosophic *Dis*beliefs:

8–   Learning is the sum of impressions made on the mind as a result of presentation of material to be known.

Educational *Dis*beliefs:

TABLE 13A. (*Continued*)

2—	Organizes learning around questions posed by the teacher or the textbook.
12—	Faithfully follows a planned schedule in order to get in the number of minutes each week allotted to each subject in the curriculum.
42—	Considers suggestions by pupils are appropriate only when closely related to the topic being studied.

Table 13A shows that teachers who provided pupils with situations of experience were relativistic (P.B. 1 and 29) in outlook and were consistently in agreement with experimentalism on both philosophic and educational beliefs: they believed that pupils should be encouraged to both formulate (E.B. 14+) and to reason out (E.B. 43+) hypotheses. In contrast, Table 13B shows that teachers who did not provide opportunities for pupils to have direct experiences in the classroom believed in learning as *ac*quisition (P.B. 8+) and were in agreement with traditional religious beliefs as to the source of authority for moral law (P.B. 19—). Teachers who tended to neglect direct experience believed that a good teacher should be very much in control of the classroom situation (E.B. 32— and 42—) and directive of the pupils' learning (E.B. 2— and 12—). Obviously, the teacher-type described on Table 13B is thoroughly and consistently in disagreement with John Dewey.

TABLE 13B. *Teachers Who Neglected Direct Experience*

Observed Classroom Practices:

32—	Since children cannot be trusted to "behave themselves" she takes steps to limit their opportunities for misbehavior.
37—	Once work has begun, insists that children remain in their places and concentrate on the task at hand.
48—	Arranges things in such a way that a child can spend much of his time listening, watching, or waiting his turn.

Positive Correlations

Philosophic Beliefs:

8—	Learning is the sum of impressions made on the mind as a result of presentation of material to be known.
19—	The laws which should regulate human conduct have been determined by the superior intelligence of an ultimate Being.

TABLE 13B. (*Continued*)

Educational Beliefs:

2—   Organizes learning around questions posed by the teacher or the textbook.

12—   Faithfully follows a planned schedule in order to get in the number of minutes each week allotted to each subject in the curriculum.

32—   Since children cannot be trusted to "behave themselves" she takes steps to limit their opportunities for misbehavior.

42—   Considers suggestions by pupils are appropriate only when closely related to the topic being studied.

Negative Correlations

Philosophic *Dis*beliefs:

None

Educational *Dis*beliefs:

1+   Frequently asks children to choose among several alternatives.

14+   Encourages children to suggest what might be done—to make "hypothetical leaps" into the unknown.

30+   Encourages children to catch hold of ideas and "run with them" beyond what is, as yet, known for sure.

43+   Has pupils compare the value of alternative courses of action and pass judgment upon their relative desirability.

47+   Provides pupils a chance to discover by experiencing actual effects whether their choice of this rather than that idea was a judicious one.

Looking at the negative side of these tables we see that teachers who provided pupils situations of experience rejected three out of four of the educational beliefs held by teachers who neglected direct experience. Likewise, the latter rejected all three of the educational beliefs subscribed to by the former. In short, what one accepted the other tended to reject.

Teachers who organized learning experiences around problems of genuine concern to pupils, shown in Table 13C, believed that this is a world of relative change (P.B. 14+ and 29+). Their belief in E.B. 15+ indicates that such teachers deliberately or knowingly allowed children to work on their own problems. Furthermore, they believed in providing situations of direct experience (E.B. 45+) and in encouraging pupils to hypothesize about their problems

TABLE 13C. *Teachers Who Organized Learning Around Problems of Genuine Concern to Pupils*

Observed Classroom Practices:

1+   Frequently asks children to choose among several alternatives.

15+   Puts pupils to work on what they see as their own problems, rather than something that is the teacher's or textbook's problem.

28+   Encourages children to adventure into "deep water," to tackle problems that appear to be "over their heads."

52+   Uses "feedback" from pupils to diagnose the changing state of affairs in the class, and revises original plans to meet new circumstances.

58+   Makes unplanned changes when a particular lesson is not getting an enthusiastic response from children.

Positive Correlations

Philosophic Beliefs:

14+   Nothing is or can be unchanging—absolutely certain.

29+   You can never prove that any fact is unconditionally true.

Educational Beliefs:

4−   Treats each lesson as an independent whole.

14+   Encourages children to suggest what might be done—to make "hypothetical leaps" into the unknown.

15+   Puts pupils to work on what they see as their own problems, rather than something that is the teacher's or textbook's problem.

43+   Has pupils compare the value of alternative courses of action and pass judgment upon their relative desirability.

45+   Focuses attention on what the children do or say, rather than on what the teacher does or says.

Negative Correlations

Philosophic *Dis*beliefs:

8−   Learning is the sum of impressions made on the mind as a result of presentation of material to be known.

Educational *Dis*beliefs:

2−   Organizes learning around questions posed by the teacher or the textbook.

5−   Frequently calls for the undivided attention of the group and scolds those who do not respond.

12−   Faithfully follows a planned schedule in order to get in the number of minutes each week allotted to each subject in the curriculum.

Table 13C.   (*Continued*)

28+	Encourages children to adventure into "deep water," to tackle problems that appear to be "over their heads."
37—	Once work has begun, insists that children remain in their places and concentrate on the task at hand.

(E.B. 1+ and 43+). They clearly rejected the notion that knowledge is something to be impressed upon the minds of men from without (P.B. 8—). Remaining completely consistent, they also rejected beliefs that teachers should make learning a direct and conscious end in itself (E.B. 2—), that teachers should follow the prescribed steps of an established method (E.B. 12—), and that a restrictive and inactive method of instruction should be imposed on all pupils in the class (E.B. 5— and 37—).

Teachers typed according to the kinds of problems around which they organized instruction were in contradiction with our framework of experimentalism on their beliefs and disbeliefs regarding the scope and depth of problems (E.B. 4— and 28+). This means that experimentalist teachers showed a preference for pupils to work on short and shallow problems, and the non-experimentalist teachers showed a preference for academic problems of greater breadth and challenge.

Apparently, teachers who are otherwise thorough-going experimentalists have confused the teachings of Rousseau and Froebel with those of Dewey regarding the nature of problems appropriate for school pupils. In Chapter 16 we will examine in greater detail the questions raised by these findings.

Table 13D shows that teachers who encouraged pupils to develop and refine hypotheses were also relativists (P.B. 14+ and 29+). Although such "hypothesizing" or "hypothetical mode" teachers believed in pupils working on problems of genuine concern (E.B. 1+), they saw no conflict in believing that all students should work on the same questions (E.B. 17—). Teachers of this type rejected the belief that learning is primarily a matter of acquiring mental impressions (P.B. 8—). As good experimentalists they believed in engaging pupils in direct experiences (E.B. 37—), and turned down, as Dewey would, the belief that learning should be a direct and conscious end in itself (E.B. 42—). However, they inconsistently

TABLE 13D. *Teachers Who Encouraged Development and Refinement of Hypotheses*

Observed Classroom Practices:

14+   Encourages children to suggest what might be done—to make "hypothetical leaps" into the unknown.

30+   Encourages children to catch hold of ideas and "run with them" beyond what is, as yet, known for sure.

43+   Has pupils compare the value of alternative courses of action and pass judgment upon their relative desirability.

Positive Correlations

Philosophic Beliefs:

14+   Nothing is or can be unchanging—absolutely certain.

29+   You can never prove that any fact is unconditionally true.

Educational Beliefs:

1+   Frequently asks children to choose among several alternatives.

17−   Holds all students equally responsible for answering certain questions about the subject being studied.

Negative Correlations

Philosophic *Dis*beliefs:

8−   Learning is the sum of impressions made on the mind as a result of presentation of material to be known.

Educational *Dis*beliefs:

42−   Considers suggestions by pupils are appropriate only when closely related to the topic being studied.

52+   Uses "feedback" from pupils to diagnose the changing state of affairs in the class, and revises original plans to meet new circumstances.

---

rejected the experimentalist belief that plans should be flexible enough to take into account the changing interests and concerns of pupils (E.B. 52+).

Teachers who provided pupils opportunity to test their own ideas experimentally, as shown in Table 13E, were firmly in agreement with three relativism items (P.B. 1+, 14+, and 29+). Although they were experimental in their educational beliefs with respect to the desirability of hypothesizing on the part of pupils (E.B. 14+ and 43+), they were inconsistent in accepting the belief that each lesson should be treated as an independent whole

TABLE 13E.   *Teachers Who Encouraged Pupils to Test Ideas Experimentally*

Observed Classroom Practices:

27+   Lets children go ahead with plans based upon foresight, observation, and consideration of several alternatives—even when she is sure their judgment is mistaken.

36+   Has children test their "guesses" by acting upon them.

39+   Encourages children to put their suggestions to a test with such remarks as, "You'll never know unless you try it."

Positive Correlations

Philosophic Beliefs:

1+   All "truths" are relative.

14+   Nothing is or can be unchanging—absolutely certain.

29+   You can never prove that any fact is unconditionally true.

Educational Beliefs:

4−   Treats each lesson as an independent whole.

14+   Encourages children to suggest what might be done—to make "hypothetical leaps" into the unknown.

43+   Has pupils compare the value of alternative courses of action and pass judgment upon their relative desirability.

Negative Correlations

Philosophic *Dis*beliefs:

8−   Learning is the sum of impressions made on the mind as a result of presentation of material to be known.

22−   Truth exists ready-made somewhere; the task of the scholar is to find it.

Educational *Dis*beliefs:

37−   Once work has begun, insists that children remain in their places and concentrate on the task at hand.

42−   Considers suggestions by pupils are appropriate only when closely related to the topic being studied.

(E.B. 4−). They were thoroughly in agreement with experimentalism in their disbeliefs, however. They rejected traditional conceptions of the nature of knowledge (P.B. 8− and 22−), and they did not believe teachers should impose restrictions on the activities of pupils in the pursuit of learning for learning's sake (E.B. 37− and 42−).

TABLE 13F. *Teachers Who Encouraged Pupils to Form Conclusions Based on Experimental Evidence*

Observed Classroom Practices:

47+ Provides pupils a chance to discover by experiencing actual effects whether their choice of this rather than that idea was a judicious one.

Positive Correlations

Philosophic Beliefs:

1+ All "truths" are relative.
14+ Nothing is or can be unchanging—absolutely certain.

Educational Beliefs:

None

Negative Correlations

Philosophic *Dis*beliefs:

None

Educational *Dis*beliefs:

None

Like all other types of teachers in agreement with experimental classroom practices, teachers who encouraged pupils to form their own conclusions based on experimental evidence were clearly relativists (P.B. 1+ and 14+), as shown in Table 13F. There were no positive correlations with educational beliefs characteristic of this teacher-type, and no negative correlations of any kind.

In analyzing the characteristics of teachers who were observed to teach experimentally, we used all of the "positive" theoretical categories (i.e., "essential features of reflective thinking") given in Chapter 6 except the category entitled "Involved Pupils in Collection of Data." None of the items in this category survived the item analysis. Apparently teachers involve their pupils in the collection of data to such an extent that this activity cannot be differentiated as a unique feature of experimentalism. Although we can argue that there are subtle and vital differences in the ways experimentalists and nonexperimentalists treat the collection of data, obviously our observers in this study were not sensitive to them.

It is not easy to talk about teachers who behave experimentally in classrooms without comparing them with their opposite number.

In the remainder of this chapter we will look at the "negative" theoretical categories representing what Dewey called "some evils in education." These will help us describe teachers who do *not* teach experimentally.

The first of the categories based on Dewey's evils, "Neglected Direct Experience," was dealt with in connection with our earlier discussion of the "positive" category "Provided Situations of Experience." The second of Dewey's evils, "Relied Upon Extrinsic Motivation," contained no items which survived the analysis for discriminating power. Apparently the use of extrinsic motivation was so widespread among our subjects that items in this category were not useful in discriminating among them. Therefore, let us

T A B L E 13G. *Teachers Who Made Learning a Direct and Conscious End in Itself*

Observed Classroom Practices:

2—   Organizes learning around questions posed by the teacher or the textbook.

34—   Insists that each child be responsible for his own work only and does not allow them to ask each other for help.

42—   Considers suggestions by pupils are appropriate only when closely related to the topic being studied.

Positive Correlations

Philosophic Beliefs:
  None

Educational Beliefs:

42—   Considers suggestions by pupils are appropriate only when closely related to the topic being studied.

Negative Correlations

Philosophic *Dis*beliefs:

1+   All "truths" are relative.

14+   Nothing is or can be unchanging—absolutely certain.

Educational *Dis*beliefs:

4—   Treats each lesson as an independent whole.

14+   Encourages children to suggest what might be done—to make "hypothetical leaps" into the unknown.

48—   Arranges things in such a way that a child can spend much of his time listening, watching, or waiting his turn.

move on to consideration of the "Learning for Learning's Sake" teacher.

Teachers who made learning a direct and conscious end in itself were characterized by what they did not believe rather than by what they believed Table 13G shows that such teachers consistently opposed relativistic beliefs (P.B. 1+ and 14+). Furthermore, they did not believe in providing direct experiences (E.B. 42−), or in encouraging pupils to formulate hypotheses (E.B. 14+). The negative correlations with E.B. 4− and 48− indicate they rejected the nonexperimentalist belief that each lesson should be treated as an independent whole and that children should spend much time listening, watching, or waiting.

The items in the category, "Followed the prescribed steps of an established method," identifies the teachers who have accepted a method sanctioned by tradition or experts or authorities (usually the planners of curriculum guides or authors of textbooks). They act like they know exactly what students should learn and exactly what steps should be followed in learning it. Such teachers might be called "prescription" teachers. These teachers were "mind-molders" or "mind-fillers" (P.B. 2−, 8−, and 15−) in their philosophic beliefs. Educationally, they believed in organizing learning around problems pre-selected by some external authority (E.B. 2− and 59−). The significant correlation with E.B. 12− indicates that such teachers were consciously and intentionally "faithful followers."

To help us interpret the negative correlations in Table 13H, let us assume that these beliefs describe teachers who did *not* follow

T ABLE 13H. *Teachers Who Followed the Prescribed Steps of an Established Method*

Observed Classroom Practices:

12−	Faithfully follows a planned schedule in order to get in the number of minutes each week allotted to each subject in the curriculum.
25−	Directs children's learning in short, sure steps.
53−	Tells children where to start and what to do to accomplish the task at hand.
59−	Clearly defines the study problem for pupils so they will have no doubts as to exactly what they are to do.

TABLE 13H. (*Continued*)

Positive Correlations

Philosophic Beliefs:

2—   The mind is a group of "contents" which come from having certain material presented to it from without.

8—   Learning is the sum of impressions made on the mind as a result of presentation of material to be known.

15—   The mind can be formed from without, just as one molds and shapes a piece of clay.

Educational Beliefs:

2—   Organizes learning around questions posed by the teacher or the textbook.

12—   Faithfully follows a planned schedule in order to get in the number of minutes each week allotted to each subject in the curriculum.

59—   Clearly defines the study problem for pupils so they will have no doubts as to exactly what they are to do.

Negative Correlations

Philosophic *Dis*beliefs:

29+   You can never prove that any fact is unconditionally true.

Educational *Dis*beliefs:

15+   Puts pupils to work on what they see as their own problems, rather than something that is the teacher's or textbook's problem.

17—   Holds all students equally responsible for answering certain questions about the subject being studied.

32—   Since children cannot be trusted to "behave themselves" she takes steps to limit their opportunities for misbehavior.

---

the prescribed steps of an established method. Accordingly, teachers who were not followers were relativists (P.B. 29+) and believed (E.B. 15+) students should work on their own problems rather than problems chosen for them by someone else. It is interesting to note, however, that nonfollowers saw no inconsistency in believing that there are certain questions all pupils should be required to answer. In addition, they believed in keeping a tight rein on the behavior of students (E.B. 32—).

The items in the category, "Imposed a General Method on All Alike," differentiated between teachers who provided for individual

TABLE 13I. *Teachers Who Imposed a General Method on All Alike*

Observed Classroom Practices:

5−	Frequently calls for the undivided attention of the group and scolds those who do not respond.
16−	Expects all children to finish a given assignment within a definitely fixed time limit.
17−	Holds all students equally responsible for answering certain questions about the subject being studied.
56−	Frequently has all pupils working on the same page of the same book at the same time.

Positive Correlations

Philosophic Beliefs:

22−	Truth exists ready-made somewhere; the task of the scholar is to find it.

Educational Beliefs:

2−	Organizes learning around questions posed by the teacher or the textbook.
5−	Frequently calls for the undivided attention of the group and scolds those who do not respond.
32−	Since children cannot be trusted to "behave themselves" she takes steps to limit their opportunities for misbehavior.
42−	Considers suggestions by pupils are appropriate only when closely related to the topic being studied.

Negative Correlations

Philosophic *Dis*beliefs:

5+	Knowledge is artificial and ineffective in the degree in which it is merely presented as truth to be accepted, held, and treasured for its own sake.
14+	Nothing is or can be unchanging—absolutely certain.
29+	You can never prove that any fact is unconditionally true.

Educational *Dis*beliefs:

14+	Encourages children to suggest what might be done—to make "hypothetical leaps" into the unknown.
15+	Puts pupils to work on what they see as their own problems, rather than something that is the teacher's or textbook's problem.
43+	Has pupils compare the value of alternative courses of action and pass judgment upon their relative desirability.
45+	Focuses attention on what the children do or say, rather than on what the teacher does or says.

TABLE 13I.   (*Continued*)

47+	Provides pupils a chance to discover by experiencing actual effects whether their choice of this rather than that idea was a judicious one.

differences and those who did not. Table 13I indicates that this is a powerful category (lots of significant correlations) which consistently comply with our theoretical framework.

Teachers who imposed a general method on all alike were in disagreement with experimentalism on both philosophic and educational beliefs in all cases. They believed (P.B. 22−) in ready-made knowledge, and (E.B. 2−) in organizing learning around teacher's or textbook's problem. They also believed (E.B. 5− and 32−) in keeping pupils under firm control, and in not letting their interest and attention stray from the assigned task (E.B. 42−).

In contrast, the negative correlations show that teachers who did *not* deal with all pupils alike were consistently in agreement with experimentalism. They believed in relativism (P.B. 14+ and 29+) and that knowledge has little value in and of itself (P.B. 5+). On educational beliefs such teachers were in across-the-board agreement with Dewey in five different categories. They believed in providing situations of experience (E.B. 45+), in having pupils work on genuine problems (E.B. 15+), in generating hypotheses (E.B. 14+), in reasoning out refined hypotheses (E.B. 43+), and in pupils forming their own conclusions on the basis of experimental evidence (E.B. 47+).

On the basis of the foregoing analyses, we can summarize the relationship between observed classroom practices and philosophic beliefs as follows:

1. Classroom practices were in agreement with experimentalism when teachers held the following types of philosophic beliefs:

    (a) Belief that we live in a world of relativity and change.

    (b) Belief that there is a continuity of doing and knowing (learning-as-*in*quiring).

2. Classroom practices were in disagreement with experimentalism when teachers held the following types of philosophic beliefs:

    (a) Belief that there is a dualism of change vs. certainty (absolutism).

(b) Belief that there is a dualism of doing vs. knowing (learning-as-*ac*quiring).

(c) Belief that there is a dualism of mind vs. body.

(d) Agreement with traditional religious beliefs regarding spiritual being and the source of moral authority.

Likewise, the relationship between observed classroom practices and educational beliefs can be summarized as follows:

1. Classroom practices were in agreement with experimentalism when teachers held the following types of educational beliefs:

(a) Belief that teachers should encourage pupils to initiate and develop hypotheses.

(b) Belief that teachers should give pupils opportunity to form conclusions on the basis of tested evidence.

2. Classroom practices were in disagreement with experimentalism when teachers held the following types of educational beliefs:

(a) Belief that teachers should neglect direct experiences.

(b) Belief that teachers should follow the prescribed steps of an established method.

(c) Belief that teachers should impose a general method on all pupils alike.

3. Classroom practices were in both agreement and disagreement with experimentalism when teachers held the following types of educational beliefs:

(a) Belief that teachers should provide situations of experience.

(b) Belief that learning should be organized around problems of genuine concern to pupils.

(c) Belief that learning should be a direct and conscious end in itself.

14

CHANGE AND CERTAINTY

IF YOU WANT to find out whether a teacher is likely to use teaching practices advocated by Dewey or teaching practices criticized by Dewey, try to discover what that teacher believes about philosophic questions regarding change and certainty. In the study described in Chapter 12 it was found that items in the *Personal Beliefs Inventory* involving "permanence and change" or "change and certainty" were most often significantly related to educational beliefs and observed classroom practices. Dewey's thesis that issues involved in philosophic notions about change and certainty are reflected in issues concerning teaching practices seems to be borne out.

In the study of the relationship of experimentalism to classroom practices the change—certainty issue was represented by three statements of belief: (1) All "truths" are relative, (2) Nothing is or can be unchanging—absolutely certain, and (3) You can never prove that any fact is unconditionally true. According to the theoretical framework drawn from Dewey, an experimentalist will agree with all three of these statements and a nonexperimentalist will disagree with all three of them. The subjects in this study were most clearly differentiated on these items.

Based on the intercorrelations of these three items of philosophic beliefs with items of educational beliefs and observed classroom practices, we are able to draw from the population of our study a hypothetical "change" teacher and a hypothetical "certainty" teacher. The "change" teacher is, of course, open to the possibility of change and able to evaluate changes in the context of the experimental method, and wants things kept flexible, relative to changing conditions. While the experimentalist teacher is reasonably confident and comfortable with change, the nonexperimentalist teacher believes his security is threatened by it, and so he joins in the quest for certainty. The "certainty" teacher wants situations closed, settled, nailed down, fixed with absolute certainty.

The philosophic beliefs of our "change" teacher were significantly related to three educational beliefs. She (the subjects were all women) believed that the teacher should: (1) Encourage children to suggest what might be done—to make "hypothetical leaps" into the unknown, (2) Make unplanned changes when a particular lesson is not getting an enthusiastic response from children, and (3) Arrange things in such a way that a child can spend much of his time listening, watching, and waiting his turn.[1] The philosophic beliefs of our "certainty" teacher were significantly related to five educational beliefs. She believed that the teacher should: (1) Organize learning around questions posed by the teacher or textbook, (2) Encourage children to adventure into "deep water," to tackle problems that appear to be "over their heads,"[2] (3) Consider suggestions by pupils appropriate only when closely related to the topic being studied, (4) Frequently have all pupils working on the same page of the same book at the same time, and (5) Clearly define the study problem for pupils so they will have no doubts as to exactly what they are to do.

Neither the "change" teacher nor the "certainty" teacher was completely consistent in her educational beliefs. As noted, there were cross-overs or contradictions. However, these contradictions do not seem to be closely knitted with the change-certainty issue. Although the "change" teacher held the "minus" belief that children should spend much time listening, watching, and waiting, it did not carry over into practice. Similarly, the "certainty" teacher's belief in encouraging students to tackle problems that appear to be over their heads, a "plus" item, was not significantly correlated as an observed classroom practice.

[1] This last belief represents an inconsistency or contradiction of the theoretical framework. A complete experimentalist is not supposed to hold such a belief.

[2] A contradiction of the theoretical framework. This is supposed to be an experimentalist belief.

The mode of teaching observed to be characteristic of teachers holding philosophic beliefs accepting of change was distinctly different from that of teachers rejecting such beliefs and presumably holding philosophic beliefs favoring the quest for certainty. The philosophic beliefs of the "change" teacher were correlated positively with classroom practices which are compatible with experimentalism and negatively with those which are in conflict with experimentalism. In sharp contrast, the philosophic beliefs of the "certainty" teacher were correlated positively with practices in conflict with experimentalism and negatively with those compatible to it. Tables 14A and 14B list the observed classroom practices of our hypothetical "change" and "certainty" teachers. From these tables it seems safe to conclude that philosophic beliefs about change and certainty can very effectively differentiate experimental teachers from nonexperimental teachers.

TABLE 14A. *The "Change" Teacher*

Educational Beliefs

1. T should encourage p to suggest what might be done—to make "hypothetical leaps" into the unknown.
2. T should arrange things in such a way that p can spend much of his time listening, watching, or waiting his turn.
3. T should make unplanned changes when a particular lesson is not getting an enthusiastic response from p.

Classroom Practices

1. T asked p frequently to choose among several alternatives.
2. T put p to work on what they saw as their own problems, rather than something that was T's or textbook's problem.
3. T encouraged p to catch hold of ideas and "run with them" beyond what is, as yet, known for sure.
4. T had p test their "guesses" by acting upon them.
5. T encouraged p to put their suggestions to a test with such remarks as, "You'll never know unless you try it."
6. T had p compare the value of alternative courses of action and pass judgment upon their relative desirability.
7. T provided p a chance to discover by experiencing actual effects whether their choice of this rather than that idea was a judicious one.
8. T used "feedback" from p to diagnose the changing state of affairs in the class, and revised original plans to meet new circumstances.
9. T made unplanned changes when a particular lesson was not getting an enthusiastic response from p.

TABLE 14B. *The "Certainty" Teacher*

Educational Beliefs

1. T should organize learning around questions posed by T or textbook.
2. T should encourage p to adventure into "deep water," to tackle problems that appear to be "over their heads."
3. T should consider suggestions by p are appropriate only when closely related to the topic being studied.
4. T should frequently have all p working on the same page of the same book at the same time.
5. T should clearly define the study problem for p so they will have no doubts as to exactly what they are to do.

Classroom Practices

1. T organized learning around questions posed by T or the textbook.
2. T treated each lesson as an independent whole.
3. T followed faithfully a planned schedule in order to get in the number of minutes each week allotted to each subject in the curriculum.
4. T expected all p to finish a given assignment within a definitely fixed time limit.
5. T held all p equally responsible for answering certain questions about the subject being studied.
6. T insisted that each p be responsible for his own work only and did not allow them to ask each other for help.
7. T considered suggestions by p are appropriate only when closely related to the topic being studied.
8. T arranged things in such a way that p can spend much of his time listening, watching, or waiting his turn.
9. T had all p frequently working on the same page of the same book at the same time.
10. T clearly defined the study problem for p so that they had no doubts as to exactly what they were to do.

Before anyone goes about probing into beliefs about change and certainty which teachers or prospective teachers may hold, he needs to take some precautions. This can be dangerous ground. For example, such notions are, indeed, considered personal and private. Legally, one cannot be required to divulge such beliefs. Officially, at least, questions in this area are "off limits" for school administrators when interviewing and hiring new teachers or reviewing the tenure status of experienced ones. What teachers believe or do not believe—about anything—is not supposed to be reflected in their teaching. It is a widely accepted maxim (some may call it a *myth*) that the "professional" teacher is "ethically" obligated to be impartial or objective, especially in areas where philosophic beliefs and value judgments are involved. The code of professional ethics demands that teachers "put aside" their personal views on such issues and not let them affect or bias their teaching. But can they?

To ask questions of this nature is, in the opinion of many of our colleagues in education, like opening Pandora's box. We are well advised to take care, lest our questions turn around and bite us.

However, the fact that certain personal beliefs of teachers have been outlawed in various segments of our society is evidence that there is in some quarters a fear that what teachers believe can make a difference in how a teacher teaches. Many states have laws which require teachers to disclaim belief in communism or in any other political philosophy which advocates overthrow of our democratic system of government by force or subterfuge. Many local communities have unwritten policies against employing teachers of certain religious beliefs. It is common knowledge—though seldom spoken of in polite company—that Catholics, or Jews, or openly confessed atheists are rarely employed as superintendents of public school systems. Likewise, the teacher who is a known believer in free love, nudism, intermarriage of Negroes and whites, or world government is likely to experience difficulty in securing or retaining a position in the schools of many communities. If we really believe that what teachers believe does not make any difference, why do we repeatedly see evidence of this kind to the contrary?

Of course, someone may say, *some* beliefs make a difference—beliefs about communism and democracy, about God and morality, that sort of thing—the really *fundamental* issues. Teachers may hold even some controversial beliefs *privately*. It doesn't matter much what teachers believe if they keep their beliefs to themselves. And it is precisely this tradition for keeping one's personal beliefs private which makes any study of the relationship of beliefs and practices a difficult and hazardous business.

Beliefs about change and certainty are especially sensitive, particularly when probed along the line of Dewey's philosophy of experimentalism. Dewey's views in this region come into direct conflict with the hallowed traditions of a number of our firmly established religious and social institutions. So much so, in fact, that Dewey has sometimes been denounced as that "relativistic atheist" whose philosophy has poisoned the minds of educationists who have ruined the American public school system with their progressive education practices. Whether or not such charges are well-founded, it is important for us to look more closely at what Dewey had to say about change and certainty.

THE QUEST FOR CERTAINTY

Living in a changing and hazardous world of nature, man is compelled to seek protection, safety, security. According to Dewey, he has sought to attain security in two ways: One is to try to appease the powers that control his world and his destiny. Man then relies upon prayer, sacrifice, ceremonial rite, and magic cult either to win the powers of nature to his side or to win a place for himself on their side. "If man could not conquer his destiny," Dewey pointed out, "he could willingly ally himself with it; putting his will, even in sore affliction, on the side of the powers which dispense fortune, he could escape defeat and might triumph in the midst of destruction." This way, of course, was rejected by Dewey. Instead, he advocated that man "turn the powers of nature to account" and construct "a fortress out of the very conditions and forces which threaten him." Man then relies upon the sweat of his own brow or "the method of changing the world through action" and "builds shelters, weaves garments, makes flame his friend instead of his enemy." Dewey felt that by using art, skill, and invention "man might establish a kingdom of order, justice and beauty through mastery of nature's energies and laws."[3]

By and large, man has chosen the first method over the second. Of his own skills in adapting things in the natural world to his own purposes and uses, man has wavered between thinking of them as the gift of the gods and thinking of them as an invasion of the prerogatives of the gods. Such abilities (or arts) are something either supernatural or unnatural. Dewey pointed out that although men have been glad enough to enjoy the fruits of their own arts, and have increasingly devoted themselves to their multi-

[3] John Dewey, *The Quest for Certainty* (New York: G. P. Putnam's Sons, 1929), pp. 3–4.

plication, there has been maintained a profound distrust of the arts as a method of dealing with the serious perils and problems of life. Characteristically, man has tried to escape from the peril of uncertainty rather than to attempt to cope with it by means of intelligent action.

As a result, Dewey observed, man has depreciated his own activities and exalted the activity of higher powers. He has elevated knowledge above making and doing, regarding his own practical activities as useful only to deal with changing, individual, and unique situations about which no complete certainty is possible. Only the higher and purer activity of the mind, so this pattern of thought has gone, can grasp what is universal, fixed, immutable. As Dewey put it, "man's distrust of himself has caused him to desire to get beyond and above himself; in pure knowledge he has thought he could attain this self-transcendence."[4]

Dewey argued that the sharp divisions or dualism between theory and practice, mind and matter, knowledge and action, which are embodied in traditional doctrine are "fundamentally connected with the quest for a certainty which shall be absolute and unshakable."[5] It was this hopeless search for absolute certainty and immutable truths which was at the heart of Dewey's objections to traditional idealistic and realistic systems of thought.

For example, Dewey deplored the idealistic concept of a remote and inaccessible absolute, or goal of perfection, saying that "It is empty; it represents a vague sentimental aspiration rather than anything which can be intelligently grasped and stated."[6] Likewise, he condemned the realistic doctrine that reduces what can be known to a fixed and unchangeable reality which exists prior to and independently of, and unaffected by, man's acts of observation and inquiry.[7] Such are the "traditional beliefs which stand in the way of acceptance of the solution that is proposed," by Dewey.[8]

Dewey traces the development of these dualisms from Plato and Aristotle who "glorified the invariant at the expense of

[4] *Ibid.*, p. 7.

[5] *Ibid.*, p. 6.

[6] John Dewey, *Democracy and Education* (New York: The Macmillan Company, 1916), p. 68.

[7] Dewey, *The Quest for Certainty, op. cit.*, pp. 22–23.

[8] *Ibid.*, p. 106.

change." According to Dewey the notion that "the office of knowl-edge is to uncover the antecedently real, rather than, as is the case with our practical judgments, to gain the kind of understanding which is to deal with problems as they arise" has ruled philosophy ever since the time of the Greeks. Thus, the predisposition of the entire classic philosophic tradition . . . toward the universal, invari-ant, and eternal was firmly fixed. Dewey outlined the line of argu-ment of this classic scheme as follows: True Being or reality is complete; in being complete, it is perfect, divine, immutable, the "unmoved mover." Then, there are things that change, that come and go, that are generated and perish, because of lack of stability which participation in ultimate Being alone confers.[9] Although this Greek formulation was made long ago and much of its terminology now sounds strange and unfamiliar, its basic features are as relevant to present modes of thought as they ever were. In spite of the tremendous changes wrought by the content and method of the modern sciences, it was Dewey's observation that the main tradition of western culture has retained intact this frame-work of ideas laid down by Plato and Aristotle. He concluded that "Perfect certainty is what man wants," and "It cannot be found by practical doing or making." Practical activities have "an uncer-tain future, and involve peril, the risk of misadventure, frustra-tion and failure."[10] Of all such beliefs about permanence and change and their related notions about the nature of the "real" world and about the nature of mind and "its organs of knowing," Dewey says, "They all flow—such is my thesis—from the separa-tion (set up in the interest of the quest for absolute certainty) be-tween theory and practice, knowledge and action."[11]

The quest for certainty and immutable reality should be ex-changed, Dewey urged, for something he called a "search for security by means of active control of the changing course of events." A haven of serenity and safety filled with permanent-but-useless fixtures were not for him. Instead he believed "Intelligence in operation, another name for method, becomes the thing most worth winning."[12]

[9] *Ibid.*, pp. 17–20.
[10] *Ibid.*, p. 21.
[11] *Ibid.*, p. 24.
[12] *Ibid.*, p. 204.

Dewey makes his case for change by showing that the "scientific man" is interested in change instead of isolated and complete fixities. He makes the point that the method of inquiry in the physical sciences "is to introduce some change in order to see what other change ensues," adding that the desired object of scientific knowledge is "the correlation between these changes, when measured by a series of operations." The notion of a natural science which should turn its back upon the changes of things, upon events, is simply incomprehensible to a scientific man. What he is interested in knowing, in understanding, Dewey emphasizes, are precisely the changes that go on. These changes set the scientist's problems—problems which are solved "when changes are interconnected with one another." Although Dewey recognizes that "constants and relative invariants figure" in the work of science, he calls them "relations between changes, not the constituents of a higher realm of Being."[13]

The scientific or experimental mind is always on the alert for problems, regarding every new question as an opportunity for further experimental change. In contrast to the "prescientific" or "nonscientific" mind which seeks the heavenly bliss of absolute certainty, Dewey suggested "There is nothing which the scientific mind would more regret than reaching a condition in which there were no more problems."[14]

In showing the changes in modes of investigation in science and philosophy from the prescientific analysis of the classic and middle ages to the ways of thought characteristic of modern science and philosophy, Dewey points out that modern man has inherited his desire for absolute certainty "through the medium of Hebraic and Christian religion." He adds that although "thinkers deeply influenced by modern science often ceased to believe in divine revelation as supreme authority," many "modern men of science" have attempted to save a portion of the older moral and religious tradition. They do this, Dewey explained, by creating a "division of territory" in which "science is limited to phenomena in space and time in order that the world of higher and noumenal realities may be appropriated by ideals and spiritual values," each with "complete jurisdiction and undisputed sovereignty in its own

[13] *Ibid.*, pp. 83–84.
[14] *Ibid.*, p. 101.

realm." This division or dualism depends, in Dewey's view, on the "adjustment to each other of two unquestioned convictions: One, that knowledge in the form of science reveals the antecedent properties of reality; the other, that the ends and laws which should regulate human affection, desire and intent can be derived only from the properties possessed by ultimate Being."[15]

Dewey clearly rejects all such forms of philosophic and religious absolutes. He believed that the concept of an experimental, open, democratic society "repudiates the principle of external authority."[16] In place of such a principle he "projects the hypothesis" that "the pattern supplied by scientific knowing" shows "it is possible for experience, in becoming genuinely experimental, to develop its own regulative ideas and standards," without "recourse to some reality beyond experience."[17] The moral impact of the "scientific pattern" is dramatized in C. P. Snow's novel, *The Search*. This is something of an account of what it is like to be a scientist. Snow charts the career of a young physicist who seeks to find himself in the discipline of science—including the tension and excitement of laboratory research and the difficult moment when a scientist must choose between violating a basic scientific principle or covering up the error that will destroy a friend's reputation and a woman's love. After much agonizing, of course, the "regulative ideas and standards" of science win out.[18]

In passing, it should be made clear that while Dewey did not believe in the existence of a supernatural Being and was extremely critical of established religions, he did *not* advocate the burning of churches, or doing away with religious experience, or destroying the values which we have inherited through our religious tradition. Quite the contrary. Dewey seemed anxious to preserve certain "religious" experiences. He even devoted a little volume to this effect called *A Common Faith*. In this work he makes the point that "there is a difference between religion, *a* religion, and the religious."[19] It was his line of argument that "a religion (and as I

[15] *Ibid.*, pp. 51–59.
[16] Dewey, *Democracy and Education, op. cit.*, p. 101.
[17] Dewey, *The Quest for Certainty, op. cit.*, p. 107.
[18] C. P. Snow, *The Search* (New York: Signet Books, 1960).
[19] John Dewey, *A Common Faith* (New Haven: Yale University Press, 1934), p. 3.

have just said there is no such thing as religion in general) always signifies a special body of beliefs and practices having some kind of ·institutional organization, loose or tight." In contrast, Dewey suggested that "the adjective 'religious' denotes nothing in the way of a specifiable entity, either institutional or as a system of beliefs . . . as one can point to this and that historic religion or existing church." Instead, "it denotes attitudes that may be taken toward every object and every proposed end or ideal."[20]

Dewey condemns organized, institutionalized religions as "A body of beliefs and practices that are apart from the common and natural relations of mankind," which "must in the degree in which it is influential, weaken and sap the force of the possibilities inherent in such relations." Instead of destroying religion it was his expressed desire to bring about "the emancipation of the religious from religion."[21] He wanted to save the elements and outlooks he called "religious" from the dogmas and sacraments of institutionalized religions which, in his analysis, agree on one point: "the necessity for a Supernatural Being and for an immortality that is beyond the power of nature."[22] It was his conviction that because of the weight of beliefs and practices based on their historic supernatural encumbrances "religions now prevent . . . the religious quality of experience from coming to consciousness and finding expression that is appropriate to present conditions, intellectual and moral." Undoubtedly, he was projecting his own sentiments in stating that "many persons are so repelled from what exists as a religion by its intellectual and moral implications, that they are not even aware of attitudes in themselves that if they came to fruition would be genuinely religious."[23]

Dewey describes a genuinely religious experience in saying: "Any activity pursued in behalf of an ideal end against obstacles and in spite of treats of personal loss because of conviction of its general and enduring value is religious in quality." Just in case someone might be deceived into thinking that he might be proposing a new kind of religion or that he might see himself as a twentieth-century "Christian Reformer," Dewey concludes his dis-

[20] *Ibid.*, pp. 9–10.
[21] *Ibid.*, p. 27.
[22] *Ibid.*, p. 1.
[23] *Ibid.*, p. 9.

cussion of "Religion Versus The Religious" with the following statement, which leaves no doubt about his position on this issue:

> If I have said anything about religions and religion that seems harsh, I have said those things because of a firm belief that the claim on the part of religions to possess a monopoly of ideals and of the supernatural means by which alone, it is alleged, they can be furthered, stands in the way of the realization of distinctively religious values inherent in natural experience. For that reason, if for no other, I should be sorry if any were misled by the frequency with which I have employed the adjective "religious" to conceive of what I have said as a disguised apology for what have passed as religions. *The opposition between religious values as I conceive them and religions is not to be bridged. Just because the release of these values is so important, their identification with the creeds and cults of religions must be dissolved.*[24]

RELIGION AND TEACHING

Related to this discussion is a factor which came up in our study of the relationship of experimentalism to classroom practices. Two beliefs items not originally categorized with beliefs about change and certainty turned out to have obvious religious connotations. Informal comments volunteered by many of the subjects indicated that they responded to the following statements with their various religious convictions foremost in mind: (1) "Man doesn't really have a spirit which is separable from his body and the world," and (2) "The laws which should regulate human conduct have been determined by the superior intelligence of an ultimate Being." The first item was meant to deal with the mind vs. body dualism, and the second was designed to differentiate between those who view emotions as something untrustworthy, something which can be controlled only by the force of the highest supernatural authority, and those who view emotions as something which can be dealt with intelligently by man himself, relying on the method of the natural sciences.

Teachers who agreed with the second item also disagreed with the first item regarding man's "spirit" to such an extent that we felt these items should be examined together. In doing this, it

[24] *Ibid.,* pp. 27–28. The italics are mine, not Dewey's.

was apparent that teachers who believed in a supernatural Being also believed there is a supreme supernatural Being who determines moral and natural law. This, of course, is entirely consistent with the traditional institutionalized religions of the culture from which the subjects of this study were drawn. What is interesting here, however, are the educational beliefs and classroom practices characteristic of those teachers who agreed with these traditional religious beliefs. These beliefs of our hypothetical "religious" teacher were significantly related to the educational belief that a good teacher "Tells children where to start and what to do to accomplish the task at hand" and to the observed classroom practice in which the "Teacher takes steps to limit pupils' opportunities for misbehavior, since they cannot be trusted to 'behave themselves.' "

For those who did not agree with these traditional religious beliefs, there were no significantly related classroom practices. There was only a limited and contradictory pattern of relationship with educational beliefs. On one hand they agreed with experimentalism that "children should be encouraged to adventure into deep water, to tackle problems that appear to be over their heads." On the other hand, they held the nonexperimentalist belief that "teachers should arrange things in such a way that a child can spend much of his time listening, watching, or waiting his turn."

At best, these results constitute only fragmentary evidence. However, they provide some insight into the influence of traditional modes of thought and practice which come to teachers through their religious training and commitments. There is no evidence to support any notion that the experimentalist is necessarily not religious in a traditional sense or that the person who holds established religious beliefs cannot also hold experimentalist beliefs and practice experimentalist practices. However, there are some grounds for conjecturing that the degree to which one feels compelled to apply in practical situations (like teaching) his religious beliefs that there is a supernatural Being who is the absolute source of moral authority, such views will *to that degree* get in the way of his belief in and use of teaching practices compatible with Dewey's philosophy of experimentalism. Furthermore, the extent to which a teacher believes in and puts into practice those ideas advocated by Dewey, such modes of thinking and acting will tend to lessen the chances that the teacher will hold traditional religious beliefs about God and morality. From the point of view of the person desirous of preserving the traditional doctrines of religion, Dewey's philosophy of experimentalism poses a dangerous threat, indeed. It is little wonder that his philosophy and its educational implications have encountered fierce opposition!

The highly charged nature of the issues involved does much to explain the power of philosophic beliefs in this category to differentiate so sharply between types of teaching practices. The differences between the experimentalist and nonexperimentalist teaching were found to be closely bound up with the change-certainty issue, and the related controversy between modes of investigation and thought of traditional religious and modern science, in accord with the foregoing discussion of Dewey's views.

15

ACQUISITION VERSUS INQUIRY

WHAT A TEACHER believes about the nature of knowledge makes a difference in what he believes good teaching is and in what kinds of practices he actually uses in the classroom. In the investigation reported in Chapter 12 we found that teachers who agreed with Dewey about the continuity of knowing and doing (knowledge as inquiry) also agreed with him about educational beliefs and in their observed classroom practices. On the other hand, teachers who disagreed with Dewey by holding beliefs in the dualism of knowing versus doing (knowledge as acquisition) also held beliefs about education and used classroom practices which were in conflict with experimentalism. Thus, our theoretical framework regarding the relation of knowledge and action seemed to be given further support.

In the study of the relationship of experimentalism to classroom practices the "Acquisition versus Inquiry" issue was represented by two statements of belief which are compatible with Dewey's philosophy and four statements of belief which are in conflict with it. The "plus" items were: (1) The value of knowledge lies in its use in the future, in what it can be made to do, and (2) Knowledge is artificial and ineffective to the degree that it is presented as truth to be accepted, held, and treasured for its own sake. The "minus" items were: (1) Learning is the sum of impressions made on the mind as a result of presentation of material to be known, (2) Truth exists ready-made somewhere; the task of the scholar is to find it, (3) Knowledge is the sum total of what is known as that is handed down by books and learned men, and

(4) Inquiry into the accumulated body of knowledge must necessarily precede intelligent inquiry into practical social problems. We identified those who agreed with the plus items and rejected the minus items as "inquiry" teachers. Those who rejected the plus items and agreed with the minus items were called "acquisition" teachers. For the "inquiry" teachers who believed knowing and doing to be closely and inseparably related, knowledge was viewed as a vital part of the process of inquiry. For the "acquisition" teachers who believed knowing and doing were distinctly different affairs, knowledge was seen as having a special existence and value in and of itself, quite apart from the means by which it is acquired or the use to which it may be put—it is something to be acquired for its own sake.

Using the significant intercorrelations of the above items of philosophic beliefs with educational beliefs and observed classroom practices, we were able to describe the educational beliefs and classroom practices which are characteristic of our hypothetical "inquiry" and "acquisition" teachers. As Tables 15A and 15B show,

T A B L E 15A. *The "Inquiry" Teacher*

Educational Beliefs

1. A good teacher has pupils compare the value of alternative courses of action and pass judgment on their relative desirability.
2. A good teacher focuses attention on what the children do or say rather than on what the teacher does or says.
3. A good teacher provides pupils a chance to discover by experiencing actual effects whether their choice of this rather than that is a judicious one.

Classroom Practices

1. The teacher was observed to put pupils to work on what they saw as their own problems rather than on the teacher's or textbook's problem.
2. The teacher was observed to provide children a number of starting places and a number of different ways of getting at a task.
3. The teacher was observed to encourage children to catch hold of ideas and "run with them" beyond what is, as yet, known for sure.
4. The teacher was observed to encourage children to put their suggestions to a test with such remarks as, "You'll never know unless you try it."
5. The teacher was observed to use feedback from pupils to diagnose the the changing state of affairs in the class and to revise original plans to meet new circumstances.

T A B L E 15B. *The "Acquisition" Teacher*

Educational Beliefs

1. A good teacher organizes learning around questions posed by the teacher or the textbook.
2. A good teacher frequently calls for the undivided attention of the group and scolds those who do not respond.
3. A good teacher directs children's learning in short, sure steps.
4. Since the children cannot be trusted to "behave themselves," a good teacher takes steps to limit their opportunities for misbehavior.
5. A good teacher, once work has begun, insists that children remain in their places and concentrate on the task at hand.
6. A good teacher tells children where to start and what to do to accomplish the task at hand.
7. A good teacher clearly defines the study problem for pupils so they will have no doubts as to exactly what they are to do.

Classroom Practices

1. The teacher was observed to call frequently for the undivided attention of the group and to scold those who did not respond.
2. The teacher was observed to hold all pupils equally responsible for answering certain questions about the subject being studied.
3. The teacher was observed to tell the children where to start and what to do to accomplish the task at hand.
4. The teacher was observed to define clearly the study problem for pupils so they would have no doubts as to exactly what they were to do.

teachers who saw knowledge as inquiry were thoroughgoing experimentalists who provided classroom situations that were inclined to be open and free, emphasizing participation of the pupils as actors as well as reactors. Teachers who saw knowledge as acquisition were decidedly nonexperimental, providing somewhat restricted or tightly controlled classroom situations in which pupils participate primarily as respondents to plans and purposes impinging upon them from without.

Obviously, whether acquisition or inquiry is given primary emphasis makes a dramatic difference in classroom practices. These findings should cause us to look more closely at the simple but subtle difference between the verbs *acquire* and *inquire*. *To acquire* means to come into possession or control of, either by some uncertain and unspecified means or by sustained effort. *To inquire* means to seek to know by asking or questioning, to search into, investigate, examine. With respect to knowledge, *acquiring* emphasizes getting and keeping what is known or already answered; *inquiring* emphasizes questioning and searching into what is problematic or unknown, not fully answered. In knowledge-as-acquisition the answer one ends up with is what is most important. In knowledge-as-inquiry the question or the process used in the questioning is at least as important as any answer it may tease out. Acquisition places the highest value on the golden eggs, although it obviously appreciates the function of the goose as a means; inquiry, while it covets golden eggs, places greater value on the goose that lays them.

Teachers we have studied generally agree that education ought to include both acquisition of and inquiry into knowledge. But which ought to take precedence, acquisition or inquiry? This is a critical issue which clearly divides one type of teacher from another. And it is usually passed over much too lightly. Looking at the hearts or roots of things can be unpleasant business compared to the more comfortable preoccupation with the skins and fringes of things. Most of us in education seem all too content to limit our differences to opinions about what ought to be acquired, when, where, how, and by whom. To limit our deliberations in this way assumes that knowledge exists ready-made somewhere and is something to be discovered, accumulated, and handed down by generations of scholars. Such limitation assumes a closure of the philosophical question, "What is the nature of knowledge?" And such a closure implies acceptance of the popular but nonexperimental belief in knowledge as something to be acquired and possessed.

The experimental mind resists the notion that inquiry is merely a means to the acquisition of knowledge. Instead, the experimentalist agrees with Dewey's theory of knowledge in which acquisition is always secondary and instrumental to free and open inquiry.

When inquiry is made but a means to the acquisition of a certain predetermined body of knowledge, according to the experimentalist, it ceases to be free, open, experimental inquiry. "Inquiry" is a mockery when it is controlled from the outside to produce answers already known, settled upon, or desired and demanded by those who run the schools. If we insist that learners acquire, above all, a predetermined set of answers, concepts, and generalizations, then we have to give up our pious lip service to the glories of open inquiry.

The experimentalist fears missing the play of the game—not engaging in inquiry—more than he fears the failure to acquire something or the loss of some precious possession. His attitude is somewhat like the old sportsman's saying that "What matters is not whether you win or lose, but how you play the game." If he is permitted the freedom to play in the game of inquiry, the experimentalist feels that he cannot lose. He feels sure that there will be acquisition of some kind and amount of knowledge, as inquiry cannot proceed without it. The only risk is certainty as to just how much of what kind. He is content simply to concentrate on developing and experiencing the process of inquiry, trusting that the fruits—his winnings—will follow as the just consequences of his efforts. Such a point of view, of course, horrifies the non-experimentalist. A conclusion that the experimentalist is an incurable optimist and the non-experimentalist is a cautious pessimist would not be entirely unjustified.

A characteristic feature of the Experimental Mind is the rejection of traditional theories that knowledge is truth to be accepted, held, and treasured for its own sake. John Dewey viewed knowledge as inquiry—as something *within* inquiry, not as a terminus outside or beyond inquiry.[1] He stressed the instrumental character of knowledge rather than the permanent or final character customarily attributed to it. By closely relating knowing and doing, and by making knowing secondary to conduct, doing, and enjoying everyday activities, Dewey's experimental theory of knowledge seems made-to-order for the practical and energetic American mind and its characteristic predisposition for *doing* things.

However, Dewey was no more sympathetic with doing for doing's sake than he was with knowing for knowing's sake. He carefully distinguished intelligent doing from mere doing. He emphasized the importance of perfecting *methods* of doing, making it clear that simply adding "more activity, blind striving, gets nothing forward." He made a plea for "doing which has intelligent direction, which takes cognizance of conditions, observes relations

[1] John Dewey and Arthur F. Bentley, *Knowing and the Known* (Boston: Beacon Press, 1949), p. vi.

of sequence, and which plans and executes in the light of this knowledge." Any notion that separates thought from action "makes no contribution to the central problem of development of intelligent methods of regulation." Instead, it "depresses and deadens efforts in that direction." The experimental procedure advocated by Dewey "is one that installs doing as the heart of knowing."[2]

Dewey's objection to the acquisition of knowledge for its own sake should not be mistaken as a blanket rejection of accumulated knowledge or a depreciation of its value. He accepted *knowledge* as a fitting designation for the outcome of inquiry, saying, "That which satisfactorily terminates inquiry is, by definition, knowledge; it is knowledge because it *is* the appropriate close of inquiry."[3] It is only when knowledge is supposed to have some meaning of its own apart from connection with and reference to inquiry that the use of the word *knowledge* caused Dewey to see red. Perhaps it was for the sake of his blood pressure, among other reasons, that he preferred the words "warranted assertibility" to designate the objective and close of inquiry. If so, it was an effective precaution, as he lived to the ripe old age of 93.

The position taken by Dewey was that knowledge, when conceived as the outcome of inquiry, is part of the continuing process of inquiry itself. He points out that just because something is settled or becomes knowledge as a result of a particular inquiry we have "no guarantee that *that* settled conclusion will always remain settled." The attainment of knowledge is a progressive matter; there is no knowledge "so settled as not to be exposed to further inquiry." In defining knowledge as the "convergent and cumulative effect of continued inquiry," Dewey explains: "In scientific inquiry, the criterion of what is taken to be settled, or to be knowledge, is being *so* settled that it is available as a resource in further inquiry; not being settled in such a way as not to be subject to revision in further inquiry."[4]

As indicated in our item in the Experimentalism Scale, the value of knowledge lies in its use in the future, in what it can be

[2] John Dewey, *The Quest for Certainty* (New York: G. P. Putnam's Sons, 1929), p. 36.

[3] John Dewey, *Logic: The Theory of Inquiry* (New York: Holt, Rinehart and Winston, 1938), p. 8.

[4] *Ibid.*, pp. 8–9.

made to do. For Dewey, knowledge is something which *comes about* as the result of experimental operations, and its object is prospective and eventual rather than something which existed before the act of knowing.[5] Its function, in general, is to make one experience readily available in other experiences. Knowledge is supposed to facilitate intelligent action. "An ideally perfect knowledge," from Dewey's viewpoint, "would represent such a network of interconnections that any past experience would offer a point of advantage from which to get at the problem presented in a new experience."[6]

While Dewey recognizes that the "content of knowledge is what *has* happened, what is taken as finished and hence settled and sure," he emphasizes that "the *reference* of knowledge is future or prospective." It is the function of knowledge to furnish "the means of understanding or giving meaning to what is still going on and what is to be done." He uses the knowledge of a physician as an example. What he has found out by study and personal acquaintance constitutes his knowledge of medicine, but it is knowledge to him *because* it furnishes the resources by which he successfully deals with the unknown things which confront him in the practice of medicine. "When knowledge is cut off from use in giving meaning to what is blind and baffling," Dewey suggests "it drops out of consciousness entirely or else becomes the object of aesthetic contemplation."[7]

Dewey criticized various systems of philosophy with characteristically different conceptions of knowledge, particularly those which state or imply certain basic divisions, separations, or antitheses, technically called dualisms. For example, he singled out such antithetical conceptions involved in the theory of knowing as empirical versus rational knowing, objective versus subjective knowing, activity versus passivity in knowing, and intellect versus emotions in knowing.

The opposition of empirical and rational theories of knowing is perhaps best known. Theories of knowledge like those of Plato and Descartes are called "rational" because they believe that only

[5] Dewey, *The Quest for Certainty, op. cit.,* p. 171.

[6] John Dewey, *Democracy and Education* (New York: The Macmillan Company, 1916), p. 396.

[7] *Ibid.,* p. 397.

through reason can we discover "real" or "true" knowledge, which can under no conditions be false. Such knowledge is, according to rationalist philosophers, found only in the higher realm of the mind, in the form of innate ideas which we do not learn, but are born with. Theories of knowledge like that of John Locke are called "empirical" because they hold that the only possible knowledge comes to us through our senses. Empirical knowledge is based on "factual" information gained strictly by observation and experimentation, rather than through speculation and "pure reason." On one hand it is argued that rational knowledge is superior because it is found above and beyond the contamination of the imperfect visible world. On the other hand it is argued that empirical knowledge is more reliable precisely because it is capable of being confirmed, verified, or disproved by earthly observation and experiment.

The trouble with using observation and experiment as the basis for establishing the truth of knowledge, argue the critics of empirical knowing, is that our sense perceptions are not reliable. They trick us and fool us. Plato believed that we can have absolutely certain knowledge of only those aspects of the world which never change. All that we can really know are the "universals" or "forms" (or as they are sometimes called, *Platonic Ideas*) which cannot be discovered through our ordinary sense experience. Our sense perceptions give only images of the shadowy, half-world of what appears to us or seems to be. Only through the use of reason, from ideas, can we know what is unchanging, eternal, absolutely certain. Most often this certainty is believed to be backed by divine guarantee.

Some empiricists deny that the sensations from which empirical knowledge is gained have any reference to an objective, absolutely certain world existing independently of the sensation. More commonly, however, empiricists usually believe in the existence of such a world. The latter breed of empiricist holds that the objects actually given to us in experience are not the physical things themselves but only mental representations of them. On this view, man cannot directly experience real physical objects; all he can directly experience are his perceptions of them at the end of a causal series that terminates in his brain. For the traditional empiricist this causal theory of perception establishes a split between the physical world and the mental world, sharply distinguishing physical reality from the private experiences which it *causes* in the minds of individual perceivers. Dewey, of course, objected to any such dualism, and it was on this account that he was critical of both rational and the traditional empirical theories of knowing.

However, Dewey's theory of knowledge *is* empirical, in that he claims observation and experience are the only possible sources of the content of knowledge. Even so, it differs by also claiming that absolute certainty is not possible, that the best we can hope for is probable knowledge. Instead of seeking absolutely true knowledge about an alleged "real" or "ideal" world, empiricists of Dewey's type try to establish the degree of reliability we can ascribe to our knowledge of the world of nature. This view of knowledge gets considerable support from developments in science and mathematics. It argues that we never need or use absolutely certain knowledge, even if it were attainable. We seem to be able to live out the course of our lives quite securely without knowledge which could not possibly be false. Obviously we can deal with the problems which confront us, with the help of scientific information about the observable world, even though such knowledge may some day prove inadequate or entirely false. Probable knowledge is all we have, and that seems good enough.

Dewey rejected the idea that man's knowledge results from having impressions made on the mind by sense data. Such a belief serves to maintain a metaphysical puzzle, or dualism, built upon the notion that there is an unobservable something—a "force," "power," "disposition," or even a "spirit" which "causes" or "brings about" the necessary connection between the world of physical objects and the world of our mental representations. This is the basis of the claim of "pure" empiricists that such a causal theory is the foundation of scientific knowledge.

The subject-predicate structure of our language plays right into the hands of the dualistic notion of cause—which is not surprising when we remember that English has been developed by a people whose way of living and thinking has been dominated by a belief in supernatural beings and forces. The scientist has been unable to completely rid himself of the dualism built into the language he must use and the culture within which he works and communicates his results. It is difficult for anyone who uses

English to keep from tripping over this "incorporated" dualism.

When natural science was first struggling to achieve its independence, those who wanted to promote the new movement borrowed the idea of an absolute, all-embracing causal force from the dominant theology. The nature of the force and the way it worked were considerably altered by the philosophers most closely associated with the development of science, but as Dewey says, "the requirements of habit were satisfied in maintaining the old forms of thought—just as the 'horseless carriages' kept the shape of the carriages they displaced." By building the new structure of science on the old foundation of a causal force, "The void left by the surrender first of a supernatural force, and then of Nature (which had replaced Deity during the periods of Deistic rationalism) was thus made good."[8]

Dewey challenged the causal theory of perception, and denied that it deserves to be called the foundation of scientific knowledge. In an historical sense, however, there can be no question that it has served as a basic assumption of a great many scientists and philosophers of science. Bertrand Russell, for example, gave it "cornerstone" status, saying, "Epistemologically, physics might be expected to collapse if perceptions have no external causes."[9]

The view that a causal theory of perception is a necessary postulate of scientific inquiry is dated. A century ago the view went almost unchallenged as the notion of necessity and search for a single all-comprehensive law was typical of the scientific and intellectual atmosphere. In contrast, probability and pluralism are the characteristics of science in this century. Even so, were we to question the first hundred scientists (or persons who think of themselves as being of a "scientific" mind) to be encountered in the nearest laboratories and classrooms, there is a strong likelihood that a sizeable percentage of them would say that the aim of science is to discover what things really are apart from the bias and deception of the human senses. This is the view held by the so-called "pure" scientist (including many educational psychologists and the educational sociologists) who rigidly divides the realm

---

[8] John Dewey, *Freedom and Culture* (New York: G. P. Putnam's Sons, 1939), pp. 84–85.

[9] Bertrand Russell, *Analysis of Mind* (London: George Allen and Unwin Ltd., 1921), p. 197.

of nature into two parts, limiting his efforts to dealing with the measurable physical qualities of size, shape and motion; taking "human qualities" and the secondary qualities of colors and smells and other subjective appearances out of the picture.

From an experimentalist position it is ironical for the "pure" scientist to be so hot to take as the aim of his science the search for the absolute reality underlying appearances—an aim built on a notion that is metaphysical and *extra*-scientific. By putting this dualistic interpretation on science, the reality he is seeking gets pushed back across the horizon where it is impossible for him to get at it or observe it directly. Having pushed reality beyond the reach of human faculties, he invents an unseen causal force to bring it back, covered all over from head to foot with mysticism.

This kind of scientist seeks causal laws of nature by which everything that turns up in experience can be reduced to their underlying causes. He makes a philosophical mistake, from the point of view of a relativistic experimentalist, in assuming that he has gone from mere appearance to reality by his reductions. And once he gets everything reduced to unobservable constructions (such as atoms, electrons, etc.), which he calls the absolute physical substances, he *unnecessarily* denies the reality of what he started out with. He *chooses* to treat the laws of nature *as if* they were causal.

Long ago David Hume pointed out in his famous argument that our attitude toward causality ought to be changed. Following an example of Hume's argument, suppose we have just finished striking a match against the friction paper on the cover of a matchbook and there is now a bright flame burning. The striking of the match is the cause and the resulting flame is the effect. If this had never happened before in the history of our knowledge we would never associate the striking of the match and the flame with each other. The reason we say that striking the match caused the flame is that we have observed these two events together a countless number of times. Whenever we strike a match against the friction paper (providing the matches are not wet and the friction paper has not been rubbed smooth), a flame follows. This sentence says everything that is of factual significance. Whenever event *A* takes place it is always followed by event *B*. If we add anything about event *A* causing event *B*, there is certainly nothing in our experience that warrants the assumption. The statement that an event of type *A* is always followed by an event of type *B* is a true general proposition and is a law of significance to Science. For example, if we strike a match in the future under proper circumstances, we can predict that a flame will follow. There is no need whatsoever to assume that some mysterious force connects the two events. And even if there were such a force, if we cannot observe it in any way, who cares about its existence? Hume does not object to calling one event a cause and the other one the effect, as long as it is clearly understood that this means no less and no more than that *A* is always followed by *B*.

In Hume's analysis of cause there is no such thing as a power or force which "causes" or "brings about" the effect. Nothing was said about the match or the paper or the striking motion being physical realities and the flame being merely a flickering effect. Those who wish to avoid the metaphysical dualism of a causal theory of perception use language and thinking of the sort suggested by Hume. Dewey, of course, accepted Hume's argument and used it to support his rejection of the several antithetical conceptions of knowledge which spring directly out of the notion that physical objects somehow stamp themselves upon the mind by means of the sense organs.

Perhaps the most notable antithesis suggested by the causal theory of perception is the one between objective knowing and subjective knowing. Objective knowledge is supposed to be something external and subjective knowledge is supposed to be something purely internal and psychical. One depends upon a body of ready-made truth, and the other upon a ready-made mind equipped with a faculty of knowing. Such an antithesis gives us two senses of the word "learning." As Dewey describes such a dualistic conception of learning: "On the one hand, learning is the sum total of what is known, as that is handed down by books and learned men. It is something external, an accumulation of cognitions, as one might store material commodities in a warehouse. Truth exists ready-made somewhere. Study is then the process by which an individual draws on what is in storage. On the other hand, learning means something which the individual *does* when he studies. It is an active, personally conducted affair."[10] Dewey repeatedly points out that the separation between subject matter

[10] Dewey, *Democracy and Education, op. cit.,* pp. 389–390.

and method is the educational equivalent of this dualism between external or objective knowledge and internal or subjective knowing.

Objective knowledge is supposed to be purely empirical knowledge which results from externally "caused" impressions. On the contrary, subjective knowledge is supposed to be purely rational knowledge which springs from activity carried on strictly within the mind, "an activity carried on better if it is kept remote from all sullying touch of the senses and external objects." According to Dewey, such a division leads to a dualism of activity and passivity in knowing. "The distinction between sense training and object lessons and laboratory exercises and pure ideas contained in books, and appropriated—so it is thought—by some miraculous output of mental energy, is a fair expression in education of this distinction."[11]

Along the same line, Dewey also objects to the unnecessary opposition between the intellect and the emotions. From the point of view of purely empirical objective knowledge "the emotions are conceived to be purely private and personal, having nothing to do with the work of pure intelligence in apprehending facts and truths." Accordingly, "The intellect is a pure light; the emotions are a disturbing heat. The mind turns outward to truth; the emotions turn inward to considerations of personal advantage and loss." Dewey accuses such notions as being responsible for the "depreciation of interest" and reliance upon "extraneous and irrelevant rewards and penalties in order to induce the person who has a mind (much as his clothes have a pocket) to apply that mind to the truths to be known."[12]

Employing his usual gambit, Dewey traces all such dualisms back to the root dualism between mind and matter, which he sees as the fountainhead of both realistic and idealistic philosophies. In epistemological theory, the separation of mind and matter breeds the necessity for conceiving a so-called objective reality which can be known only by means of subjective ideas, representations, images, or sense data. In educational theory, the mind vs. matter dualism is equivalent to the subject matter vs. method dualism, which in this work we have categorized as "knowledge as acquisition" in contrast to "knowledge as inquiry" which is used to

[11] *Ibid.*
[12] *Ibid.*, p. 391.

hold beliefs about knowing consistent with Dewey's philosophy.

Looking at the relationship of this theoretical discussion to practical implications in the classroom, it is obvious that all inquiry and no acquisition could make Jack as dull a boy as all acquisition and no inquiry. While one must be given up to get the other, Dewey's experimentalism does not require that we give up either completely. Although both cannot be emphasized at the same time, experimentalism suggests a method by which we can switch back and forth between emphasis on acquisition at one time and emphasis on inquiry at another time.

Consider the child who is struggling to learn how to tie his shoe laces. What is a problem worthy of experimental inquiry for the four-year-old ought to have long since been reduced to a satisfactorily acquired skill for the fourteen-year-old. Likewise, when a child first encounters multiplication, inquiry may profitably be emphasized, but it is absurd that forever after he should have to engage in experimental inquiry every time he needs to know the product of 7×5. Somewhere along the line the emphasis needs to shift to acquisition to reduce the basic multiplication facts to the automatic and routine so that the pupil is free to move on to mathematical problems more deserving of his experimental effort.

Thus, the emphasis on acquisition and inquiry (within the experimental framework of knowing as inquiry) is a cyclical, pulsating, rhythmic process. It works something like the carefully balanced blade of a rotary lawnmower, with acquisition at one end of the blade and inquiry at the other end. As we push the mower across the lawn, first one end and then the other cuts into the grass, each new cut clearing the way for the advance of the next. Let the two ends get out of balance and you cut nothing.

There is a popular notion that acquisition of a certain amount and kind of knowledge must precede inquiry into practical, personal, professional, and social problems; that one must possess knowledge before one can put it to intelligent use. This idea would indicate that the acquisition end of the blade should always cut ahead of the inquiry end. Dewey, of course, challenged this assumption.

Dewey proposed a contrary notion, considerably less popular, that knowledge is possible only through experimental inquiry;

that one should first become involved in the process of inquiry into problems of concern and interest and let knowledge follow as it will or as it is needed. Some interpreters of experimentalism would conclude that the inquiry end of the blade should always cut ahead of the acquisition end. This leads, of course, to the same silly argument as to which came first, the chicken or the egg.

The experimental method (an educative experience or the process of experimental inquiry) can begin with either inquiry or acquisition. It does not matter which comes first. What does matter to the experimentalist is that in education the emphasis shift from one to the other and back again, over and over, in some sort of harmonious and balanced *continuity*.

Typically in American education, even in the heyday of the progressive movement, acquisition has overbalanced inquiry. Progressives differed only in what they wanted pupils to acquire and in the manner in which they thought they should acquire it. The experimentalist teachers described earlier who see knowledge as inquiry do not emphasize inquiry at the expense of acquisition. Instead, they tend simply to bring inquiry somewhat more into balance with acquisition. The differences noted between the classroom practices of the teachers who see knowledge as inquiry and those of the teachers who see knowledge as acquisition illustrate the difference it makes when overemphasis on acquisition is corrected by bringing inquiry into somewhat better balance with acquisition.

16

INQUIRY INTO WHAT?

THE MOST PERSISTENT discrepancy between what teachers believe is good teaching practice and what they are observed to do in the classroom concerns the kind of problems around which teaching-learning is organized. In our study of the relationship of experimentalism to classroom practices we found that while many teachers believed that students should work on what they saw as their own problems rather than something that was the teacher's or textbook's problem, only a handful of the most thoroughgoing experimentalists actually organized learning around students' problems. Although experimentalist teachers organized learning around problems of genuine concern to students, these same teachers showed a preference for problems short in scope and shallow in depth. While nonexperimentalist teachers tended to choose instructional problems which are remote from the concern and interest of students, they showed an experimentalist's preference for problems of greater scope and challenge to students.

In the study the issues involving the nature of problems around which teachers should organize in classroom activities was represented by five statements of belief which are in agreement with Dewey's philosophy: (1) A good teacher puts pupils to work on what they see as their own problems, rather than something that is the teacher's or textbook's problem, (2) Frequently asks children to choose among several alternatives, (3) A good teacher encourages children to adventure into "deep water," to tackle problems that appear to be "over their heads," (4) A good teacher uses "feedback" from pupils to diagnose the changing state of affairs in the class, and revises original plans to meet new circumstances, and (5) A good teacher makes unplanned changes when a particular lesson is not getting an enthusiastic response from children.

We computed intercorrelations of the above items of educational beliefs with items of philosophic beliefs and observed classroom practices. These intercorrelations revealed that teachers who agreed with experimentalism on the importance of organizing learning around problems which are of genuine concern and interest to pupils were strong in their denial of the belief that "The mind is a group of 'contents' which come from having certain material presented to it from without" ($r = -.55$), and also disagreed with the philosophic proposition that "The laws which should regulate human conduct have been determined by the superior intelligence of an ultimate Being" ($r = -.36$).

A most notable finding regarding teachers who believed students should work on problems of genuine concern is the fact that in actual practice they did *not* "put pupils to work on what they saw as their own problems" (an insignificant r of .21). This is a good example of discrepancy between educational beliefs and teacher practices.

Another interesting finding was that the belief that "A good teacher encourages children to adventure into deep water, to tackle problems that appear to be over their heads," was rather consistently rejected by teachers otherwise in agreement with Dewey's experimentalism. For example, this item was negatively correlated with the experimentalist belief that "You can never prove that any fact is unconditionally true" ($r = -.38$) and the experimentalist practice of "putting pupils to work on what they see as their own problems, rather than something that is the teacher's or textbook's problem" ($r = -.42$). Perhaps the tone of this item was too strenuous or "tough" for some experimentalists. This raises the question of whether there might be both a "soft" and a "hard" experimentalism. The fact that many teacher-subjects with strong leanings to experimentalism also showed a tendency to "softness" or "protectiveness" toward children may be the result of Dewey's philosophy having been confused with the notions of Rousseau and Froebel, as discussed in Chapter 5.

We found that teachers who were observed to organize learning experiences around problems which students saw as their own believed in such relativistic items as "Nothing is or can be unchanging—absolutely certain" ($r = .37$), and "You can never prove that any fact is unconditionally true" ($r = .41$). In addition, they believed in providing situations of direct experience and in encouraging children to hypothesize about their problems.

In contrast, our findings show that nonexperimentalist teachers who were observed to organize learning activities around problems predetermined by the course of study or some similar external entity rather than the pupils' problems believed "Learning is the sum of impressions made on the mind as a result of presentation of material to be known" ($r = .39$). Such teachers also tended to believe that teachers should (1) make learning a direct and conscious end in itself, (2) follow the prescribed steps of an established method, (3) call for the undivided attention of pupils and scold those who do not respond, and (4) insist that pupils remain in their places, once work has begun, and concentrate on the task at hand.

As touched upon earlier, teachers typed according to the kinds of problems around which they organized instruction were in contradiction with our theoretical framework on their beliefs regarding the scope and depth of problems. The experimentalists showed a preference to have children work on short, shallow problems which they treated as independent wholes rather than on longer, more comprehensive problems (four significant contradictory intercorrelations ranging from $-.36$ to $-.43$). The nonexperimentalist showed a preference for academic problems of greater breadth and challenge. It would appear that the question of the source, size, and strength of instructional problems represents ground on which both the experimentalist and non-experimentalist are confused. Must problems of genuine concern and interest to students necessarily be short, small, and gentle? Must problems of substantial breadth and depth necessarily be predetermined academic or society-centered problems which are divorced from the immediate wants and worries of school youngsters?

There needs to be clarification for the would-be experimentalist of the fact that Dewey's philosophy of education is very positive in its demands for difficult, disturbing, and troublesome problems that are essential for stimulating students to reflective thinking. To miss this is to miss the whole point of Dewey's equating an educative experience with a reflective experience. The trick for the experimentalist teacher is to discover the kinds of problems of significant breadth and depth that have aspects of concern and interest for both *students* and *society*. This trick is complicated by the difficulties involved in bringing the limited and immature wants and worries of students into focus with problems the adult society desires and demands them to be able to deal with successfully.

Whether one agrees or disagrees with Dewey's experimentalism, one still must deal with the question of the subject matter of education. What is most important for youngsters to acquire or learn in school has been a subject for debate throughout the history of mankind. Even if the emphasis in education were to shift suddenly from acquisition to inquiry, the question would remain: "Inquiry into what?"

A curriculum which focuses primarily on the processes of inquiry must have some kind of content or subject matter. Inquiry operates in a context; it is inquiry *into something*. An inquiry-centered curriculum ought to provide areas or fields of inquiry, and locate possible points of entry into these. Whether these are called subjects, topics, ideas, interests, needs, projects, problems, or what have you, they constitute curriculum content.

Since it simply is not possible to inquire into everything, decisions need to be made about the comparative value of what should be included in the school curriculum. Then, too, decisions are needed regarding *when* this *what* should be dealt with as the child progresses through school—decisions about difficulty and sequence. Prior to such decisions, however, we need to ask: "*Who* makes these decisions? On what basis? What philosophic predispositions lead to what decisions?"

Granting that the legal responsibility for making such decisions rests with the states, and that these are often delegated to local school districts, school administrators, curriculum committees, and the like, our assumption is that, in the final analysis, *it is the teacher who makes such decisions*. When the teacher closes the door to his classroom and faces his students, he is free, often without realizing it, to carry out or undo most of the previous decisions made regarding the education of his students. The question may not be so much who makes the decisions, but who the decision maker pays attention to, what points of view he listens to, what influences him in making decisions. Such questions are as relevant to the selection of curriculum content as they are to teaching methods.

In dealing with such questions, there are three easily identified positions or predispositions which are likely to influence teachers' decisions about curriculum content.

First, there is the notion that curriculum should be determined by the needs and interests of the individual child. The subjects of inquiry should be of genuine and immediate concern to the inquirers. Therefore, those who hold this position look to the personal-social problems of childhood for curriculum "entrees." Second, there is a notion that the curriculum is best determined by the broader concerns and aspirations of the adult society, which, more than incidentally, foots the bill for the educational enterprise. The subjects of inquiry should have genuine significance to the present and future life of the society into which the child is being inducted or "civilized." Therefore, those holding this position are predisposed to look to the social scene for problematical situations worthy of inquiry in the school curriculum. Third, there is a notion that the inherent nature and structure of knowledge constitutes the most fertile ground for the development of intellectual inquiry. The subjects of inquiry should include not only the fundamental ideas and general principles of the established subject matter fields but also the "attitudes of inquiry" and the "problem of solving problems" on one's own. Therefore, those holding this position are inclined to look to the content and methodology of the academic disciplines or subject matter fields for the problems of inquiry to be tackled in the school curriculum.

Figure 1 illustrates the three distinct points of view competing to determine the nature of the problems of inquiry or subject matter which should be the organizational focus of the curriculum. A triangular situation is represented, with the nature of the individual child impinging upon curriculum decisions from one side, the nature of society from another side, and the nature of systematized knowledge from still another side.

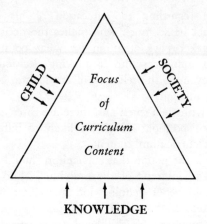

FIGURE 1. *Influences on the determination of curriculum content.*

John Dewey, of course, has been popularly associated with the child-centered curriculum, rightly or wrongly. In any event he would not deny that the individual child, his interests and his concerns, has to be an important—an inescapable—referent for selecting the content of effective educative experiences. Any proposed subject for inquiry, no matter how essential from the standpoint of adult society or the logical structure of knowledge, is doomed to failure unless it touches the intended learner's *wants* and *worries*. As the old saying goes, "You can lead a horse to water, but you can't make him drink." So it is with school children and learning. The subject must matter to the student or he will not inquire into it, not profitably, regardless of what is done to entice him or to force him to do so. He will profitably make inquiry only into something he cares about or can be stirred to care about.

Consistent with Dewey is the notion that to be an effective stimulant to thought the school subject must be a problem. It must affect the child, move him, arouse him, hit him where it counts. Whatever the content does to the pupil, it must make him *feel* something—then he will care. Youngsters are likely to feel and care about only what involves them directly, and this poses a problem for curriculum planners. It makes the installation of a set body of prescribed content difficult, if not impossible.

Thinking they have captured the whole of Dewey's educational ideas, a relatively small band of educators (composed mainly of theoreticians rather than practitioners) fervently advocate something called the "emerging" curriculum. Those who regard the child and his emerging needs and interests as *the* focal point of the school program, make no detailed list of specific objectives to be achieved or content to be covered (taught) or discovered (learned). Instead, the staff of a school spends much time trying to understand each child as an individual, and to help him identify, define, and deal with his personal-social problems. These "felt needs" of children become the basis for determining the learning experiences or content of the curriculum. Just what these so-called needs are, and the important "abilities, attitudes, and understandings" judged necessary to deal with them, cannot be predicted far in advance; instead they must *emerge* from the on-going experiences of the children. As uncertain as this may seem, the contention is that there is no alternative. The perceived needs and interests of the learner are the only possible "centers," "forces," or "ideas" around which to organize learning experiences that have any meaning and significance for him. Another important idea involved in this approach to curriculum making is that the needs and interests of a group of children, if developed properly, will necessarily cut across all the important problems of a society, without respect for the arbitrary lines which separate the various divisions or disciplines into which the accumulated knowledge of mankind has been organized.

Advocates of the child-centered curriculum tend to overestimate the difficulty of finding something that is of concern and interest to children. This position overlooks the commonly observed fact that children are normally interested in just about anything and everything. The difficulty is to find something which children are *not* interested in, a trick which teachers through the ages seem to have mastered with uncanny ability. Less facetiously, the real problem facing teachers with respect to children's needs and interests is to *select* those things children will be permitted to deal with on school time, to decide which are trivial and which are nontrivial—from the standpoint of the adult society and the nature of organized knowledge as well as the children themselves. Errors in perception and judgment on this score are difficult and, perhaps, impossible to avoid. Nevertheless, such errors constitute one of the greatest failings in the determination of the content of the educational program.

A mistaken notion about the inevitability of the child's needs and interests playing a key role in the determination of curriculum content is that children *do the deciding* themselves. This notion envisions children "voting on," "choosing," "picking," or "dreaming up" whatever it is that they want to "study," or "experience." Such may or may not be the case. Children may *influence* the determination of the curriculum content without taking over the responsibility of teachers, representing the adult society and knowing something of the structure of knowledge, to make such decisions. Children are excited by new ideas—things which never occurred to them before, and things which they might not have thought of on their own. Teachers can make some choices and suggestions, throw out some challenges, and even make some demands without damaging the tender little psyches of their pupils.

Speaking of tenderness, another predisposition of the child-centered approach is to believe that the younger the child the softer and more gentle should be his educational subject matter. Apparently, little children should be permitted to deal only with little problems, and big, hard, ugly problems should be postponed until the bloom of childhood is off the bush. This notion has led to grinding up the content of the school curriculum into an insipid, predigested, pablum. No chunks are left which might be large enough for any child to choke on—or sink his teeth into. However, child-determined content need not be namby-pamby. For example, Bruner contends "that any subject can be taught effectively in some intellectually honest form to any child at any stage of development."[1] Although this is a bold hypothesis, Bruner asserts that "No evidence exists to contradict it; considerable evidence is being amassed that supports it."

More appropriate, perhaps, are the observations of Sylvia Ashton-Warner, the brilliant novelist and teacher, who tells of making effective use of content in her Maori Infant Room which the faint-hearted consider downright gory. In teaching her "little ones" beginning reading, she looks for words that have intense personal meaning, words bound up with the security and inner

[1] Jerome S. Bruner, *The Process of Education* (Cambridge, Mass.: Harvard University Press, 1962), p. 33.

world of the child. She seeks to help youngsters learn to read and write a "Key Vocabulary, common to any child in any race," which "centers around the two main instincts, fear and sex."[2] The private Key Vocabularies developed in school by her pupils typically include such words as: kiss, knife, kill, jail, fight, yell, hit, crack, beer, bomb, drunk, crying, dead, bed, darling. Such words are rarely permitted in American primary rooms.

Obviously, one can take the child, his nature and needs, into account in the selection of content for inquiry without necessarily swallowing the questionable assumptions and narrow interpretations of Rousseau, Froebel, and their "gentle" followers. It should be just as obvious that while the concerns and interests of the pupil are important considerations in selecting problems of inquiry, there is more to it than just that.

Historically, American society has demanded and supported a system of formal or deliberate education. Although some effort has been made in the schools to secure the assent of the pupils to the ordeal, we have forced the young to attend school so that they will be taught the things we adults have decided they should know. Such a procedure is common in one form or another to all societies in the upbringing of their children. People, having organized themselves as a society or state, deliberately set about to see to it that their young learn things which will preserve and perpetuate the established way of life. Education, by origin and definition, is the practice by which the young are "civilized" or inducted into the ways of living that adults in their society consider right and good.

People are likely to continue to go right on exercising this traditional influence on the content of their children's education. Those who develop grand theories and plans for quick and drastic "improvements" in education too frequently overlook this fact of life, which contributes to their inevitable failure. This was the difficulty with those who misinterpreted and overemphasized Dewey's efforts to get schools to relate learning to the child's world of experience. It is likewise the difficulty with those who these days are attempting to reinstate in schools an overemphasis on the nature of logically organized or "disciplined" knowledge.

[2] Sylvia Ashton-Warner, *Teacher* (New York: Simon and Schuster, 1963), pp. 35–42.

While there should be little question of the right and power of the adult society to influence the curriculum of the schools, there is much debate about what content or problems of inquiry American society most values. This, of course, gets us back to the acquisition versus inquiry issue. A principal figure in this issue at present is Jerome S. Bruner, a Harvard psychologist. Interestingly, Professor Bruner has chosen to debate this question with Dewey in a little piece titled "After John Dewey, What?"[3]

The implied answer to the question, of course, is: "Jerome Bruner." In comparing his pedagogic creed with the one Dewey wrote in 1897, Bruner appears to share Dewey's preference for inquiry over acquisition. Bruner prefers teaching which is done in the "hypothetical mode" to that done in the "expository mode" because "it is largely the hypothetical mode which characterizes the teaching that encourages discovery."[4] However, Bruner disagrees sharply with Dewey about what constitutes the appropriate subject matter for inquiry and discovery. He concedes that Dewey's belief that problems rising out of the pupil's own social activities and experiences ought to be the subject matter of the school may have been appropriate in the 1890s, but not today. In the two thirds of a century between 1897 and today, Bruner suggests that modern psychology has produced revolutionary changes in "our understanding of man, his intelligence, his capabilities, his passions, and the forms of his growth." These changes, plus all the accompanying social and technological changes between Dewey's day and ours, makes Dewey's philosophy of education inappropriate. Bruner suggests the need to construct a new philosophy of education "guided by what we know today of the world and of human nature."[5] And he volunteers to start the ball rolling by junking all that old-fashioned nonsense about the social problems of the child, and, instead, make something called the "structure of knowledge" the focus of inquiry in education.

What Bruner means by the "structure of knowledge" is not made entirely clear. Although he says "The issue of subject matter in education can be resolved only by reference to one's view of

[3] Jerome S. Bruner, *On Knowing: Essays for the Left Hand* (Cambridge, Mass.: Harvard University Press, 1962), pp. 113–126.

[4] *Ibid.*, p. 83.

[5] *Ibid.*, p. 115.

the nature of knowledge," the definitions and examples Bruner offers for his uses of the term *knowledge* lack recognizable epistemological referents. Instead, he talks about knowledge as a "model" which gives "meaning and structure to regularities in experience," and as the "organizing ideas" which render "experience economical and connected." He offers as examples such concepts as "force in physics, the bond in chemistry, motives in psychology, style in literature."[6] Obviously, Bruner confuses theories *in* knowledge with theories *of* or *about* knowledge.

For Bruner, the nature of knowledge is essentially academic, in the sense that he shows very little concern for the practical or useful significance of knowledge to the outside-of-school wants and worries of students or the non-academic society from which they come and to which most of them will return. He describes the structure of knowledge variously as the "fundamentals," "basic principles," "ideas," "models," "rules," "foundations," "attitudes," and "generalizations,"[7] which are peculiar to the familiar subdivisions of organized knowledge. In the academic tradition, Bruner chooses to call these "disciplines."

Bruner offers examples of how grasping the structure of a discipline is understanding it in a way that enables many other things to be related to it meaningfully. He describes a set of observations of an inchworm traveling along a plane inclined to different degrees, from which students can discover the rule that the locomotion of such simple organisms as worms is regulated to a fixed or built-in standard. As the result of such observations the student is supposed to grasp the basic relation between external stimulation and locomotor action, presumably in general. From this discovery, according to Bruner, it is only a short logical leap to other highly related information such as "the swarming of locusts where temperature determines the swarm density in which locusts are forced to travel," and the fact that we find different species of insects "at different altitudes on the side of a mountain where crossbreeding is prevented by the tendency of each species to travel in its preferred oxygen zone." He offers similar examples from the disciplines of mathematics and language to illustrate his

[6] *Ibid.,* p. 120.

[7] Jerome S. Bruner, *The Process of Education, op. cit.,* chaps. 1 and 2.

point that "to learn structure, in short, is to learn how things are related."[8]

Such examples also illustrate Bruner's tendency to slide off discussions of *what* the structure of knowledge is to discussions of *how* it is grasped. This is very distressing, as he closely follows Dewey on questions of method while contradicting him diametrically on questions of content. For example, he agrees with Dewey's experimentalism in his rejection of specific transfer of training in favor of transfer of general principles and attitudes, arguing that students should not initially learn a specific fact or skill "but a general idea, which can then be used as a basis for recognizing subsequent problems as special cases of the idea originally mastered." He stresses, however, that the transfer of principles "is dependent upon mastery of the structure of subject matter."[9]

Continuing his discussion of what structure of knowledge is, Bruner says that the school curriculum ought to reflect clearly the basic or underlying principles of various fields of inquiry. He believes that the basic subjects in the school curriculum ought to be rewritten and their teaching materials revamped "in such a way that the pervading and powerful ideas and attitudes relating to them are given a central role." Furthermore, he believes that the decision as to what should be taught to school children "is a decision that can best be reached with the aid of those with a high degree of vision and competence in each of these fields."[10]

Bruner wants an academic curriculum made by academicians. But he is worried that such a curriculum may be academic in content only, and overlooks the fact that academicians, in the best sense, produce this content through attitudes and methods of intellectual inquiry. He cautions those who would undertake a large-scale revision of the school curriculum that "Mastery of the fundamental ideas of a field involves not only the grasping of general principles, but also the development of an attitude toward learning and inquiry, toward guessing and hunches, toward the possibility of solving problems on one's own."[11] He wants the young physics student, for example, to learn physics by "some working

[8] *Ibid.*, pp. 6–7.
[9] *Ibid.*, pp. 17–18.
[10] *Ibid.*, pp. 18–19.
[11] *Ibid.*, p. 20.

version" of the processes of inquiry, attitudes, convictions, and excitement of discovery the physicist experiences in plying his discipline.

Bruner's position on this issue is premised on the following central conviction:

... that intellectual activity anywhere is the same, whether at the frontier of knowledge or in a third-grade classroom. What a scientist does at his desk or in his laboratory, what a literary critic does in reading a poem, are of the same order as what anybody else does when he is engaged in like activities—if he is to achieve understanding. The difference is in degree, not in kind. The schoolboy learning physics *is* a physicist, and it is easier for him to learn physics behaving like a physicist than doing something else.[12]

With respect to teaching method there is no conflict on this point with Dewey's experimentalism. In fact, Bruner follows up with a criticism of ingrained educational practices of the 1960s which is very similar to Dewey's criticism of school instruction in the 1890s:

The "something else" usually involves the task of mastering what came to be called at Woods Hole a "middle language"—classroom discussions and textbooks that talk about the conclusions in a field of intellectual inquiry rather than centering upon the inquiry itself. Approached in that way, high school physics often looks very little like physics, social studies are removed from the issues of life and society as usually discussed, and school mathematics too often has lost contact with what is at the heart of the subject, the idea of order.[13]

The beauty of this statement and its essential agreement with Dewey's views on educational method should not hide the fact that Bruner is no experimentalist. Dewey, I am sure, would find Bruner's thinking rampant with philosophic dualisms. It is obvious that Bruner views academic pursuits as far more valuable than practical or social activities. His curriculum is designed to produce physicists, political scientists, poets, and psychologists, as opposed to plumbers, politicians, printers, and psychologically well-adjusted people.

Bruner rejects Dewey's idea that education is primarily a social

12 *Ibid.*, p. 14.
13 *Ibid.*

process and that the school is simply that form of community life in which the child is to be brought to share in the inherited resources of the race, and to use his own powers for social ends. Instead Bruner believes that "the school is an entry into the life of the mind." Even though he agrees with Dewey that school is, to be sure, life itself and not merely a preparation for living, Bruner insists that it is primarily a special form of life "where one experiences discovery by use of intelligence, where one leaps into new and unimagined realms of experience, experience that is discontinuous with what went before." It is his contention that Dewey's insistence upon the continuity of the school with the community overlooks the special function of education as a force in moving beyond the practices of what he calls "preliterate societies" to "new realms of experience, the discovery and exploration of new mysteries, the gaining of new Powers."[14]

In contrast to Dewey's belief in the continuity of knowledge and action (or subject matter and method) is to be found in a conception of knowledge as inquiry, it is Bruner's conviction that "the unity of knowledge is to be found within knowledge itself, if the knowledge is worth mastering." Although he agrees with Dewey on the virtues of inquiry *as method,* he sees it not as its own end as Dewey does but as a means to the acquisition of the structure of knowledge. Whatever it is, Bruner's structure of knowledge is precious for its own sake.

For Bruner the answer to the question of "Inquiry into what?" turns out to be the answer to the question "What is nontrivial?" He states that "If one can first answer the question, 'What is worth knowing about?' Then it is not difficult to distinguish between the aspects of it that are worth teaching and learning and those that are not."[15] And to the question "Who decides what is worth knowing?" he implies the answer "Knowledgeable men like me and the group of thirty-five scientists, scholars, and educators who attended the famous conference at Woods Hole on Cape Cod to discuss how education might be improved in primary and secondary schools." Dr. Bruner's quarter of a century of research on perception should have taught him that what is perceived as nontrivial by such a select group may be perceived as

[14] Bruner, *On Knowing: Essays For the Left Hand, op. cit.,* pp. 118–119.
[15] *Ibid.,* pp. 121–122.

very trivial indeed by the remaining ninety-some percent of the adult society, to say nothing of the children to be taught.

Bruner's position calls for the leaders in each of the various fields of inquiry to sit down and decide (1) what is the nontrivial content of their field, and (2) what are the modes of inquiry most suitable to the pursuit of their discipline, and (3) what are the features of the structure of their discipline which distinguishes it from other disciplines. His illustrations seem to imply that the content and methodology of each discipline is discretely unique, that they are not modeled around a skeleton of inter-related principles which are common to all disciplines. With Bruner's idea of a structure of a discipline much seems to depend on what discipline one is talking about, and on one's individual perception of what is fundamental to that discipline. It would be foolish to claim that all mathematicians are in agreement regarding the basic concepts, principles, insights, and attitudes which exemplify mathematics as a discipline, or that historians are of one mind as to what the structure of history is or how it should be approached.

In a criticism of the development of Bruner's "structure of the disciplines" as an educational slogan, Professor Herbert Kliebard points out that there is currently much debate among academicians themselves concerning the relative merits of the "new" curriculums prepared by select groups of academic experts.[16] For example, Samuel Eliot Morison has recently criticized the approach to teaching history developed by Educational Services, Incorporated, an organization of academicians from Harvard and MIT. Historian Morison expresses a preference for the narrative tradition in history, even though he recognizes such views are outside of what he calls "the 'Brunerian' frame of reference."[17] Likewise, a professor of physics, in a recent interview, makes a scathing attack on some of the new "structured" courses in science and mathematics. Referring to these new curriculums as a form of "educational carpet baggery" and to the local school officials who implement them as "scalawags," Professor Alexander Calandra sharply criticizes what he sees as a decided overemphasis on theory in

[16] Herbert M. Kliebard, "Structure of the Disciplines as an Educational Slogan," *Teachers College Record* (April 1965), pp. 598–603.

[17] S. E. Morison, "The Experiences and Vistas of a Historian," in *Vistas of History* (New York: Random House–Knopf, 1964).

programs like the ones sponsored by PSSC and CBA and an "unfortunate divorce of pure mathematics from applied mathematics" in the new mathematics programs.[18]

John Dewey would most certainly have shared Kliebard's concern that "overemphasis on theoretical abstractions and the creation of a dichotomy between theory and practice, in turn, may serve to obscure the relevance of school to the world of affairs."[19] In Chapter 5 we noted Dewey's emphasis on the importance of subject matter in education. While Bruner concurs with Dewey that education best proceeds through the process of inquiry and discovery, he seems impatient with Dewey's belief that the learner's *initial* subject matter should be at least to some degree, identified and selected by the learner in the course of his "active doing." He lacks Dewey's confidence that such apparently willy-nilly basis for content selection is likely to be "enlarged and worked over into rationally or logically organized material—that of the one who, relatively speaking is expert in the subject."[20]

Dewey would reject Bruner's proposals for a "structure-centered" curriculum as nothing more than a sophisticated warming over of the traditional subject-centered curriculum. He would re-emphasize our need to develop curriculum around problems, social and personal, of significant breadth and depth so that they could be "plugged into," or have plugged into them, considerations relevant to the "structure" of organized subject matter disciplines. Instead of engaging in unprofitable debate as to whether the child, society, or subject matter should be the dominant influence on curriculum content, Dewey would urge that teachers consider the kinds of practices which are useful in bringing the limited wants and worries of pupils into focus with problems both the adult society and the structure of disciplines demand them to be able to handle successfully.

[18] Alexander Calandra "The New Curriculums: A Sharp Dissent," *School Management* (1964), No. 8, pp. 76–82.

[19] Kliebard, *op. cit.,* p. 602.

[20] Dewey, *Democracy and Education, op. cit.,* pp. 116–117.

part V

Using Knowledge of Beliefs and Behavior

T HE STORY of our efforts to date to investigate *The Experimental Mind in Education* is nearly told. Concern for better understanding the relationships between beliefs and practices has been established as the setting for the study. In order to carry this study forward it has been necessary to develop and test instruments for measuring both beliefs and practices of teachers along a common theoretical dimension—in this case, Dewey's Experimentalism. These instruments, along with the results of testing them, have been described in considerable detail. Now, we have reached the point of deciding what can and should be done with them.

Chapter 17 discusses the potential of such instruments for bringing a much-needed philosophic honesty to educational research. Several proposals are offered for demonstrating the usefulness of philosophy in educational research on such problems as teacher competence and teacher education. Chapter 18 examines the responsibility of theorizers to test their beliefs empirically, and suggests that the procedures used in this study constitute one approach for accomplishing this. Chapter 19 asks the value-loaded question, "What *should* we do with knowledge of teachers' beliefs and practices?"

17

PHILOSOPHIC HONESTY
IN EDUCATIONAL RESEARCH

STUDY OF THE RELATIONSHIP between philosophy and teaching practices has not generally been considered indispensable to either the preparation of teachers or school curriculums, or to the conduct of educational research. In teacher education programs philosophy has been taught separately from and unrelated to courses in teaching methods. Educational philosophers haven't seemed to know or care much about classroom practices. And instructors in teaching methodology have been equally oblivious of philosophy and how it relates to classroom practice. Likewise, curriculum makers have shown no inclination to publicize the philosophic biases underlying their prescriptions as to what should be taught and how. As for those who have done most of the research in education, their avoidance of problems relating to pedagogical practice has been exceeded only by their shyness in the face of problems which involve questions of value.

Research in education has been conducted for the most part within the tradition of psychology; rarely has it been attempted within a theoretical framework that has an explicit philosophic orientation. In fact, its psychological tradition has encouraged educational researchers to make a deliberate effort to avoid, if at all possible, any contamination from philosophic positions, especially those involving value or ethical judgments.

Psychologists, particularly educational psychologists, are anxious to be considered scientists. "True" scientists, unlike ordinary human beings, are supposed to be impartial. In the name of "pure" science they strive for absolute accuracy through perfect disinterestedness or objectivity. Affiliation with some partisan interest results in the loss of the scientific spirit. Such a radical requirement makes it awfully tough to be both scientific and human. Happily, most men of science disclaim or ignore this extreme view. Unhappily, too many researchers in education and the other social sciences are still being sucked in by it. Apparently, the outright rejection of anything faintly smelling of philosophy helps them feel more "scientific"—and, therefore, more respectable.

Under pressure to be scientifically clean, it is not uncommon for researchers in education to kid themselves and others into believing that they are capable of suspending their partialities or philosophies during their performances as researchers. This, of course, is nonsense. People are partial. We favor some things over others. Only if we do our favoring in a partisan manner with undue joy, sorrow, or passion can it be called unfair or unscientific. Unreasoned partiality we call prejudice or bias. However, when partiality is unmarked by antipathy or suspicion we call it preference or inclination. Either way, to be partial is to be human. The predisposition to favor one side of a question or conflict is an inescapable ingredient in any personality system. And, as we have indicated throughout, a person's partial preferences influence his perceptions and his behavior—even though he may *wish* that they did not.

To this point former Supreme Court Justice Arthur Goldberg offers his favorite quotation:

We cannot be impartial. We can only be intellectually honest; that is, aware of our own passions, on guard against them and prepared to warn our readers of the dangers into which our partial views may lead them. Impartiality is a dream and honesty a duty.[1]

One needs only to glance through back issues of educational research journals to see that research in this field is, despite the desires and denials, filled with value judgments. One is struck time and again by the frequency and naivete with which researchers use value-loaded terms. Examples are research on "creativity," "effective" teachers, "gifted" students, "academic excellence," problems of relating subjects "appropriately" in order to

---

[1] Gaetano Salvamini, in "My Favorite Quotation," *Saturday Evening Post* (December 1, 1962).

obtain "valid" experiments and "significant" findings, establishing a "favorable" intellectual climate, providing "adequate" financial support, developing "legitimate" investigations into "basic" or "fundamental" areas where "reliable" or "warranted" evidence is highly "desirable." In all research studies the researcher drops such clues to the fact that he is consciously or unconsciously committed to value judgments of some kind.

Researchers in educational psychology are captives of their own passion for objectivity. They discuss theories of teaching and learning (calling them "models") which they claim are value-free. They invent "operational" definitions, which describe the inter-action that supposedly takes place between teacher and pupil when teaching and learning happens. Numerous flow charts based on an elaborate computer model are required equipment for the explanation of such theories. The clank of metal is deafening, but the ghost behind the machine is discernible though not spoken of. Despite their pretense of objectivity, they succeed only in postponing by several steps the uncovering of the philosophic assumptions involved. For example, dominant in American psychology are the assumptions of philosopher John Locke (1) that the mind of an individual is *tabula rasa* at birth, (2) that the human mind is a passive thing which acquires content and structure only through the impact of sensation and the criss-cross of associations, (3) that the human organism is governed from without rather than from within, and (4) that it is mechanically determined rather than in some degree spontaneous. Variants of the Lockean point of view, according to psychologist Gordon Allport, "are found in associationism of all types, including environmentalism, behaviorism, stimulus-response (familiarly abbreviated as S-R) psychology, and all other stimulus-oriented psychologies, in animal and genetic psychology, in positivism and operationism, in mathematical models—in short, in most of what today is cherished in our laboratories as truly 'scientific' psychology."[2]

Our quarrel is not with *what* these assumptions imply, but with the denial on the part of researchers in education that they have any obligation for making them known to their audience.

[2] Gordon W. Allport, *Becoming* (New Haven: Yale University Press, 1955), p. 8.

Instead of warning us that their theories of teaching and learning are indeed built upon controvertible philosophic notions concerning the nature of man, they try to persuade us to accept them as the purest products of objective empiricism. This is an unforgivable breach of intellectual honesty.

In a review of educational research, Scriven found that researchers make many philosophic assumptions but usually neither recognize nor test them. He suggests the following explanation:

A strong tradition in the history of psychology separates empiricism from ethics and the average researcher feels completely insecure when he discovers that his criteria involve ethical variables. Either he does not allow himself to perceive this fact, or, if he does perceive it, he says nothing about it.[3]

Within the tradition of psychology educational researchers have turned their attention to variables which do not appear, immediately at least, to involve philosophic positions. This, of course, rules out the most interesting problems in education and encourages a concentration of research effort on easily measured but trivial variables, adding fuel to the criticism that research in education is much ado about nothing.

Psychology's obsession with objectivity is itself a value judgment stemming from a well-known philosophic position. It is the bias of science, speaking loosely, which favors knowledge which has objective or external validity; i.e., knowledge of "real stuff" observable and verifiable in a sensible public world independent of what is personal and private in the fears and feelings and the minds of knowers. The notion of objective knowledge has played a crucial role in the advance of science, particularly the physical sciences. However, carried to extremes as it is by radical empiricists, it restricts what is allowable scientific knowledge so very narrowly that one is forced to deny knowledge of atoms on the same grounds one disallows knowledge of leprechauns. Without diminishing the importance of or desirability for a reasonable degree of objectivity in research in the social sciences, including education, it should be clear to anyone who attempts to study human behavior that subjectivity is an observable and measurable natural phenomenon

[3] Michael Scriven, "The Philosophy of Science in Educational Research," *Review of Educational Research*, XXX, No. 5 (December, 1960), 423.

which will not go away no matter how intently we try to ignore it. Human beings are subjects as well as objects, and research involving human beings cannot progress very much farther without facing up to and accounting for the subjectivity of both the researchers and the researched.

The thoughtful researcher should recognize that freeing oneself from any and all subjective value positions—getting into a presuppositionless frame of mind—is an enormously difficult if not impossible assignment. Any belief except the belief in the desirability of investigating the problem at hand is an undesirable belief which may interject itself between the researcher and his research problem. Therefore, achievement of objectivity means getting rid of all beliefs, at least for the time being—and this makes it necessary first off to discover what beliefs one already holds.[4] In other words, we must become aware of our beliefs and biases even if for no better reason than merely to expunge them for the purpose of achieving objectivity in research.

Where do we turn for help in discovering what our beliefs are and how to talk sense about them? Since value judgments, logical analyses, and systems of thought are involved, one would think that the experience of philosophers in such matters might prove helpful. But that apparently does not often occur to the researcher in education. Instead, he maintains his shyness of philosophers and philosophies, and attempts to describe and classify his beliefs or assumptions within "home-made" frameworks. Into this latter category fall what has come to be called socio-psychological theories.

Among researchers in the social sciences there is a growing emphasis on the need for theoretically oriented research. To fill this need more and more of them are turning to "theory building," producing social interaction theory, learning theory, teaching theory, curriculum theory, and even metatheory or theory of theory. Such theories have merit and promise. Generally, they are built up by induction from "factual" evidence. Their socio-psychological orientation gives them a supposedly value-free or "pure" status not enjoyed by theories contaminated by philosophic considerations of metaphysics, epistemology, ethics, axiology, and the like. Such theories—and those who build them—are oblivious to the known

[4] James K. Feibleman, "Some Problems in the Philosophy of Education," *Harvard Educational Review*, 26, No. 2 (Spring 1956), 151–152.

theories and familiar language conventions in philosophy and to the accumulated experience and skill of trained philosophers.

The characteristic weakness of most of these socio-psychological theories is that they have been devised by amateur philosophers and are consequently naive from the standpoint of philosophy of science. Obviously, this new band of theorizers is totally unaware, either by accident or by design, that both philosophers and other scientists have already been over the road ahead of them. They seem not to know that there are modern philosophies of science which enjoy enough precision and sophistication to command the respect of both science and philosophy. They could save themselves much time and trouble, and the rest of us much bewilderment, if they would just get over the "thing" which compels them to go to ridiculous lengths to avoid the accumulated knowledge, experience, and the conventions of philosophy, especially the nomenclature all other intelligent men have agreed to use when talking about theory and theory making. Socio-psychological frameworks for research on teaching are drenched in detail which is made as complex as possible in concept. They are couched in strangely-minted language which confuses and obscures rather than clarifies and simplifies (like good theory should). These theories invariably are built upon several elementary philosophical assumptions which lie half-hidden and hopelessly tangled in logical contradictions one or more steps back—out of the easy reach of analysis.

All researchers in education and the human subjects they study have beliefs which affect choices made in the performance of their respective tasks. As we have already pointed out, beliefs operating in a particular situation are not always recognized. Our beliefs about the fundamental questions of philosophy often lie beneath and are disassociated from the surface beliefs we consciously see involved in specific teaching and research settings. These implicit underlying beliefs may be in conflict with the explicit beliefs we recognize as operating on the surface. When this is the case, confusion and inconsistency are likely to be the predominant characteristics of our theoretical formulations.

Those who develop theoretical frameworks in education (whether to guide research, the education of teachers, curriculum development, or instructional procedures) *have a responsibility to raise their basic beliefs to the level of critical self-consciousness.* By basic beliefs we mean beliefs which have been acquired about the meaning of life, the nature and destiny of man, the nature of the world in which we live and the nature of our knowledge of it.

For example, Fattu recognizes that those who study teacher effectiveness "should be aware of, and state explicitly as evidence of that awareness, the implicit value assumptions involved."[5] However, the explicit statement of the value assumptions requires more than a superficial treatment of philosophy. Morse and his colleagues,[6] using a multiple-criterion approach, developed instruments to discriminate teachers' classroom behavior along four different theoretical viewpoints in educational psychology: (1) Growth and Development, (2) Mental Health, (3) Subject Matter Content, and (4) Group Dynamics. This group of researchers recognized that these diverse psychological viewpoints to some extent parallel philosophical arguments. They made a conscientious effort to study the different philosophical approaches to classroom instructional design which appeared to them to be dictated by the four different viewpoints of educational psychology. However, their search for parallel viewpoints in educational philosophy lacked any orientation to fundamental philosophical considerations, i.e., theory of knowledge (epistemology), theory of existence or being (ontology), or theory of value (axiology). This may explain why they found a perplexing lack of significant relationship between the teacher's general classroom practice and what was called the teacher's "philosophy."

Let us treat the problem of deciding "Who's a Good Teacher" more thoroughly. More than half a century of research effort has failed to yield meaningful criteria for measuring teacher effectiveness.[7] The trouble is that this effort has centered on the search for a single, all-inclusive, universally applicable, and preferably value-free

[5] William J. Ellena, Margaret Stevenson, and Harold V. Webb, editors, *Who's a Good Teacher?* (Washington, D.C.: American Association of School Administrators, 1961) p. 42.

[6] William C. Morse, Richard Bloom, and James Dunn, *A Study of School Classroom Behavior from Diverse Evaluative Frameworks: Developmental, Mental Health, Substantive Learning, Group Process* (Ann Arbor, Mich.: University of Michigan, 1961).

[7] A. S. Barr and R. E. Jones, "The Measurement and Prediction of Teaching Efficiency," *Review of Educational Research 28* (June, 1958), 256–264.

standard of teacher "goodness" around which the majority of the nation's educators could rally. It couldn't help but fail.

Two major trends appear to influence researchers recently engaged in the study of teacher effectiveness: (1) they attempt operationally to define behavior and/or characteristics of teachers, without reference to any theoretical framework, or (2) they are guided by a supposedly value-free framework that is socio-psychologically oriented.

The ten-year study by Ryans is an example of the trend to define operationally the characteristics of teachers and their behavior.[8] Ryans' work related three dimensions of teachers' classroom behavior (friendly vs. aloof, systematic vs. unplanned, stimulating vs. uninspiring) to a teacher characteristic schedule which is a self-report inventory of three hundred verbal and pictorial items relating to personal preferences, self-judgments, biographical data, frequently-engaged-in activities, and so forth. This schedule is a detailed collection of diverse characteristics (such as generosity toward others, interest in reading, participation in high school activities, number of years' experience, and the like) without any explicit theoretical framework to tie them together in patterns with meaningful implications for educational practice.

Jensen identified the need for a framework of concepts that could be used to analyze teachers' classroom behaviors systematically and offered a promising socio-psychological framework in which to assess the influence of social interactions in the classroom and the individual and group learning which resulted.[9] In another socio-psychologically oriented study, Getzels and Thelen described three different styles of teaching: (1) nomothetic, (2) ideographic, and (3) transactional. They identified the transactional style as striking a balance between requirement of students' mastering subject matter and promotion of their achieving personal goals in the classroom situation.[10]

[8] David G. Ryans, *Characteristics of Teachers* (Washington, D. C.: American Council on Education, 1960).

[9] Gale E. Jensen, "The Socio-psychological Structure of the Instructional Group," *The Dynamics of Instructional Groups.* Fifty-Ninth Yearbook of the National Society for the Study of Education, Part II. (Chicago: The National Society for the Study of Education, 1960), pp. 83–114.

[10] Jacob W. Getzels and Herbert A. Thelen, "The Classroom Group as a Unique Social System," *ibid.,* pp. 53–82.

The studies by Anderson,[11] Withall,[12] and Flanders[13] are additional examples of investigations of patterns of teacher behavior carried on within sociopsychological frameworks. Anderson looked at teacher behavior along a dominative-integrative dimension. Withall focused on teacher-centered versus pupil-centered classroom climate, classifying teachers' verbal statements into seven categories. Flanders' twelve-category observational technique was used to look at the patterns of social interactions in classrooms. From an assessment of teachers' responding or initiating behavior, Flanders was able to quantify the behaviors that contribute to the dynamic interaction of the participants in the teaching-learning process.

While such operational or sociopsychological approaches may yield interesting descriptions of teaching behavior they do nothing whatsoever to help anyone solve the problem of deciding which teachers are good and which are not so good. Their deliberate effort to avoid contamination from philosophy leaves them high and dry. The user of these approaches has no way (except to leap in the dark clutching his own blind and unspoken of faith) to get from the described characteristics of teachers to judgments regarding the relative merits of the differentiated types of teachers.

If we are to research the question "Who's a Good Teacher?" and make any sense of it, we must answer the prior question: "Good in terms of what value position?" The literature is full of abortive attempts to define criteria for judging good teaching. Almost without exception these criteria are stated in terms of what a teacher ought to do or be like—without any reference to underlying assumptions. In order to be meaningful, any referent for "goodness" ought to be recognizable philosophy, i.e., logically compatible with assumptions regarding fundamental questions of philosophy.

[11] Harold H. Anderson, Joseph E. Brewer, and Mary Frances Reed, *Studies of Teachers' Classroom Personalities, III. Follow-Up Studies of the Effects of Dominative and Integrative Contacts on Children's Behavior,* Applied Psychology Monographs No. 11 (Stanford, Calif.: Stanford University Press, 1946).

[12] John Withall, "The Development of a Technique for the Measurement of Social-Emotional Climate in Classrooms," *Journal of Experimental Education, 17* (March 1949), 347–361.

[13] Ned A. Flanders, *Teacher Influence, Pupil Attitudes, and Achievement: Studies in Interaction Analysis,* Final Report, Cooperative Research Project No. 397 (Minneapolis: University of Minnesota, 1960).

Our bases for judging what is "good" or "competent" or "effective" needs to be defined in terms of logical structures intelligent men can talk together about with some degree of common meaning and understanding.

In our pluralistic, open, democratic society, universal agreement on a single criterion or set of criteria is neither possible nor desirable. For this reason, studies on teacher competence need to have judgments made by observer-judges using individual criteria identifiable in terms of explicitly stated and measured positions on relevant value continua. Judgments should be relative to described value positions and described circumstances, rather than based on absolute values and universal circumstances.

There is, of course, no way to differentiate effective and ineffective teachers without making a value judgment. Looking for a single, absolute, value-free standard for judging teacher competence is as pathetically fruitless as searching for a single set of religious principles upon which all Americans can agree. An equally absurd notion is that, because the study of teacher effectiveness involves questions of values, it is necessarily a fanciful or whimsical kind of enterprise which lies completely outside the realm of empirical science. Either way teacher effectiveness remains a matter of irresponsible opinion, subject to the authority or caprice of prevailing powers.

We think the study of *The Experimental Mind in Education* offers an intelligent alternative to the extremes of either authority or caprice. We have developed procedures for making logical connections between theory and practice, or, between value judgments and observable facts or happenings. Utilizing both the method and the supporting system of thought proposed by Dewey, we have demonstrated that value judgments (beliefs) can be measured and compared with *logically congruent* observable behavior (teachers' classroom practices). We have used Dewey's comprehensive framework of experimentalism *as a means* for looking at teaching practices *in correspondence to* value positions regarding what is "good." Philosophic systems such as this constitute the connecting threads, the avenues upon which we can get back and forth from practices to beliefs in some meaningful fashion.

The value of our instruments to research on teacher effectiveness is not that they measure agreement-disagreement with Dewey's

philosophy but that they permit *comparable* measurements of beliefs and classroom practices *in terms of a common referent.* It is
this *connection* between criteria for effectiveness (beliefs or values)
and observable evidence of effectiveness in the classroom (teacher
practices) which has been missing from previous efforts to measure
and predict teacher effectiveness. It is desirable that philosophic
honesty (and responsibility) in research on teaching not be burdened
on Dewey's experimentalism alone. It is not the only philosophy
relevant to the problem—by a long shot. Similar instruments are
needed for measuring agreement-disagreement with such other
pertinent value dimensions as Classical Realism, Existentialism,
Liberal Christian Idealism, Neo-Thomism, and so forth. Continued
effort in these directions will increase our ability to bring sense
and order to the discussion and study of teacher effectiveness.

In an effort to demonstrate the usefulness of philosophy in
educational research, we are currently using the Experimentalism
Inventories in "An Investigation of Observer-Judge Ratings of
Teacher Competence," a four-year research project funded by the
U. S. Office of Education. In this study we use the measures of experimentalism to establish the value positions of both the teachers
and the observers who make judgments regarding their teaching
competence. It is our contention that in order to understand what
is meant when someone says, "This is a good teacher" or "This
is a poor teacher" we must know who the observer-judge is, what
he values, where he stands when he observes and judges. Furthermore, we need to have this same sort of information about and
from a number of different and differing observer-judges, including
repeated observations under varying conditions. When we also
know something about the teacher's values and viewpoint we are
then able to explore more adequately the relative positions of the
judge and the teacher and the possible relationships and interactions affecting judgments of the teacher's effectiveness.

In addition to opening this sort of door to the problems of
judging teacher competence, instruments for measuring agreement-
disagreement with relevant philosophic dimensions can profitably
be used in research designed to study what effects, if any, the values
of others have upon the values and practices of teachers. For example, we might measure the beliefs of college students at the time
of their admission to teacher education programs, with periodic

remeasurement at strategic stages of their preservice training, following them through the first few years of their experience in the field. Such studies could identify influencing factors (people, courses, field experiences and the like) in the evolvement of their teaching characteristics, or they could reveal that teacher education programs have little or no effect in influencing the kind of teacher one becomes. How one teaches may prove out to be a matter of sheer accident or chance, or to be a matter of personality or beliefs largely determined long before one enters a school of education.

The kind of data which our instruments make available could also be useful in studying the selection of college supervisors of student teachers and cooperating public school "master" teachers with whom student teachers are placed. An even more interesting study would involve the placement or pairing of student teachers with supervisors and master teachers. There was evidence in our original study of the relationship of experimentalism to classroom practices to indicate that supervisors and master teachers in some cases are in serious value conflict with their students, as well as with the objectives of the teacher education programs of which they are an important part. Perhaps such a conflict constitutes a healthy divergence which is both desirable and unavoidable.

Considering the effectiveness of basic philosophic beliefs in differentiating among groups of teachers, teacher education programs might well afford to spend more time and effort examining the philosophic roots of specific educational issues and problems. This implies that teachers be given greater opportunity for developing and understanding basic systems of philosophy, including elementary logic, as well as understanding the lines of relationship connecting fundamental philosophic positions with educational points of view, and, in turn, the connections of these to decisions teachers must make regarding classroom methods and procedures. With this kind of background, subsequent generations of teachers could become more astute in uncovering hidden or silent biases involved in recommendations to them to subscribe to passing fads in curriculum and instruction, or in the findings of educational research.

18

THE EMPIRICAL TESTING
OF BELIEF

ANYONE WHO VENTURES into the study of the relationship between beliefs and behavior soon finds himself caught between opposing factions. Psychologists, who consider the study and explanation of behavior their exclusive province, tend to distrust the intrusion of philosophy into empirical research. The problems presented by the apprehensions of psychology were dealt with in the last chapter. These are rivaled by those created by philosophers who regard beliefs as strictly philosophical or religious concerns and resent their submission to the empirical procedures of psychology. Therefore, the builder of attitude, beliefs, or personality inventories, questionnaires, or scales (by whatever name one chooses to call such things) had better be prepared to face criticism from both directions.

From the psychological side the challenges most often concern questions of reliability, validity, experimental design, procedures used in the collection and analysis of data, and the like. The alarm signals from that direction have rung loudly, indeed. Much effort and anguish has been spent in trying to harmonize that noise, for it could not and *should* not be completely silenced.

From the philosophical side, the challenges are of an entirely different nature. They concern questions of epistemology, ethics, intellectuality, scholarship—even honesty, propriety, and personal integrity. For example, one philosopher friend made the accusation that the inventories (or their maker; it was never made clear which) reflected a "shocking anti-intellectual and anti-philosophical attitude." Recalling that the charge of anti-intellectualism has been leveled against John Dewey, that part of the criticism may be further validation that the inventory items reflected Dewey's philosophy! However, the "anti-philosophical" charge was taken seriously as an instance of a prevalent notion that it is improper to deal with philosophy via quantified responses on a paper and pencil test. From the very outset, I was cautioned on this score by my principal adviser in philosophy, who although quite sympathetic to both Dewey's philosophy and the idea that it should be tested empirically, doubted the value of reducing any philosophy to a handful of personal opinion statements. Thus, I am most conscious of the charge that the development of the Personal Beliefs and Teacher Practices Inventories may not be "good philosophy."

Let us get a bit more specific in examining the objection that the inventories do not represent good philosophy. The *Personal Beliefs Inventory* presents questions which according to the introductory description have no right or wrong answers—questions about which people have legitimately different beliefs or opinions. The questions concern such fundamental philosophical matters as "change," "knowledge," "truth," "mind," and "spirit." To answer these questions appropriately (from the standpoint of "good philosophy") would require a great deal of careful philosophical analysis. And the jotting down of numbers from 1 to 6 in response to the inventory items falls far short of full-scale philosophical consideration.

According to one of my philosopher friends, the questionnaire fails to make a proper distinction between opinion and knowledge about complex philosophical matters. He points out that the questionnaire calls for an opinion "or an automatic, unreflective response—something off the top of one's head." Knowledge about such matters implies a careful, critical understanding of the problems, ambiguities and dilemmas inherent in them. While knowledge in this connection should not imply final answers it would seem that opinion implies only a lack of understanding. What my philosopher friend means is that nothing short of a complete essay could possibly be an appropriate response to these questions. Or, as he says it: "What the questionnaire demands of me is that I not puzzle over responses to items but give my first or immediate response—in other words, my opinion. But this is precisely what I cannot do! My habit of mind compels me when I see questions about "truth" or "mind" to pause and ask how the word is being used, what does it mean. I could no more answer these questions which use vague and ambiguous terms than I could write with my toes."

Even after repeated item analyses to eliminate vague and ambiguous terms, such terms still remain. However, we have discovered an interesting lack of agreement about which terms are which. What is vague and ambiguous for one person is precisely what makes an item crystal clear for another. How any given person works out these inescapable language problems in his pattern of responses (i.e., his acceptance or rejection of the items) is not irrelevant to his agreement—disagreement with John Dewey.

With respect to the demand for quick off-the-top-of-the-head responses, the inventories share much in common with psychological tests of the free-association variety. A good example is the analysis of opposites in which the tester reads a list of stimulus words such as "black," "day," "mother," and expects relatively rapid-fire responses such as "white," "night," and "father." A break or departure in the chain of style or content of responses, such as a hesitation, may be taken as a clue to emotional involvement. For instance, if the subject takes a long time to respond to the word "mother" the psychologist may suspect parental relationships as a promising entry to dealing with his problem, particularly if other similar stimulus words produce similar responses, building into a pattern. Likewise, we are interested in the pattern of responses to the range of inventory items. Confusion or contradiction on a few isolated items does not seriously affect the overall results.

Philosophers seem to be intrigued by the *items* but dislike the form and limitations placed upon the *responses* called for, while we get just the opposite reaction from psychologists who seemingly would be content with the answers if only they could be more sure of the questions. Short, quick responses which lend themselves to easy categorization and quantification make sense to psychologists, but succeed only in frustrating and infuriating philosophers. Our experience in administering the inventories to large numbers of college professors suggests that this division regarding the adequacy of responses can be viewed as an instance of the larger division which separates the scientist and the nonscientist. For example, professors from the natural and social science fields, as well as from mathematics, generally have responded more easily and more enthusiastically than have their colleagues from the fields of language, literature, and philosophy. Apparently the scientist-type accepts the checking of quantified responses as a familiar and legitimate mode of operation—at least in the realm of physical phenomena. The nonscientist who has very little understanding or patience with such procedures even when limited to the study of the physical world is often incensed when they are extended as an encroachment upon the noumenal realm which he considers his own private preserve.

For example, a professor of classical languages recently agreed to serve as observer-judge in our study of teacher competence. During a training session in which we were demonstrating the use of the *Teacher Practices Observation Record,* this man raised a series of agitated questions regarding both the procedures and the useful-ness of the information yielded. He failed to see the value of what he called "a bunch of check marks and numbers" to the problem of deciding who is a good teacher. He said he was perfectly willing to sit down and observe a teacher's performance and then to tell us whether he thought it was good or bad, and why, but he would have no part of our system of recording those observations and judgments. In the exchange which ensued it was made clear that the professor saw nothing wrong with observing teacher behavior, holding a wet finger up in the wind, and passing judgment on what he saw. What he objected to was our efforts to force him to bring some precision to his observations and assign quantitative weights to his judgments. Announcing that he could not com-promise with such "lunacy" he stomped out of the room.

A similar objection was made, somewhat less heatedly and much more eloquently, by a former colleague Herbert M. Howe, Chairman of the Department of Classics at the University of Wis-consin. Professor Howe declined to respond to the inventories on the grounds that the entire field of psychological or objective testing seems filled with pitfalls. He protested against our particular ques-tionnaires as seeming to be "a welter of appeals to prejudice," and felt that "attempting to produce answers to them can only give an appearance of nonexistent precision." Although he thought such a project as this may be very useful and conceded that some of the answers "might serve to reveal a good deal about the person taking the test," he added the reservation: "But I doubt very much whether the fact that 68.1% of the test subjects turn out to feel a particular way means very much." Like that of his fellow classicist, the meat of Professor Howe's objection centers around his concern about reducing information about a human being's personality or belief structure to mere numbers and the lumping of individuals into groups described by the average of those numbers. This, coupled with a dislike of questionnaires in general, is summed up in Professor Howe's concluding remarks: "I hope you do not mind these ill-natured maunderings of a curmudgeon whose ulcers start effervescing at the sight of all questionnaires, but I have never yet seen one which, treated scientifically, was worth the time it required to fill out."

What the nonscientist objects to about having scientific procedures imposed upon him is that they restrict the freedom to which he is accustomed. They cramp his style. A good illustration of this occurred one evening in a social gathering in which a number of us non-scientific philosopher-types were engaged in the sport of hypothesizing an elaborate theoretical construct—some nonsense about the inter-relationship of the stars in the universe. As this scheme and the playful argument over it grew to greater and greater proportions, the pleasure of those involved increased to a fever pitch. Then, a single, unsolicited comment by one of the heretofore disgruntled but silent wives, brought our castle in the air crashing to the ground. She simply pointed out that the premise on which the whole theoretical argument was built did not square with well established scientific fact. Whatever the cited fact was, it was something any seventh grade science student knows. The point is, this suggestion of the lack of correspondence with empirical evidence ruined our fun. And any person who endeavors to test theory empirically is bound to be shunned from the inner circle of theorists as unceremoniously as was the uncalled-for wife in this case.

A classic example of this can be found in the case of William H. Sewell, a research oriented sociologist who dared to subject to empirical test the well entrenched psychoanalytic doctrine stemming from Freud's theory concerning the significance of infantile "oral" and "anal" experience in later personality adjustment. Despite a carefully conceived and a laborious effort to give the theory a fair scientific test, he failed to find empirical verification for the theory that the specific channeling of infantile physiological urges by the child's parents is reflected in the later personality adjustment and traits of the individual.[1]

This Freudian doctrine was simply too widely and too deeply held to expect that Sewell's work would be permitted to knock it into a cocked hat without a strong counterattack against him, his theorizing, his design, his procedures, and the weight of his evidence. The most serious of the criticisms argued that Sewell's evidence was not appropriate to the theory. For example, let us quote La Barre:

Sewell dreams up an ignorant and silly hypothesis, that of "High Sleep Security," which he then imputes to the Freudians, only to find it roundly disproved. No person oriented in psychoanalysis has ever stated that sleeping with the mother, Sewell's "High Sleep Security," is conducive to later personality adjustment. On the contrary, all would agree that this is an index of maternal overprotection that bodes ill for later personality adequacy and adjustment. Who can be surprised, then, that chi-square negates his absurd hypothesis; and what informed person can see it as other than establishing the actual position of psychoanalysis? Sewell is manifestly ignorant of the real position of his opponents.[2]

Although Sewell was able to answer La Barre on this score to the satisfaction of his fellow social scientists,[3] it should be obvious by now that very little dent has been made in the armor of the psychoanalysts. Sewell's study and its reverberations has been used by Hyman as an illustrative case of the problems encountered in the elaboration of variables to comprehend and verify a complex and discursive theory. Hyman uses the fascinating story of Sewell's study, which he reviews in detail, to make the point that "tests of discursive theories despite maximum care, permit of considerable disagreement as to the weight of the evidence."[4]

[1] Wm. H. Sewell, "Infant Training and the Personality of the Child," *American Journal of Sociology*, LVIII:2 (September, 1952), 150–159.

[2] W. La Barre, "Sewell's Infant Training and the Personality of the Child," Letters to the Editor, *American Journal of Sociology*, 58 (1952), p. 419.

[3] Wm. H. Sewell, Letter to the Editor, *American Journal of Sociology*, 58 (1952), 419–420.

[4] Herbert H. Hyman, *Survey Design and Analysis* (Glencoe, Ill.: The Free Press, 1955), pp. 357–363.

I think it was Voltaire who once commented to the effect that "Dogs to whom you present food for which they have no liking are likely to bite you." Despite the compelling evidence compiled by Sewell, and the exhausting care with which he conducted his research, the "dogs" didn't like it. Likewise, there are some dogs which do not like the stuff produced by the study of the *Experimental Mind* reported in this book. However, there are some important differences between Sewell's work and mine.

First of all, the work here lacks the precision and sophistication Sewell was able to bring to the design of his empirical research. Second, I did not set out to test Dewey's theory as Sewell set out to test Freud's. I got onto Dewey's experimentalism primarily as a conveniently available vehicle for investigating possible relationships between theory and practice. Only after I was already quite a way down the road did it dawn on me that if empirical evidence were found of the relationships Dewey said should be found, in a sense I would be validating the theory that guided me. Thus, it was too late to incorporate Sewell's null hypothesis procedure. I was already committed to the positive hypothesis that Dewey's theory would work. This fact may be the major reason why evidence was found which succeeded in supporting Dewey rather than failing to do so as Sewell's study did to Freud.

In contrast to the hostility toward Sewell's study by the psychoanalysts one might expect that Deweyites, to the last man, would welcome a study which empirically verifies much of Dewey's theory concerning the relationship of beliefs and practice. But such has not always been the case. It turns out that not all Dewey enthusiasts are interested in having this particular aspect of Dewey's theory verified. Many Dewey scholars are interested only in his social and political philosophy, or his theory of art, or theory of valuation, or some of the more general aspects of his philosophy of education. Philosophers show a predisposition to ignore Dewey's theory of instruction—the pedagogical aspects of his philosophy. The latter has been relegated to the practitioners or educationists. And while educationists have given Dewey's descriptions of reflective thinking (the method of education) much attention, they have shown almost no interest in its connection with underlying philosophic beliefs. In summary, some philosophers who specialize in Dewey are inclined to the view that I have overemphasized a relatively minor aspect of Dewey's experimentalism, and some educationists are inclined to feel that I have unnecessarily made too much of the relationship between specific teaching practices and the more controversial aspects of Dewey's general philosophy— particularly his unconventional views on religion and the nature of knowledge.

The "true believers" of John Dewey's philosophy don't like having their pet interpretations of his theory upset. There is a prevalent notion among teachers that they are or should be experts on Dewey's educational philosophy. Such is not always the case. Generally, the ordinary teacher's knowledge of Dewey is vague, incomplete, and often incorrect. When such people find themselves in low agreement with Dewey on the inventories, they often engender guilt feelings and resentment. In such cases there is an understandable anxiousness to conclude (1) that the inventories grossly misinterpret Dewey's theory, or (2) that something is very much wrong with our empirical procedures, or, failing to knock us down on the first two, (3) that empirical validation is not the best way to test the truth of a theory.

What is the right way to validate or test the truth of theories? For some the validation of a theory—or of any other belief is settled by the deliverance of a solemn judgment on the part of established authority. Reliance is placed on the judgment of those "who are in a position to know" or "who are empowered to decide." It must be kept in mind, however, that the validation of a theory—in the scientific community, at least—is never a matter of official decision. It is a mistake to assume that "science" is a single, self-contained entity which possesses a universal standard by which theories can be proved or disproved "scientifically." Instead, science is the outcome of the activities of countless individuals working in a wide variety of ever-changing contexts. At any given moment a particular theory will be accepted by some scientists and not by other scientists. A given scientist may accept a theory for one purpose and not for another.

For some people the test of truth is a popularity contest. They go along with "what is generally accepted." But men of science have often rejected theories, or expressed dissatisfaction with them, long after the views in question had won widespread acceptance. For instance, Huygens was not satisfied by Newton's mechanics, and Einstein doubted the underlying validity of quantum indeterminacy. In an open, pluralistic society, whether we are speaking of science, politics, philosophy, or religion, *very few theories are generally accepted*. The acceptability of a theory is always a matter of degree—more or less weight will be assigned to it, and it will have a more or less limited range of justified application.

Common sense tells us that truth ought to correspond with fact. We say that a theory is true if it "fits the facts," that is, if predictions made on the basis of the theory come true. Truth depends on a relation between a belief and experience in the real world. My belief that I have gasoline in the tank of my automobile is true because it corresponds to the facts about the tank; the belief that there is a tiger in my tank is false because it fails to correspond to the facts about the tank.

Science is governed fundamentally by the reality principle. When we hold a belief about the physical world the belief is made true or false not by other beliefs but by something in the physical world to which it refers. Thinking so does not make it so. In science thought is checked and controlled by information derived from experience, observation, and experimentation. Thought is put into correspondence with its object. The only alternative to the recognition that our will must be submitted to an objective world—a world not of our own making—is what Bertrand Russell has aptly called "subjectivist madness."

This appeal to "the facts" rests on a bedrock of common sense which seems only too obviously true. Yet it cannot be forgotten that how we conceptualize facts in turn depends on theories which play a part in their perception. We must guard against the possibility that the facts may be wholly constituted by the theory they are used to verify. Beliefs, lacking a sound observational core, can make facts out of whole cloth.

Such perversions against the empirical test of truth have aroused some to seek another criterion which does not require any correspondence with facts—the coherence theory of truth. This theory holds that truth is not determined by a relation between a belief and something else, a fact or reality, but by the relations between beliefs themselves. Accordingly, to say a belief is true means that it fits into a coherent system with other beliefs. Even in science it is as important that theories cohere as that they fit the facts. All of us are familiar with the "shock of recognition" or the "click of relation" when unknowns suddenly become familiar or when widely different and separate phenomena suddenly fall into a recognizable pattern—like pieces in a puzzle. Many theories fail largely because there is no way in which they can be fitted into the body of theory already established. There is, for example, quite a lot of direct evidence to support the existence of extrasensory perception (E.S.P.). Yet, putting aside the question whether such evidence is acceptable (whether research designs and statistical analysis were sound, whether adequate controls were used, and so on), it remains that E.S.P. runs contrary to everything else we know about the transmission of information.

Obviously, it would be foolish to put too much reliance on the test of coherence. To do so would prevent any real breakthroughs in our thinking. "Coherence is a conservative principle," as Kaplan reminds us, "which ruthlessly suppresses as rebellion any movement of thought which might make for a scientific revolution. The unyielding insistence that every new theory must fit those theories already established is characteristic of closed systems of thought, not of science."[5] To avoid this difficulty, it is obvious that we need a more permissive and more practical norm for the validation of theories.

Charles Sanders Peirce, the founder of modern pragmatism, is credited with introducing the view that the truth of a theory or thought should be tested by its practical consequences, the difference it makes in practice, its bearing upon the conduct of life.[6] For a pragmatist truth is the quality of an insight that makes it accurately predictive of subsequent behavior. Those who find fault with this view leap to the unwarranted conclusion that any beliefs which "work" are true. Accordingly, if a lie "works" it is proven to be true. Nonsense! It is quite conceivable that a theory might work well and yet not be true or work badly and yet be true. Furthermore, what works for one man may not work for another, and

[5] Abraham Kaplan, *The Conduct of Inquiry* (San Francisco: Chandler Publishing Company, 1964), pp. 314–315.

[6] C. S. Peirce, *Popular Science Monthly* (January, 1878), 286–302. Also published in Charles S. Peirce, "Values in a Universe of Change," in *Selected Writings of Charles S. Peirce,* Philip P. Weiner, ed. (Garden City, N.Y.: Doubleday & Company, Anchor Books, 1958).

what works for him at one time may not work for him at another. If such were Peirce's view, the pragmatic position would indeed end up squarely between the horns of its own dilemma.

There is a tendency to take the pragmatic test outside the context of scientific inquiry to something that might be called "homely" applications, which hardly qualify as satisfactory conditions for validation. For instance, we hear people say about the minister, "Why doesn't he practice what he preaches?" Or to the economist, "If you're so smart why ain't you rich?" Application may fail for many reasons external to the theory, just as success may be due to factors external to the theory. Success or failure in the working of a theory raises certain questions about its value, but what it contributes to validation must be carefully assessed in each case.

William James, in his attempts to popularize Peirce's pragmatism, undoubtedly aided the widespread misconception that pragmatists hold truth to be the "cash value" of an idea. He used the term "cash value" only to illustrate figuratively the "instrumental" function of truth and did not intend that it be taken literally. According to the more serious epistemological writings of Peirce and Dewey, the pragmatic position is that a belief or theory (they would say "insight" or "proposition") is true if it predicts events (or consequences) with accuracy. If it "works" *in this way,* then it is true. If a lie works in this way it is not the lie that is proven true but the theory that the telling of the lie will get the liar out of his present or anticipated jam. Thus, no dilemma is involved here. The theory being tested is proven to be accurately predictive, therefore true.

So, the pragmatic test of truth turns out to be simply a specific version of the correspondence theory of truth discussed a few pages back. The pragmatist does not quarrel with the need for truth to *correspond* with reality. He differs with traditional philosophers about the nature of reality and his quarrel is with those who seek absolute truth in correspondence with a fixed and unchanging reality.

The pragmatic method of testing for truth should not be difficult for today's Americans to understand, because it is precisely the truth-testing method of modern science. While science has its unproven theories, beliefs, and conjectures, it asserts as true only what is experimentally or experientially warranted.

"The trouble with the scientific method," it has often been said, "is that it does not leave room for belief without empirically warranted evidence." Lots of people insist upon the right to believe their beliefs without any interference from the empirical requirements of science. For them truth is plainly a case of "What I most deeply feel to be true is indeed true." It is simply a matter of belief or faith. The only warrant that is required is having a belief and having the conviction of its truthfulness.

This view stems in considerable measure from the religious conviction that faith rather than works constitutes the best or most proper test of truth. I recently heard an Episcopalian minister state that "If Christians had to be judged on the basis of their observable behavior, then none of us would turn out to be Christians. There would be no Christians." He candidly pointed out that if you put before you a Christian and a non-Christian it is conceivable that there will be no behavioral difference between them. Their empirically observable acts may be the same. Yet there is a difference, according to my minister friend. What a person believes influences what he is open to, the story he listens to, the pattern of his inner life, how he defines himself. There is no empirical criterion by which to measure such subjective differences. This is essentially the argument given by those who regard our study of beliefs and practices "anti-intellectual" and "anti-philosophical." They might as well add "anti-religious" to the charges.

A striking similarity can be seen between the empirical vs. rational and objective vs. subjective tests of truth, discussed earlier in this chapter, and the age-old issue of works vs. faith as a test of the valid Christian life. On one hand in this issue is the Pelagian camp which favors works over faith. The teachings of Pelagius, condemned as heretical, maintain that a person's salvation depends not upon redemption through faith but on the exercise of his freedom of will not to sin—how he behaves. On the other side stands the Augustinian camp which values faith over works. It was St. Augustine who synthesized diverse Christian doctrines to proclaim that the basis of Christian life is the trust or faith one has in God. And whether a particular person has this faith, only he can tell. It is strictly a matter between him and God. My Episcopalian minister puts himself clearly in the Augustinian camp.

Much of the faith vs. works controversy can be traced back

to the teachings of Paul, who had difficulty reconciling his theology with his practical interests. Paul complained, "Every time I try to do good, I do bad," confessing that "If we were to hold a sinner's contest, I would win hands down." He handled this problem by mystically placing man in God's hands. It was an article of faith for Paul that God is, ultimately, the cause of everything that happens. God not only knows what is going to happen; he is also the agent who brings it about. Following this line Paul argued that if God is the cause, I am not. If God does everything, man does nothing. With human free will ruled out, our sense of at least some control over our environment, our destinies, and our behavior is an illusion.

Carrying Paul's doctrine forward, Augustine held that even if we believe we have led a blameless life we cannot be certain of salvation. None of us is free from temptations of the flesh. A relapse is possible at any time. Our life is a desperate hazard full of traps and snares. Nothing seemed to Augustine more obvious than the misery of the human situation. It was clear to Augustine that he could do nothing to extricate himself from this terrible situation. He struggled for years to lead a good life, and all in vain. When he did experience salvation, it was none of his doing; it was something which came to him, a free gift from God. A voice spoke to him and the whole world was changed for him. It was something that happened to him, an event to which he contributed nothing.

If Augustine had been able to change himself and had changed himself, he would have himself to thank, not God; he would have demonstrated his own goodness and power, not God's. Instead, Augustine's personal experience supported his belief in God's omnipotence and perfection. The actual mechanics of salvation, according to Augustine, are told in the story of Jesus Christ, who became man and suffered on the cross for our sins. As he stated it, "From this hell on earth there is no escape, save through the grace of the Savior Christ, our God and Lord."[7]

Augustine believed that by this drama of the death and resurrection of Jesus, God intends to move our wills, to turn us toward Him and thus begin the process of conversion and repentance by an act of our own initiative. Of course, God could have, had He

---

[7] *City of God* (Dods), XV, 22.

chosen, saved us by divine decree. Instead, he preferred to create us with wills, and to make these wills the instruments of our salvation.[8] Thus, so the doctrine goes, sin turns out to be voluntary after all.

By this very complicated maneuver, it seems, Augustine gets hung up on a dilemma over human freedom. First he argues that man is helpless in the grip of evil and repeatedly asserts that no man acts rightly save by the assistance of divine aid. Then he turns around to point out that there is no limitation or restriction on the human will. His doctrine forces onto us an unjust God which both blames us and punishes us for sinful acts of which He is the sole author.

Pelagius, a monk of British birth who lived in Rome during Augustine's time (early fifth century), objected to this strange and mystical line of thought. He held that the doctrine of man's depravity and incompetence to do anything about it led men to be slothful in Christian living. He believed that such a denial of human freedom and worth made it much too easy to excuse giving into those very lusts of the flesh condemned by Paul and Augustine.

Pelagius was a practical man, more concerned with morality than theology. He saw that responsibility and free will seem to be connected, and that rejection of the latter seems to sweep away the former with it. If man has no control over what he does, how can he be held responsible for his acts. If God is everything, is He not responsible for our sins? If this were the case God then becomes the maker of all evil and wickedness, which we mistakenly attribute to ourselves. Why would a good God run such a sloppy universe?

The fundamental issue in the Pelagian heresy involves the importance of man's place in the world. Does his behavior make any difference? The Augustinian determination to exalt God led inevitably to the conclusion that man is worthless. The Pelagian heresy is basically a protest against such a drastic judgment of man's worth and capacity. Generally speaking, the Pelagian position is that, however small, man amounts to *something*. What he does counts.

From the Pelagian point of view, a person is judged by what

[8] W. T. Jones, *A History of Western Philosophy* (New York: Harcourt, Brace & World, Inc., 1952), p. 379.

he does—his practices or his works. What he believes can be inferred from how he behaves. According to my simple, country-folk ancestors (Pelagians all!), a man's actions speak louder than his words. It doesn't matter what he believes or says if he doesn't behave properly. Whether we are talking about religion, politics, business, everyday family living, or classroom teaching, if a person doesn't behave it, then it is concluded that he doesn't believe it. The proof of one's faith is found in his works. You have to back it up with fitting behavior. Pelagians are from Missouri—they have to be shown!

Do not be misled by the polarization of the Augustinian and Pelagian camps. Just because the Augustinians make works secondary to faith does not mean they depreciate good works. Likewise, the Pelagians value faith highly as instrumental to the avoidance of sinful behavior on the road toward divine grace and salvation. Even so, their differences regarding the relative importance of faith and works permits a clear and useful distinction. This difference helps us to understand why a study which examines the relationship of beliefs and behavior from an essentially Pelagian premise can only be regarded as blasphemous by people with a basic Augustinian point of view.

In the previous chapter dissatisfaction was expressed with psychology's obsession for objectivity. In this chapter the fondness of traditional philosophy and religion for subjectivity has come under fire. Taking the two chapters together, our complaint is against those who insist belief and behavior ought to remain separated and isolated from one another; that beliefs are unresearchable and should not be permitted to clutter up studies of human behavior; that it is all right to submit behavior to empirical research, but not beliefs, which are so personal and private that they defy measurement by any known empirical procedure. We have tried to show that orthodoxy on both the psychology and philosophy side of the fence perpetuates the unnecessary bifurcation of beliefs and behavior. A sort of "gentleman's agreement" has been reached in which the territorial imperative of the other is to be respected and cooperatively enforced against anyone who might try to establish lines of commerce across their common border.

19

CHANGING THE BELIEFS
AND PRACTICES OF TEACHERS

USING INSTRUMENTS which claim to measure people's beliefs is dangerous business. Tools of this sort are doubly dangerous when they further claim to predict what people will do. That which can be used to predict can also be used to control and change. To what extent, if any, are we justified in using the measures of *The Experimental Mind* to control or change the beliefs and practices of teachers?

Is there anyone among us who is not advocating some sort of change in American education? Each of us has his own pet theory for "improving" teaching. And the success of every such scheme is dependent upon somehow achieving the control required to produce the changes desired. We indicate our awareness of this when we jokingly say, "If I were king, such and such would be made to happen," or "If I could play God, teachers would do this rather than that." But the joke is too true to be amusing. The person who seriously engages in the business of installing changes, even though he may call them "innovations," should be aware of his own willingness to play God.

When we advocate change we imply, whether we state it or not, our dissatisfaction with some existing pattern of practices. It means that we have judged a situation to be "bad," "wrong," or "inadequate," and are now proposing changes we believe will make it "good," "right," or at least "better." We cannot plead or push for change without having made a value judgment. While there is no harm in our making value judgments, we risk playing God when we try to press our values onto others, making our beliefs their beliefs.

Advocates of change in education rarely declare their beliefs to those whose behavior they seek to change. Apparently, they prefer to take their victims unaware. Either they don't know the beliefs underlying the changes they desire, or, if they do, they consider it bad strategy to discuss them clearly, openly, or honestly. In their enthusiasm to get their innovation installed they rarely solicit more than tacit consent from the teachers whose behavior it most affects. The failure to secure the support of teachers, particularly at the beliefs level, may account for the rapidly passing parade of unsuccessful innovations (or "fads," as they used to be called) in American education. Teachers willingly—and, thus, effectively—make only those changes they themselves believe to be needed and wanted. Changes which only somebody else believes in, changes which are externally imposed upon them, are soon rejected and defeated.

If anyone is effectively to change the classroom behavior of teachers, he must also change their beliefs. Teacher education institutions (the teachers colleges) have long understood this principle. Very early in their efforts to improve teaching via the professional preparation of teachers they learned that the dissemination of information and the demonstration of new teaching techniques was not enough to produce desired changes. So they attacked the philosophic base—the classic thesis that education should be primarily concerned with the development of the mind—underlying the entrenched practices of the schools which they regarded as unsatisfactory. In its place they proposed a new twentieth-century philosophy—a confusing admixture of the thoughts of Thorndike, Rousseau, Freud, and John Dewey—which held that henceforth the major aim of education should be the development of the whole child.

Teacher education institutions over the years have been only moderately effective in changing the minds and practices of American teachers. Impatient with slow and incomplete success, some educationists have made a concerted effort to persuade the nation's diverse educational enterprise to adopt the new faith by making a captive audience of all prospective teachers. State legislatures were convinced to write certification laws which required that all teachers take a sufficient number of education courses. Once the new "science" of education had been legally established as an unavoidable ingredient in the preparation of teachers, an attempt was made to establish a national accreditation agency designed to bring all teacher education institutions into line. At this point the advocates of the rapid and complete "professionalization" of teachers were in a position to move American education forward boldly, marching in step to the same piece of beautiful music.[1]

Fortunately (or unfortunately, depending on one's point of view), educationists were never so cohesive a group as their detractors tried to make them out. They disagreed among themselves about how to use their power, and lost it before it could be effectively consolidated.[2,3] Quite apart from the long-standing philosophical quarrel about what the central focus of education should be, the rest of the academic community bitterly resented the enthusiasm of the teachers colleges for selling the controversial "truths" of an "established" dogma. Pressing one's advantage to engage in this sort of brainwashing is unacceptable in a community of scholars dedicated to the untrammeled exercise of critical intelligence.

Although we have a long tradition in our society for controlling the outward behavior of citizens, this same tradition frowns upon most forms of thought control. Our laws are concerned almost exclusively with man's overt behavior and only rarely with his private thoughts. Legally, we place many kinds of restrictions, and some prescriptions, on what man can do, but leave him pretty much free to believe what he pleases. Thus, efforts to control the beliefs of teachers may violate their civil liberties, or, at least, their democratic sensibilities.

But is man so free to believe what he will as our legal and scholarly tradition leads us to assume? All of us are the victims of our own enculturation—perhaps the most powerful teaching machine ever devised. By this process we not only learn the traditional content of the culture into which we happen to be born, we also

[1] Bob Burton Brown, "Dangers in the Misuse of NCATE Accreditation," *Journal of Teacher Education* (September 1963), pp. 326–332.

[2] John R. Mayor, *Accreditation in Teacher Education: Its Influence on Higher Education* (Washington, D. C.: National Commission on Accrediting, 1965), p. 303.

[3] Bob Burton Brown, "An Epitaph for NCATE," *Journal of Teacher Education* (September 1965), pp. 375–377.

assimilate its patterns of behavior and belief. By the time we are mature enough to bring our own critical intelligence and volition to bear upon these inherited practices and values, it is already too late. They are so firmly, if not irrevocably, rooted that we must forever after stumble over them in pursuit of any changes we come to desire.

If we are to have any effect whatsoever in influencing our own cultural design, we must bring to bear upon it all the intelligence and power at our disposal. The difficulty experienced in trying to break the mold which creates and traps the "culturally deprived" is evidence of unyielding nature of cultural impact. The most drastic and massive attacks upon it make precious little difference in its course. It seems almost to have a mind of its own.

B. F. Skinner, the father of teaching machines, thinks we now have a way of getting at the "mind" of culture and changing it as we wish. Instead of attacking it, or blasting it with counter propaganda, he recommends that we con it into doing our bidding through positive reinforcement. This sort of deliberate redesign of the culture by behavioral science, however, requires the abandonment of any pretense of democracy. But this doesn't bother Skinner, who maintains that democracy has grown obsolete anyway.

Speaking through his story character Frasier in *Walden Two,* Skinner says that "democracy is a pious fraud." People *feel* free, but they really aren't. For example, elections give people the feeling they have chosen the government they want, but voting turns out to be little more than a device for blaming conditions on the people. Skinner contends that "The people aren't rulers, they're scapegoats. And they file to the polls every so often to renew their right to the title."[4] While he agrees that democracy may have been a beautiful dream, it never really had a chance. Now it has been made obsolete by behavioral science. He argues that once we have acquired a behavioral technology we cannot leave the control of behavior to the unskilled. Continuation of an open democratic society will only perpetuate the despotism of ignorance, neglect, irresponsibility, and accident.[5]

[4] B. F. Skinner, *Walden Two* (New York: The Macmillan Company, 1948) 1962 paperback edition, p. 266.

[5] *Ibid.,* p. 268.

In place of the despotism of democracy Skinner advocates a planned society behaviorally engineered. Skinner argues that we already have a highly developed and effective science of behavior. With this new science it is now supposedly possible to control the behavior of men as one wishes. Many of us are familiar with the evidence to this effect in Vance Packard's popular book *The Hidden Persuaders*. Accordingly, the question is no longer one of achieving such controls, but rather one of deciding what to do with them. Should we outlaw them? Dump them in the ocean? Or leave them in unseen hands, pretending that no such controls exist? Skinner's view is that we must, like it or not, seize control of the controls while we still can, and then, deliberately and intelligently, engineer a society along the Utopian lines of Walden Two. The only alternative he sees is to abdicate the determination of our behavior and beliefs to the despotic interplay of "the charlatan, the demagogue, the salesman, the ward heeler, the bully, the cheat, the educator, the priest—all who are now in possession of the techniques of behavioral engineering."[6]

"Better us than them," one might agree. And why not? Since we are not really free anyway, wouldn't it be better to scientifically engineer ourselves than to placidly settle for what culture has accidentally dealt to us? Or for what suits the purposes of some hidden persuader? So long as there is no alternative to having our behavior determined in the future, why not pick our own determiner while we can?

The provocative questions raised by Skinner have not caused any great rush to abandon American democracy for a Walden Two type of society. Although we hear an occasional rumor about some would-be-Frasier having started a small behaviorally engineered community somewhere or another, very little serious consideration has been given to the idea. It is usually dismissed as one of Skinner's playful little jokes. On the other hand, there has been much clamoring to learn about and to come into possession of the techniques of behavioral programming—presumably for use within our established social framework. Lots of people, so it seems, are anxious to predict and control other people's behavior. One is forced to conclude that people prefer to string along with (or join)

[6] *Ibid.,* p. 256.

the charlatans, demagogues, salesmen, ward heelers, bullies, cheats, educators, and priests than to switch to the alternative route offered by B. F. Skinner.

I do not agree with Skinner that human behavior is, can, or should be completely determined externally. Personally, however, his Walden Two option (if it is still open) is preferable to permitting the charlatans, etc., to freely operate behavioral controls however they see fit from behind bushes. Skinner at least is intellectually honest, even to the point of recognizing that he is willing to play God and giving us public notice of what he is up to.

Much of the conflict involved in the problem of changing the beliefs and practices of teachers is created by the fact that education must be viewed as a field of professional activity as well as an academic discipline or field of intellectual inquiry: School must keep. There is action which must be taken *now*. Therefore, some sort of closure on philosophy is required as a base for decisions about what to do. To avoid responsibility for designing deliberate change in the beliefs and behavior of teachers is to settle for the status quo merely to ride the irrepressible wave of tradition.

Colleges of education have quite naturally followed in the pattern established by other professional colleges, including law and medicine, for the preparation of practitioners. By definition a professional preparation program assumes that the people who design and run them know (1) what good practice is, and (2) what is required to train people to do it. In the case of teacher education, we have been forced to do business under false pretenses.

There is no body of objective evidence that tells us the kind of competencies that all teachers should have or the kind of preparation required to develop such competencies. Furthermore, we have lacked an adequate theoretical base for clearly defining and producing competently trained teachers. We simply have been unable to agree on what good teaching is and how to prepare people to do it. There are no unchallenged grounds on which we can say that certain competencies are the ones that teacher education programs should try to produce.

Yet, we go about training teachers *as if* there were some sort of universal consensus, supported by an irrefutable body of theory and research, regarding a "one best" definition of good teaching and a "one best" teacher education program. The view that teacher education is primarily preparation for professional practice leaves us no choice but to conjure up arbitrary goals and objectives in the form of prescribed teaching behavior, practices, or competencies. Likewise, we erect an elaborate body of special knowledge, skills, attitudes, and experiences (equally arbitrary) designed to achieve such goals. Assuming incorrectly that the question "What is good teaching?" has already been settled, and that nothing further needs to be said about it, both the ends and means of such teacher education programs are fraudulent.

Teacher education programs and the people who design and run them claim knowledge they do not possess, and advertise what knowledge they do have as something other than it is. They pretend to know how to predict and control behavior scientifically, while at best they can only make intelligent guesses based on vaguely catalogued trial and error experience. The subject matter of education is more folklore than science, yet a high degree of scientific "objectivity" is claimed for it. This myth of objectivity veils untold value judgments unavoidable in the process of deciding that *this* shall constitute the proper education of teachers rather than *that*.

Any program which is conceived to train teachers to behave in certain ways and not to behave in others *is necessarily* both *subjective* and *prescriptive*. Furthermore, such a program, if it is successful, makes prospective teachers the victims of its prescription. The word *victim* is appropriate because, as things have been working, teachers in training have no alternative but to take the medicine prescribed for them, like it or not. My objection is not to the existence of bias and subjectivity in teacher education, but to keeping it a secret, pretending it is not there. While a certain amount of prescription may be desirable, I object even more strongly to giving any single prescription (program of required courses) the force of law, thereby freezing out all possible competition and experimentation. If some group wishes to run a prescriptive teacher education program, and they are in a position to do so, let them go ahead—providing they clearly stipulate and publicly announce their bias. This bias ought to be stated in the form of observable and measurable competencies and be accompanied by an understandable theoretical rationale. Anyone who follows such a program should do so voluntarily, in full knowledge of where it promises to take him, and why.

Since any "professional preparation" approach is necessarily prescriptive as to definition of teacher competence, there should be a number of alternative programs available to every teacher candidate. It is not enough that students have a choice to become an elementary or secondary school teacher, or to specialize in this subject or that. Choices with respect to differing theories of teaching and learning should also be possible. In this case, every teacher would be "some kind" of teacher, not "just" a teacher of this grade level or subject. Every teacher would have a specified point of view and in terms of which he is certified competent.

We should teach teachers which practices go with which of their beliefs. We should deliberately produce teachers who are logically consistent along a given philosophic dimension, fully aware of that bias and that it is a bias. We could have, for example, one program for the preparation of "inquiry" teachers and another for "acquisition" teachers. Perhaps we could provide a program for Existentialist teachers whose central concern and skill is dealing with individual feelings and self concepts, leaving the development of intellectual processes and the stuffing of minds to the graduates of the other programs. Likewise, if we wish to prepare teachers for Catholic schools, possibly we should turn out graduates whose competencies are defined, without apology, in terms of beliefs and classroom practices consistent with Thomism. If I were sending my children to a Catholic school, which I am not, I would expect them to get a Catholic education at Catholic hands—and not some so-called "objective" and "unbiased" education at the hands of teachers trained in terms of some confusingly defined, if defined at all, common denominator.

Teachers should be more different than alike, and so should the programs which select and train them. It is perfectly legal for teachers in America to hold diverse beliefs and to behave according to these views in the classrooms. Teacher education programs which try to train all teachers in one common mold, as is the established pattern, deserve all the criticism that has been heaped upon them.

The advocates of change in education today seem to be repeating the mistakes of the past. Characteristically, the managers of change always seem to be committed to some grand plan for reaching Nirvana in a hurry. And they are not satisfied unless all of us go there together, whether we want to or not. When change agents encourage us to be different, to believe and do different things, they don't mean different from each other. When they attack sameness, they are attacking some old or established sameness. The difference they seek to make, when established, turns out to be simply a new sameness that has taken the place of the old one.

One of the major problems in achieving sweeping educational change is the difficulty in changing basic philosophic beliefs. Since people in our traditionally open society currently hold different and differing beliefs, any change must begin at a myriad of points and proceed in all directions at once. This makes the installation of wholesale changes in harmonious concert an extremely hazardous undertaking. The failure of the teachers colleges to change the beliefs and control the behavior of anyone and everyone who came to their door has already been cited as evidence of this. Now, however, there is growing sentiment for by-passing the necessity of changing beliefs by limiting admission to those who already believe the "right" things, or who are "ripe" for change. Presumably, those who hold the "wrong" beliefs or who are the "personality types" that resist change will be screened out and denied the right to qualify for teacher certification.

Having developed and presented in this book instruments with some potential for predicting and controlling the beliefs and behavior of teachers, I worry about the propensity of educational leaders for misusing them. The fact that these instruments measure agreement-disagreement with Dewey's philosophy, beliefs which are popularly associated with educationist dogma, increases my concern. Throughout the development of these instruments it has been suggested repeatedly that they may be useful in screening prospective teachers, either prior to their admission to teacher education programs or before their successful graduation and certification. Invariably, the implication is that only those in reasonable agreement with experimentalism should be allowed into the teaching profession. Such a horrifying notion gives me nightmares!

It is perfectly legal, and highly desirable from a number of different legitimate philosophies, to disagree diametrically with

John Dewey. Should parents who hold such beliefs be forced to send their children to private or parochial schools? Should not the public schools reflect the diversity of points of view which are rightfully held in the society which supports them? Should our schools reflect only the majority beliefs, or only "safe" beliefs which incur no strong objection from any quarter? If so, it is questionable that the current enthusiasm of educators for "objective" or "research-based" truths would survive a popular election. It seems highly probable that the use of the instruments presented in this book to restrict or control admission to the teaching profession might be considered contrary to our democratic tradition and a violation of civil liberties.

It is wrong, in my opinion, for *any* group of planners of educational programs to try to change other people to *any* system of beliefs. Missionaries—people who take heathens from barbaric conditions in order to civilize them—should be outlawed in education. Their total insensitivity with respect to the rights and desirability of others to be different from themselves is unforgivable. We have a right to ask of others only that they understand their own beliefs and that they be logically consistent in their beliefs and practices. This means *internal* consistency, not *external* consistency. To have the beliefs and practices of all teachers consistent with each other would produce a monolithic dullness of catastrophic proportions.

Does this mean that I am against change? Of course not. Then, what kind of changes am I trying to stimulate in teachers? Do I want them to move toward Dewey's experimentalism or away from it? Personally, I don't really care which direction teachers move with respect to agreement-disagreement with Dewey. My concern is with the *congruity* of the relationship between beliefs and behavior. Does the teacher do what he believes and believe what he does? The measures of experimentalism were developed to help people find answers to this question. And if they don't like what they find, then they may decide to change either their beliefs or their practices, or both, in whatever directions they decide upon. My plea is for them to keep making such changes repeatedly, seeking and maintaining the greatest possible logical consistency in themselves. This is the only sort of change anyone has a right to ask, or to attempt to engineer in others. A truly *Experimental Mind* would not have it otherwise.

APPENDIX

Intercorrelations of Beliefs and Practices

AS THE RESULT of an item analysis for discriminating power, the following items were selected for the computation of intercorrelations of beliefs and practices. The item numbers listed here are those used in the tables which follow.

PHILOSOPHICAL BELIEFS

Item Number	Statement
1	All "truths" are relative.
2	The mind is a group of "contents" which come from having certain material presented to it from without.
5	Knowledge is artificial and ineffective in the degree in which it is merely presented as truth to be accepted, held, and treasured for its own sake.
8	Learning is the sum of impressions made on the mind as a result of presentation of material to be known.
14	Nothing is or can be unchanging—absolutely certain.
15	The mind can be formed from without, just as one molds and shapes a piece of clay.
16	Man doesn't really have a "spirit" which is separable from his body and the material world.
19	The laws which should regulate human conduct have been determined by the superior intelligence of an ultimate Being.
22	Truth exists ready-made somewhere; the task of the scholar is to find it.
25	Knowledge cannot be attained purely mentally—just inside the head.

Item Number	Statement
27	Knowledge is the sum total of what is known, as that is handed down by books and learned men.
29	You can never prove that any fact is unconditionally true.
30	Practical activities are intellectually narrow only insofar as they are routine or carried on under the dictates of authority for some disconnected purpose.
36	Science helps us to decide moral issues.

Educational Beliefs and Teacher Practices

1	Frequently asks children to choose among several alternatives.
2	Organizes learning around questions posed by the teacher or the textbook.
4	Treats each lesson as an independent whole.
5	Frequently calls for the undivided attention of the group and scolds those who do not respond.
12	Faithfully follows a planned schedule in order to get in the number of minutes each week allotted to each subject in the curriculum.
14	Encourages children to suggest what might be done—to make "hypothetical leaps" into the unknown.
15	Puts pupils to work on what they see as their own problems, rather than something that is the teacher's or textbook's problem.
16	Expects all children to finish a given assignment within a definitely fixed time limit.
17	Holds all students equally responsible for answering certain questions about the subject being studied.
24	Provides children a number of starting places and a number of different ways of getting at a task.
25	Directs children's learning in short, sure steps.
27	Lets children go ahead with plans based upon foresight, observation, and consideration of several alternatives—even when she is sure their judgment is mistaken.
28	Encourages children to adventure into "deep water," to tackle problems that appear to be "over their heads."
30	Encourages children to catch hold of ideas and "run with them" beyond what is, as yet, known for sure.
31	Makes "doing something" with a thing, rather than the *thing* itself, the center of children's attention.
32	Since children cannot be trusted to "behave themselves" teacher takes steps to limit their opportunities for misbehavior.

Item Number	Statement
34	Insists that each child be responsible for his own work only and does not allow them to ask each other for help.
36	Has children test their "guesses" by acting upon them.
37	Once work has begun, insists that children remain in their places and concentrate on the task at hand.
39	Encourages children to put their suggestions to a test with such remarks as, "You'll never know unless you try it."
42	Considers suggestions by pupils are appropriate only when closely related to the topic being studied.
43	Has pupils compare the value of alternative courses of action and pass judgment upon their relative desirability.
45	Focuses attention on what the children do or say, rather than on what the teacher does or says.
47	Provides pupils a chance to discover by experiencing actual effects whether their choice of this rather than that idea was a judicious one.
48	Arranges things in such a way that a child can spend much of his time listening, watching, or waiting his turn.
52	Uses "feedback" from pupils to diagnose the changing state of affairs in the class, and revises original plans to meet new circumstances.
53	Tells children where to start and what to do to accomplish the task at hand.
56	Frequently has all pupils working on the same page of the same book at the same time.
58	Makes unplanned changes when a particular lesson is not getting an enthusiastic response from children.
59	Clearly defines the study problem for pupils so they will have no doubts as to exactly what they are to do.

TABLE A1. *Intercorrelations of Philosophical Beliefs with Educational Beliefs and Teacher Practices Which were Significant at the 1 and 5 Percent Levels*

Item Number	Statement	Philosophical Beliefs					
		Educational Beliefs Item Number	r	Level	Teacher Practices Item Number	r	Level
1	All "truths" are relative.	48	.49[a]	.01	31	.36	.05
		2	−.35	.05	36	.41	.05
					42	−.43	.05
					47	.42	.05
2	The mind is a group of "contents" which come from having certain material presented to it from without.	15	−.55	.01	12	.37	.05
		59	.51	.01	52	.40	.05
		2	.37	.05			
		53	.40	.05			
5	Knowledge is artificial and ineffective in the degree in which it is merely presented as truth to be accepted, held, and treasured for its own sake.	2	−.35	.05	5	−.42	.05
		5	−.39	.05			
		45	.42	.05			
		59	−.37	.05			
8	Learning is the sum of impressions made on the mind as a result of presentation of material to be known.	53	.45	.01	24	−.46	.01
		59	.45	.01	53	.46	.01
		43	−.43	.05	59	.45	.01
					15	−.39	.05
					30	−.36	.05
					39	−.37	.05
					52	−.40	.05

	Statement	Item	r	p	Item	r	p
14	Nothing is or can be unchanging—absolutely certain.	14	.42	.05	1	.53	.01
		48	.41[a]	.05	4	-.48	.01
		56	-.40	.05	16	-.55	.01
					17	-.62	.01
					43	.59	.01
					2	-.36	.05
					15	.37	.05
					34	-.35	.05
					36	.35	.05
					39	.40	.05
					42	-.43	.05
					47	.41	.05
					48	-.35	.05
					56	-.40	.05
15	The mind can be formed from without, just as one molds and shapes a piece of clay.	17	-.36[a]	.05	53	.38	.05
		53	.38	.05			
16	Man doesn't really have a "spirit" which is separable from his body and the material world.	48	.37[a]	.05	None		
		53	-.35	.05			
19	The laws which should regulate human conduct have been determined by the superior intelligence of an ultimate Being.	28	-.36	.05	32	.42	.05
		53	.38	.05			
22	Truth exists ready-made somewhere; the task of the scholar is to find it.	45	-.51	.01	17	.36	.05
		25	.35	.05	39	-.36	.05
		37	.35	.05			
		47	-.39	.05			

TABLE A1. (Continued)

		Philosophical Beliefs					
Item Number	Statement	Educational Beliefs Item Number	r	Level	Teacher Practices Item Number	r	Level
25	Knowledge cannot be attained purely mentally—just inside the head.	None			48	.37[a]	.05
27	Knowledge is the sum total of what is known, as that is handed down by books and learned men.	32	.46	.01	None		
		5	.38	.05			
		53	.39	.05			
29	You can never prove that any fact is unconditionally true.	56	-.46	.01	17	-.46	.01
		28	-.38[a]	.05	36	.51	.01
		42	-.37	.05	39	.48	.01
		58	.38	.05	56	-.46	.01
		59	-.39	.05	4	-.43	.05
					12	-.40	.05
					15	.41	.05
					16	-.39	.05
					30	.37	.05
					31	.39	.05
					52	.38	.05
					58	.38	.05
					59	-.40	.05

30	Practical activities are intellectually narrow only insofar as they are routine or carried on under the dictates of authority for some disconnected purpose.	30 14	.45 .42	.01 .05	None
36	Science helps us to decide moral issues.	59	.36[a]	.05	None

[a] Signifies intercorrelation which contradicts the theoretical framework of experimentalism.

TABLE A2. *Intercorrelations of Educational Beliefs with Philosophical Beliefs and Teacher Practices Which were Significant at the 1 and 5 Percent Levels*

Item Number	Statement	Educational Beliefs					
		Philosophical Beliefs Item Number	r	Level	Teacher Practices Item Number	r	Level
1	Frequently asks children to choose among several alternatives.	None			32	−.44	.01
					43	.37	.05
2	Organizes learning around questions posed by the teacher or the textbook.	1	−.35	.05	16	.47	.01
		2	.37	.05	31	−.46	.01
		5	−.35	.05	12	.38	.05
					53	.43	.05
					58	−.40	.05
4	Treats each lesson as an independent whole.	None			2	−.36[a]	.05
					15	.38[a]	.05
					27	.41[a]	.05
					42	−.43[a]	.05
5	Frequently calls for the undivided attention of the group and scolds those who do not respond.	5	−.39	.05	5	.37	.05
		27	+.38	.05	15	−.36	.05
12	Faithfully follows a planned schedule in order to get in the number of minutes each week allotted to each subject in the curriculum.	None			12	.36	.05
					31	−.36	.05
					58	−.36	.05

Item							
14	Encourages children to suggest what might be done—to make "hypothetical leaps" into the unknown.	14, 30	.42, .42	.05, .05	1, 34, 37, 17, 24, 27	.44, -.44, -.46, -.38, .42, .35	.01, .01, .01, .05, .05, .05
15	Puts pupils to work on what they see as their own problems, rather than something that is the teacher's or textbook's problem.	2	-.55	.01	12, 16, 58	-.42, -.36, .37	.05, .05, .05
16	Expects all children to finish a given assignment within a definitely fixed time limit.	None			None		
17	Holds all students equally responsible for answering certain questions about the subject being studied.	15	-.36^a	.05	53, 14	-.55, .41^a	.01, .05
24	Provides children a number of starting places and a number of different ways of getting at a task.	None			None		
25	Directs children's learning in short, sure steps.	22	.35	.05	None		
27	Lets children go ahead with plans based upon foresight, observation, and consideration of several alternatives—even when she is sure their judgment is mistaken.	None			None		

TABLE A2. (Continued)

Item Number	Statement	Educational Beliefs					
		Philosophical Beliefs Item Number	r	Level	Teacher Practices Item Number	r	Level
28	Encourages children to adventure into "deep water," to tackle problems that appear to be "over their heads."	19 29	−.36 −.38[a]	.05 .05	15	−.42[a]	.05
30	Encourages children to catch hold of ideas and "run with them" beyond what is, as yet, known for sure.	30	.45	.01	48	−.35	.05
31	Makes "doing something" with a thing, rather than the *thing* itself, the center of children's attention.	None			None		
32	Since children cannot be trusted to "behave themselves" she takes steps to limit their opportunities for misbehavior.	27	.46	.01	5 25 48	.45 −.43[a] .37	.01 .05 .05
34	Insists that each child be responsible for his own work only and does not allow them to ask each other for help.	None			None		
36	Has children test their "guesses" by acting upon them.	None			None		

#								
37	Once work as begun, insists that children remain in their places and concentrate on the task at hand.	22	.35	.05	27	−.39	.05
					28	−.43	.05
					30	−.40	.05
					39	−.36	.05
39	Encourages children to put their suggestions to a test with such remarks as, "You'll never know unless you try it."		None				
42	Considers suggestions by pupils are appropriate only when closely related to the topic being studied.	29	−.37	.05	32	.58	.01
					36	−.46	.01
					39	−.45	.01
					2	.36	.05
					27	−.35	.05
					31	−.40	.05
					43	−.41	.05
					56	.37	.05
43	Has pupils compare the value of alternative courses of action and pass judgment upon their relative desirability.	8	−.43	.05	39	.45	.01
					1	.39	.05
					17	−.41	.05
					24	.35	.05
					27	.38	.05
					32	−.36	.05
					37	−.37	.05
					52	.43	.05
					56	−.42	.05
					58	.39	.05
45	Focuses attention on what the children do or say, rather than on what the teacher does or says.	22	−.51	.01	1	.45	.01
		5	.42	.05	17	−.35	.05

TABLE A2. (*Continued*)

Item Number	Statement	Educational Beliefs					
		Philosophical Beliefs Item Number	r	Level	Teacher Practices Item Number	r	Level
47	Provides pupils a chance to discover by experiencing actual effects whether their choice of this rather than that idea was a judicious one.	22	−.39	.05	5 31 32 48	−.37 .37 −.42 −.35	.05 .05 .05 .05
48	Arranges things in such a way that a child can spend much of his time listening, watching, or waiting his turn.	1 14 16	.49[a] .41[a] .37[a]	.01 .05 .05	42	−.47[a]	.01
52	Uses "feedback" from pupils to diagnose the changing state of affairs in the class, and revises original plans to meet new circumstances.		None		43	−.35[a]	.05
53	Tells children where to start and what to do to accomplish the task at hand.	8 2 15 16 19 27	.45 .40 .38 −.35 .38 .39	.01 .05 .05 .05 .05 .05		None	

56	Frequently has all pupils working on the same page of the same book at the same time.	29	-.46	.01				None
		14	-.40	.05				
58	Makes unplanned changes when a particular lesson is not getting an enthusiastic response from children.	None	None					None
59	Clearly defines the study problem for pupils so they will have no doubts as to exactly what they are to do.	2	.51	.01	59	.37	.05	
		5	-.37	.05				
		29	-.39	.05				
		36	.36[a]	.05				

[a] Signifies intercorrelation which contradicts the theoretical framework of experimentalism.

TABLE A3. Intercorrelations of Teacher Practices with Philosophical Beliefs and Educational Beliefs Which were Significant at the 1 and 5 Percent Levels

Teacher Practices

Item Number	Statement	Philosophical Beliefs Item Number	r	Level	Educational Beliefs Item Number	r	Level
1	Frequently asks children to choose among several alternatives.	14	.53	.01	14 45 43	.44 .45 .39	.01 .01 .05
2	Organizes learning around questions posed by the teacher or the textbook.	14	−.36	.05	4 42	−.36[a] .36	.05 .05
4	Treats each lesson as an independent whole.	14 29	−.48 −.43	.01 .05		None	
5	Frequently calls for the undivided attention of the group and scolds those who do not respond.	5	−.42	.05	32 5 47	.45 .37 −.37	.01 .05 .05
12	Faithfully follows a planned schedule in order to get in the number of minutes each week allotted to each subject in the curriculum.	2 29	.37 −.40	.05 .05	2 12 15	.38 .36 −.42	.05 .05 .05
14	Encourages children to suggest what might be done—to make "hypothetical leaps" into the unknown.		None		17	.41[a]	.05

15	Puts pupils to work on what they see as their own problems, rather than something that is the teacher's or textbook's problem.	8 14 29	−.39 .37 .41	.05 .05 .05	4 5 28	.38ᵃ −.36 −.42ᵃ	.05 .05 .05
16	Expects all children to finish a given assignment within a definitely fixed time limit.	14 29	−.55 −.39	.01 .05	2 15	.47 −.36	.01 .05
17	Holds all students equally responsible for answering certain questions about the subject being studied.	14 29 22	−.62 −.46 .36	.01 .01 .05	14 43	−.38 −.41	.05 .05
24	Provides children a number of starting places and a number of different ways of getting at a task.	8	−.46	.01	14 43	.42 .35	.05 .05
25	Directs children's learning in short, sure steps.		None		32	−.43ᵃ	.05
27	Lets children go ahead with plans based upon foresight, observation, and consideration of several alternatives—even when she is sure their judgment is mistaken.		None		4 14 37 42 43	.41ᵃ .35 −.39 −.35 .38	.05 .05 .05 .05 .05
28	Encourages children to adventure into "deep water," to tackle problems that appear to be "over their heads."		None		37	−.43	.05
30	Encourages children to catch hold of ideas and "run with them" beyond what is, as yet, known for sure.	8 29	−.36 .37	.05 .05	37	−.40	.05

TABLE A3. *(Continued)*

		Teacher Practices					
		Philo-sophical Beliefs			Educa-tional Beliefs		
Item Number	Statement	Item Number	r	Level	Item Number	r	Level
31	Makes "doing something" with a thing, rather than the *thing* itself, the center of children's attention.	1 29	.36 .39	.05 .05	2 12 42 47	−.46 −.36 −.40 .37	.01 .05 .05 .05
32	Since children cannot be trusted to "behave themselves" she takes steps to limit their opportunities for misbehavior.	19	.42	.05	1 42 43 47	−.44 .57 −.36 −.42	.01 .01 .05 .05
34	Insists that each child be responsible for his own work only and does not allow them to ask each other for help.	14	−.35	.05	14	−.44	.01
36	Has children test their "guesses" by acting upon them.	29 1 14	.51 .41 .35	.01 .05 .05	42	−.46	.01
37	Once work has begun, insists that children remain in their places and concentrate on the task at hand.		None		14	−.46	.01

No.		No.	r	p	No.	r	p
39	Encourages children to put their suggestions to a test with such remarks as, "You'll never know unless you try it."	29 8 14 22	.48 -.37 .40 -.36	.01 .05 .05 .05	42 43 37	-.45 .45 -.36	.01 .01 .05
42	Considers suggestions by pupils are appropriate only when closely related to the topic being studied.	1 14	-.43 -.43	.05 .05	48 4	-.47[a] -.43[a]	.01 .05
43	Has pupils compare the value of alternative courses of action and pass judgment upon their relative desirability.	14	.59	.01	1 42 52	.37 -.41 -.35[a]	.05 .05 .05
45	Focuses attention on what the children do or say, rather than on what the teacher does or says.		None			None	
47	Provides pupils a chance to discover by experiencing actual effects whether their choice of this rather than that idea was a judicious one.	1 14	.42 .41	.05 .05		None	
48	Arranges things in such a way that a child can spend much of his time listening, watching, or waiting his turn.	25	.37[a]	.05	30 32 47	-.35 .37 -.35	.05 .05 .05
52	Uses "feedback" from pupils to diagnose the changing state of affairs in the class, and revises original plans to meet new circumstances.	8 29	-.40 .38	.05 .05	43	.43	.05
53	Tells children where to start and what to do to accomplish the task at hand.	8 2 15	.46 .40 .38	.01 .05 .05	17 2	-.55[a] .43	.01 .05

TABLE A3. *(Continued)*

| | | Teacher Practices | | | | | |
| | | Philosophical Beliefs | | | Educational Beliefs | | |
Item Number	Statement	Item Number	r	Level	Item Number	r	Level
56	Frequently has all pupils working on the same page of the same book at the same time.	29 14	−.46 −.40	.01 .05	42 43	.37 −.42	.05 .05
58	Makes unplanned changes when a particular lesson is not getting an enthusiastic response from children.	29	.38	.05	2 12 15 43	−.40 −.36 .37 .39	.05 .05 .05 .05
59	Clearly defines the study problem for pupils so they will have no doubts as to exactly what they are to do.	8 29	.45 −.40	.01 .05	59	.37	.05

[a] Signifies intercorrelation which contradicts the theoretical framework of experimentalism.

DEWEY'S STATEMENTS ON THE FEATURES OF THE METHOD OF REFLECTIVE THINKING

THE FOLLOWING LIST includes seven major features of reflective thinking (or an educative experience), and represents a composite of the features described by Dewey. Each statement in this composite list is coded to identify the original list and page number in *Democracy and Education* from which it was taken. Table A4 is an analysis of reflective thinking devised to assist in the understanding of the code used to identify the source of the statements in the composite list, as well as to show graphically the variation from one of Dewey's lists to another.

Table A4. *Analysis of Reflective Thinking*

Composite List / Major Features	p. 176	p. 177	p. 177	pp. 189–191	p. 192	p. 203
				The Characteristics of Reflective Thinking Listed by John Dewey in *Democracy and Education*		
1. Situation of experience		A		I-a	First	
2. Problem	i	B	(a)	I-b	Second	(1)
3. Initial hypotheses	ii	C		IV-a		
4. Collection of data	iii	D	(b)	II	Third	(2)
5. Reasoned hypotheses	iv	E	(c)	III	Fourth	(3)
6. Experimental testing	v	F	(d)	IV-b	Fifth	(4)
7. Conclusion		G		IV-c		(5)

"Thinking"

The Features of Reflective Thinking

1. Situation of experience

A.   The stimulus to thinking is found when we wish to determine the significance of some act, performed or to be performed.

I-a.   The initial stage of . . . thinking is experience—doing and having something done to one in return.

First.   That the pupil have a genuine situation of experience—that there be continuous activity in which he is interested for its own sake.

2. Problem

i.   Perplexity, confusion, doubt, due to the fact that one is implicated in an incomplete situation whose character is not yet fully determined.

B.   Then we anticipate consequences. This implies that the situation as it stands is, either in fact or to us, incomplete and hence indeterminate.

(a).   The sense of a problem.

I-b.   The situation should present something new, uncertain, or problematic . . . so as to demand thinking.

Second.   That a genuine problem develop within this situation as a stimulus to thought.

(1).   Problem.

3. Initial hypotheses

ii.   A conjectural anticipation—a tentative interpretation of the given elements, attributing to them a tendency to effect certain consequences.

C.   The projection of consequences means a proposed or tentative solution.

IV-a.   Anticipations of possible solutions, whether they be humble guesses or dignified theories.

4. Collection of data

iii.   A careful survey (examination, inspection, exploration, analysis) of all attainable consideration which will define and clarify the problem in hand.

D.   To perfect this hypothesis, existing conditions have to be carefully scrutinized.

(b).   The observation of conditions.

II.   There must be *data* at command to supply the considerations required in dealing with the specific difficulty which has presented itself.

Third.   That he possess the information and make the observations needed to deal with it (the problem).

(2).   Collection and analysis *of data.*

5. Reasoned hypotheses

iv.   A consequent elaboration of the tentative hypothesis to make it more precise and more consistent, because squaring with a wider range of facts.

E.   . . . implications of the hypothesis (have to be) developed—an operation called reasoning.

(c).   The formation and rational elaboration of a suggested conclusion.

III.   Suggestions, inferences, conjectured meanings, suppositions, tentative explanations—*ideas,* in short, aroused by consideration of data.

Fourth.   That suggested solutions occur to him which he shall be responsible for developing in an orderly way.

(3).   Projection and elaboration of suggestions or ideas.

6. Experimental testing

v.   Taking one stand upon the projected hypothesis as a plan of action which is applied to the existing state of affairs: doing something overtly to bring about the anticipated result, and thereby testing the hypothesis.

F.   Then the suggested solution—the idea or theory—has to be tested by acting upon it.

(d).   The active experimental testing.

IV-b.   Anticipations of possible solutions are tested by the operation of acting upon them.

Fifth.   That he have opportunity and occasion to test his ideas by application, to make their meaning clear and to discover for himself their validity.

(4).   Experimental application and testing.

7. Conclusion

G.   If it (the hypothesis) brings about certain consequences, certain determinate changes, in the world, it is accepted as valid. Otherwise it is modified, and another trial made.

IV-c.   (Tested consequences) are to guide and organize further observations, recollections, and experiments.

(5).   The resulting conclusion and judgment.

INDEX